The EVERYTHING®
Italian Practice Book
with CD

Dear Reader,

I first heard Italian from my Italian-born maternal grandfather, Eugenio Savastano, while growing up in the suburbs of Providence, Rhode Island. He was my link to the Italian language. Though I learned many expressions and sayings from him, I didn't start studying it formally until high school. Learning to speak Italian fluently was not easy—it took me years of study and living in Italy to truly master the language.

This book is designed to help people who have some knowledge of the Italian language practice some of the grammar they already know and to reinforce some of the less familiar grammatical points. Keep in mind that learning a foreign language takes time, dedication, and practice. Try not to get frustrated when you don't fully understand something—with practice you'll get it right!

Ronald Glenn Wrigley

The EVERYTHING® Series

Editorial

Innovation Director	Paula Munier
Editorial Director	Laura M. Daly
Executive Editor, Series Books	Brielle K. Matson
Associate Copy Chief	Sheila Zwiebel
Acquisitions Editor	Lisa Laing
Development Editor	Katie McDonough
Production Editor	Casey Ebert
Language Editor	Daniela Gobetti

Production

Director of Manufacturing	Susan Beale
Production Project Manager	Michelle Roy Kelly
Prepress	Erick DaCosta
	Matt LeBlanc
Interior Layout	Heather Barrett
	Brewster Brownville
	Colleen Cunningham
	Jennifer Oliveira
Cover Design	Erin Alexander
	Stephanie Chrusz
	Frank Rivera

Visit the entire Everything® Series at *www.everything.com*

THE
EVERYTHING®
ITALIAN PRACTICE BOOK

Practical techniques to improve
your speaking and writing skills

Ronald Glenn Wrigley, M.A.

Adamsmedia
Avon, Massachusetts

For Ellen and Matthew

An Everything® Series Book.
Everything® and everything.com® are registered trademarks of F+W Publications, Inc.

Published by Adams Media, an F+W Publications Company
57 Littlefield Street, Avon, MA 02322 U.S.A.
www.adamsmedia.com

ISBN 10: 1-59869-382-4
ISBN 13: 978-1-59869-382-9

Printed in the United States of America.

J I H G F E D C B A

Library of Congress Cataloging-in-Publication Data
Wrigley, Ronald Glenn.
The everything Italian practice book / Ronald Glenn Wrigley.
    p.   cm. – (An everything series book)
ISBN-13: 978-1-59869-382-9 (pbk.)
ISBN-10: 1-59869-382-4 (pbk.)
1. Italian language—Textbooks for foreign speakers—
English. 2. Italian language—Self-instruction. I. Title.
PC1129.E5W75 2007
458.2'421—dc22
2007015789

This book is available at quantity discounts for bulk purchases.
For information, please call 1-800-289-0963.

Contents

Acknowledgments

I would like to thank my beautiful wife, Ellen, for her support, and my family for their inspiration. A special thanks to all of my Italian teachers —from Mr. Panone to Dr. Trivelli. Your dedication has inspired me over the years. A heartfelt thanks to Lisa Laing, and to all of the people at Adams.

Top Ten Reasons to Practice Your Italian

1. You will be able to read Dante's *Divine Comedy* in Italian.

2. You'll understand the names of different pasta shapes.

3. You'll understand when to use the subjunctive.

4. You'll learn the language of close to 60 million people in Italy.

5. You'll learn that Italian is easier to pronounce than English.

6. You'll improve your employability by being fluent in a second language.

7. You'll understand what Andrea Bocelli is singing about.

8. You'll learn the language of the world's finest art, fashion, and gastronomy.

9. You'll be able to watch *Amarcord*, *La Vita è Bella*, and *Caro Diario* in Italian.

10. You'll be able to travel to Italy without worrying about the language barrier.

Introduction

▶ THE ITALIAN LANGUAGE evolved from Vulgar Latin (*sermo vulgaris*, common speech), the spoken language of the people of the Roman Empire. In the centuries following the fall of the Roman Empire, many Latin-based dialects sprang up throughout the Italian peninsula. The earliest written evidence of these dialects dates to the 10th century A.D., in the form of legal documents found in Benevento, in the Campania region of southern Italy. Written Italian began to develop in the early part of the 14th century through the works of Dante Alighieri. In his *Divine Comedy*, Dante's native Tuscan dialect was strongly influenced by the dialects of the court poets of the Sicilian School, whom Dante admired. Given the dominant economic role of the Tuscan city-states in the 14th century, the influence of the Tuscan dialect spread. Several literary movements in the 15th and 16th centuries further solidified Tuscan Italian as the spoken and written standard for the peninsula.

The unification of Italy in 1861 brought about sweeping social and economic reforms. Mandatory schooling and the proliferation of means of mass communication and mass transit had an enormous impact on the formation of modern standard Italian. Local dialects, characterized as the language of the uneducated, began to fall out of favor in the decades following unification. As Benito Mussolini and his Fascist party rose to power in the early 20th century, the push toward a common language intensified. With the goal of solidifying his control over the Italian population, Benito outlawed the public use of dialects. Modern standard Italian was by now firmly established as the sole official language of the Italian state and the Italian people.

Despite being politically and geographically united, Italians do not possess a strong sense of national identity, as Luigi Barzini noted in his book *The Italians*. Florentines feel themselves distinct from Sicilians, who in turn feel themselves distinct from Romans. Since the end of fascism, there has been a resurgence of local identity and pride, a phenomenon in Italy known as *campanilismo* (derived from the word *campanile*, or "bell tower"). Literally speaking, *campanilismo* refers to the loyalty and pride that one would have for the bell tower in one's hometown. In contemporary Italy, it is not uncommon to find after-school or weekend programs for school-aged children taught in local dialects. In some cases, this localized pride has been harnessed by extremists, giving rise to political parties with platforms based on secession from the Italian state.

Though *campanilismo* exists in every corner of continental Italy and the islands, all Italians receive formal education in modern standard Italian. Almost all Italians are bilingual; that is, they speak Italian and their local dialect. Knowing Italian doesn't provide you with the key to one generic culture. Rather it opens the door to thousands of different cultures, each of which has made unique contributions in the areas of the visual arts, literature, science, politics, music, cinema, cuisine, and commerce. By studying Italian with the help of *The Everything® Italian Practice Book*, you will develop a new understanding of Dante's Florence, Pirandello's Sicily, Puccini's Lucca, Fellini's Rimini, Vico's Naples, Mazzei's Florence, and Ferrari's Modena.

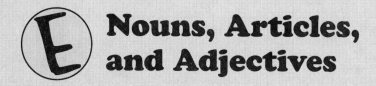

Part 1

Nouns, Articles, and Adjectives

This first part covers some basic grammatical concepts: nouns, articles, and adjectives. Mastering these topics is crucial to developing your spoken and written Italian. Even if you're at a more advanced level, reviewing these concepts can only help to reinforce what you know.

Common Nouns Versus Proper Nouns

A common noun refers to a person, place, thing, event, substance, quality, or idea.

Some Common Nouns:

libro	book
caffè	coffee
studentessa	student
pazienza	patience
anniversario	anniversary
salotto	living room

A proper noun names an individual, event, or place.

Some Proper Nouns:

Roma	Rome
Marco	Mark
Pasqua	Easter
Capodanno	New Year's
il professore Savastano	Professor Savastano
la dottoressa Bianchi	Doctor Bianchi

Exercise 1: Translation

Translate the following nouns into English, then say them aloud to practice your pronunciation.

1. *dottore* ....

2. *energia* ....

3. *stazione* ....

4. *filosofia* ....

5. *automobile* ....

6. *università di Perugia* ....

7. *prosciutto di Parma* ....

8. *ufficio postale* ....

9. *treno* ....

10. *bicicletta* ....

Masculine and Feminine Nouns

In Italian, a gender (masculine or feminine) is attributed to every noun. As a general rule, all nouns that end in –*o* are masculine.

Some Masculine Nouns:

ufficio	office
negozio	store
telefono	telephone
fratello	brother
cugino	(male) cousin
amico	(male) friend

As a general rule, nouns ending in –*a* are feminine.

Some Feminine Nouns:

amica	(female) friend
sorella	sister
casa	house
macchina	car
strada	street
chiesa	church

Exercise 2: Listening Comprehension

Listen to Track 1 and repeat aloud the nouns as read. Then listen again, writing down what you hear. Finally, go back and assign a gender—masculine or feminine—to each one.

Noun	*Gender*
1.	....
2.	....
3.	....
4.	....
5.	....
6.	....
7.	....
8.	....
9.	....
10.	....
11.	....
12.	....
13.	....
14.	....
15.	....

Nouns Ending in –e

As you probably have noticed, many nouns do not end in –o or –a in their singular form; rather, they end in –e. Nouns that end in –e can be either masculine or feminine. There are a few cues to look for in determining the gender of nouns ending in –e.

Nouns ending in –ore are masculine:

dottore	doctor
professore	professor
favore	favor
fiore	flower
odore	odor
autore	author

Nouns ending in –ione are feminine:

stazione	station
ragione	reason
lezione	lesson
conversazione	conversation
televisione	television
situazione	situation

Nouns Ending in a Consonant

Nouns ending in a consonant are masculine and are almost always borrowed from another language:

- film
- bar
- sport
- hobby
- tram
- autobus

Nouns Ending in an Accented Vowel

There are several common words that end in an accented vowel. Correct pronunciation of these words can be tricky. Make sure to stress the last syllable.

Nouns ending in an (accented) –è, –ì, or –ò are masculine:	
caffè	coffee
tassì	taxi
casinò	casino

Nouns ending in an (accented) –à or –ù are feminine:	
città	city
gioventù	youth

Nouns in the Plural

In Italian a noun is usually made plural by changing the final vowel. As a general rule, a masculine singular noun ending in –o changes to –i in the plural:

Singular	Plural
libro	libri
amico	amici
aeroporto	aeroporti
fratello	fratelli
teatro	teatri

A feminine singular noun ending in –a changes to –e in the plural:	

Singular	Plural
sorella	sorelle
pizza	pizze
casa	case

A feminine singular noun ending in –a changes to –e in the plural:

ragazza	ragazze
macchina	macchine

Singular nouns ending in –e, whether masculine or feminine, change to –i in the plural:

Singular	Plural
dottore	dottori
stazione	stazioni
fiore	fiori
televisione	televisioni
autore	autori

Nouns with Irregular Endings

There are a few important exceptions to the general rule of forming plurals. Many of these exceptions affect commonly used nouns.

A singular noun ending in –io changes to –i in the plural:

Singular	Plural
calendario	calendari
stadio	stadi
diario	diari
figlio	figli

Singular nouns ending in –co, –go, –ca, and –ga add an *h* before the final vowel to preserve the hard sound of the *c* or *g*.

Singular	Plural
tedesco	tedeschi
albergo	alberghi
amica	amiche
maga	maghe

There are some common words that are excepted from this rule:

Singular	Plural
amico	amici
politico	politici
medico	medici

Singular nouns ending in an accented vowel are invariable; that is, they do not change from the singular to the plural:

Singular	Plural
città	città
caffè	caffè
tassì	tassì
tribù	tribù

Nouns ending in consonants (that are borrowed from other languages) are invariable and do not change from the singular to the plural:

Singular	Plural
sport	sport
bar	bar
yogurt	yogurt

Nouns commonly used in their truncated (shortened) form do not change from the singular to the plural:

Singular	Plural
cinema (short for *cinematografo*)	cinema
auto (short for *automobile*)	auto
moto (short for *motocicletta*)	moto

Exercise 3: Making Nouns Plural

Give the plural form of the nouns listed.

1. *calendario* ....

2. *stazione* ....

3. *dottore* ....

4. *giorno* ....

5. *ragione* ....

6. *tedesco* ....

7. *albergo* ....

8. *auto* ....

9. *amico* ....

10. *studente* ....

11. *bar* ....

12. *caffè* ....

13. *stadio* ....

14. *attore* ....

15. *libro* ....

Exercise 4: Listening Comprehension

TRACK 2

Listen to Track 2 and repeat aloud the nouns read. Then listen again, writing down what you hear. Finally, go back and write the plural form of each noun.

Noun	Plural
1.	....
2.	....
3.	....
4.	....
5.	....
6.	....
7.	....
8.	....
9.	....
10.	....
11.	....
12.	....
13.	....
14.	....
15.	....

Exercise 5: Singular to Plural and Plural to Singular

Rewrite the nouns, making singular nouns plural and plural nouns singular.

1. *calendari* ....

2. *televisione* ....

3. *pizze* ....

4. *amiche* ....

5. *amico* ....

6. *caffè* ....

7. *autori* ....

8. *albergo* ....

9. *negozio* ....

10. *casa* ....

Indefinite Articles

The indefinite article, the equivalent of English "a" or "an," has the form *un* or *uno* for masculine nouns, and *un'* or *una* for feminine nouns. We must look at the first letter of the word in order to form the indefinite article.

If the first letter of the noun is...	*Masculine*	*Feminine*
...a consonant (other than *s* or *z*)	*un ragazzo*	*una casa*
...a vowel	*un amico*	*un'amica*
...*s* + consonant	*uno stadio*	*una studentessa*
...*z*	*uno zero*	*una zebra*

Exercise 6: Articles and Nouns

Translate the following articles/nouns into Italian:

1. A (male) friend ....

2. A (female) friend ....

3. A taxi ....

4. An apple ....

5. A (male) student ....

6. A (female) student ....

7. A zoo ....

8. A university ....

9. An actor ....

10. A conversation ....

Definite Articles

Forming the definite article (corresponds to the word "the" in English) is a bit more complicated. There are seven forms of the definite article in Italian—*il, l', lo, i, gli* (masculine), and *la, l', le* (feminine). In order to determine the correct form of the definite article, look at the initial letter, the gender (masculine or feminine), and number (singular or plural) of the noun that the definite article precedes.

If the word is masculine, and the first letter of the word is...	Singular	Plural
...a consonant (other than *s* or *z*)	*il lago*	*i laghi*
...a vowel	*l'amico*	*gli amici*
...*s* + consonant	*lo studente*	*gli studenti*
...*z*	*lo zero*	*gli zeri*

If the word is feminine, and the first letter of the word is...		
...a consonant	*la ragazza*	*le ragazze*
...a vowel	*l'amica*	*le amiche*

Exercise 7: Articles and Nouns

TRACK 3

Listen to Track 3 and repeat aloud the singular articles and nouns. Then listen again, writing down what you hear. Finally, go back and write the plural forms of the articles and nouns.

Noun	*Plural*
1.	....
2.	....
3.	....
4.	....
5.	....
6.	....
7.	....
8.	....
9.	....
10.	....

Adjectives

An adjective modifies or describes a noun. In Italian, an adjective must agree in number (singular or plural) and gender (masculine or feminine) with the noun that it modifies. There are two categories of adjectives in Italian, those with four forms and those with two forms.

The first category includes adjectives whose masculine singular form ends in –*o*. These adjectives have four possible endings:

Mario è bravo. (Mario = **masculine, singular;** *bravo* = **masculine, singular)** **Mario is good.**

Maria è brava. (Maria = **feminine, singular;** *brava* = **feminine, singular)** **Maria is good.**

Mario e Marco sono bravi. (Mario e Marco = **masculine, plural;** *bravi* = **masculine, plural) Mario and Marco are good.**

Maria e Marla sono brave. (Maria e Marla = **feminine, plural;** *brave* = **feminine, plural) Maria and Marla are good.**

The second category includes adjectives whose masculine singular form ends in –e. These adjectives have two possible endings.

Mario è intelligente. (Mario = **masculine, singular;** *intelligente* = **masculine, singular) Mario is intelligent.**

Maria è intelligente. (Maria = **feminine, singular;** *intelligente* = **feminine, singular) Maria is intelligent.**

Mario e Marco sono intelligenti. (Mario e Marco = **masculine, plural;** *intelligenti* = **masculine, plural) Mario and Marco are intelligent.**

Maria e Marla sono intelligenti. (Maria e Marla = **feminine, plural;** *intelligenti* = **feminine, plural) Maria and Marla are intelligent.**

Exercise 8: Adjectives

Complete the sentence with an adjective that has the opposite meaning of the underlined adjective. The adjective must agree in number and in gender with the noun that it modifies. Choose from the following list: *giovane, povero, basso, magro, stupido, brutto, grande, noioso, antipatico, avaro.*

1. *Stefano è alto. Suo fratello Gianni è* ....

2. *Marina è intelligente. La sua amica Grazia è* ....

3. *Zio Alberto e zia Barbara sono generosi. I miei cugini sono* ....

4. *Il capo di Monica è simpatico. Il capo di Massimo è* ....

5. *Le sorelle di Giovanni non sono vecchie. Sono* ....

6. *La casa non è piccola. È* ....

7. *I film non sono interessanti. Sono* ....

8. *Il cane di Stefano non è grasso. È* ....

9. *Le macchine non sono belle. Sono* ....

10. *Bill Gates è ricco. Tu sei* ....

Placement of Adjectives

When paired with a noun, most adjectives follow the noun:

Giulio è un ragazzo intelligente. **Giulio is an intelligent boy.**

«Il Codice Da Vinci» è un libro interessante. **The Da Vinci Code *is an interesting book.***

I bambini italiani giocano nel parco. **The Italian children are playing in the park.**

There is a group of commonly used adjectives, however, that often precede the nouns they modify:

Lui abita in una piccola casa. **He lives in a small house.**

L'ho visto l'altro giorno. **I saw him the other day.**

David e Gianni sono vecchi amici. **David and Gianni are old friends.**

Exercise 9: Adjective Placement

Give the correct form of the adjective in parentheses and place it correctly either before or after the noun it modifies.

1. *Mio zio ha due (vecchio)* .... *case* .... *in campagna.*

2. *Abita vicino a un (piccolo)* .... *lago* ....

3. *L'italiano non è una (difficile)* .... *lingua* ....

4. *Parlo di un (altro)* .... *libro* ....

5. *Ogni giorno vedo gli (stesso)* .... *studenti* ....

6. *Ieri ho visto un (stupido)* .... *film* ....

7. *Elena è una (bello)* .... *ragazza* ....

8. *Tre (ricco)* .... *signori* .... *mangiano al ristorante.*

9. *Noi abbiamo due (simpatico)* .... *amiche* ....

10. *È una (nuovo)* .... *idea* ....

Quantifying Words

As adjectives (modifying a noun), *molto* (very, much, many, a lot of), *tanto* (so much, so many), *troppo* (too much, too many), and *poco* (a little, little, few) each have four forms:

molto	tanto	troppo	poco
molta	tanta	troppa	poca
molti	tanti	troppi	pochi
molte	tante	troppe	poche

Io bevo molto vino. **I drink a lot of wine.**
Io bevo tanto vino. **I drink so much wine.**
Io bevo troppo vino. **I drink too much wine.**
Io bevo poco vino. **I drink a little wine./I don't drink much wine.**

Io bevo molta birra. **I drink a lot of beer.**
Io bevo tanta birra. **I drink so much beer.**
Io bevo troppa birra. **I drink too much beer.**
Io bevo poca birra. **I don't drink much beer.**

Io leggo molti libri. **I read many books.**
Io leggo tanti libri. **I read so many books.**
Io leggo troppi libri. **I read too many books.**
Io leggo pochi libri. **I read few books./I don't read many books.**

Io leggo molte riviste. **I read many magazines.**
Io leggo tante riviste. **I read so many magazines.**
Io leggo troppe riviste **I read too many magazines.**
Io leggo poche riviste. **I read few magazines./I don't read many magazines.**

Exercise 10: **Molto, tanto, troppo, poco**

Give the correct form of *molto, tanto, troppo, poco.*

1. *Noi abbiamo (molto)* .... *amici.*

2. *Mio padre ha (poco)* .... *pazienza.*

3. *Il mio capoufficio ha (poco)* .... *idee buone.*

4. *Non voglio mangiare (troppo)* .... *grassi.*

5. *Lui ha (tanto)* .... *cugini in Italia.*

As adverbs (modifying an adjective or a verb), *molto, tanto, troppo, and poco* are invariable:

Modifying an Adjective

La casa è molto bella. **The house is very beautiful.**
La casa è tanto bella. **The house is so beautiful.**
La casa è troppo piccola. **The house is too small.**
Luisa è poco intelligente **Luisa is not very intelligent.**

Modifying a Verb

Tu parli molto. **You talk a lot.**
Tu parli tanto. **You talk so much.**
Tu parli troppo. **You talk too much.**
Tu parli poco. **You don't talk much.**

All adjectives follow the noun when they are modified by the adverbs *molto* (very), *poco* (little, not very), *tanto* (so much), *troppo* (too much), *abbastanza* (enough, rather), *un po'* (a little):

Marco è uno studente molto bravo. **Marco is a very good student.**
Marianna è una ragazza poco simpatica. **Marianna is not a very nice girl.**

Exercise 11: Adverbs

Rewrite the sentences, incorporating the adverbs listed.

1. *Mio fratello è un uomo simpatico. (molto)*

   ....

2. *Maria è una persona sincera. (abbastanza)*

   ....

3. *Tu e Antonio siete ragazzi intelligenti. (poco)*

   ....

4. *Lui ha dei cugini curiosi. (troppo)*

   ....

5. *Lui abita in una bella casa. (tanto)*

   ....

Tutto/a/i/e

When the adjective *tutto/a* is used in the singular, it means "the whole"; when used in the plural (*tutti/e*), it means "all" or "every." The adjective *tutto/a/i/e* is always followed by the definite article.

Io studio tutto il giorno. **I study the whole day.**

Tutti gli studenti studiano molto. **All of the students study a lot.**

Io mangio tutta la pizza. **I eat the whole pizza.**

Tutte le professoresse insegnano tutti i giorni. **All of the professors teach every day.**

Exercise 12: Tutto

Write the correct form of *tutto* + the definite article in the space provided.

1. *Io studio* .... *sera.*

2. .... *vini italiani sono buoni.*

3. *Ho letto* .... *racconti di Alberto Moravia.*

4. *Mio fratello ha pulito* .... *casa.*

5. .... *ragazze sono simpatiche.*

Ogni

Ogni (each, every) is an invariable adjective and is always followed by a singular noun.

Ogni studente studia molto. **Each (or every) student studies a lot.**

You will see that this construction carries the same meaning as the following:

Tutti gli studenti studiano molto. **All the students study a lot.**

Exercise 13: Each and Every

Rewrite the expressions using *ogni*.

1. *tutti i ragazzi* ....

2. *tutte le case* ....

3. *tutte le bottiglie* ....

4. *tutti i giorni* ....

5. *tutti gli studenti* ....

Let's Practice

Try to complete the following exercises without referring back to the grammatical explanations.

Exercise 14: Indefinite Articles

Give the indefinite article for the following nouns.

1. .... *libro*

2. .... *casa*

3. .... *amico*

4. .... *amica*

5. .... *zoo*

6. .... *zebra*

7. .... *studente*

8. .... *studentessa*

Exercise 15: Definite Articles

Give the definite article for the following nouns, then give the plural form of both the article and noun.

1. .... *giardino* ....

2. .... *albero* ....

3. .... *zero* ....

4. .... *studio* ....

5. .... *casa* ....

6. .... *autostrada* ....

Exercise 16: Correct or Incorrect?

Rewrite the words and phrases, correcting the grammatical and spelling errors.

1. *lo stessa ragazza*

....

2. *uno città europea*

....

3. *l'altra giorno*

....

4. *due fiore gialle*

....

5. *tre giovane fratelli*

....

6. *un bello città*

....

7. *i nuovi calendarii*

....

8. *una dottore intelligenta*

....

9. *li ragazzi simpatico*

....

10. *un libro interessanto*

....

Exercise 17: Il Signor Gori

TRACK 4

Listen to Track 4, and then answer the questions.

1. *Dove abita il signor Gori?*

....

2. *Di che colore è la casa del signor Gori?*

....

3. *Quanti piani ha la casa?*

....

4. *I suoi vicini di casa sono simpatici?*

....

5. *Com'è la macchina del signor Gori?*

....

6. *Quanti figli ha?*

....

7. *Come sono i figli?*

....

Exercise 18: Opposites

Answer the questions using an adjective whose meaning is opposite to the adjective in the question.

1. *Sono noiosi i film di Robin Williams?*

....

2. *L'italiano è una lingua difficile?*

....

3. *Sono bassi gli edifici di Manhattan?*

....

4. *Sono pigri i giovani di oggi?*

    ....

5. *Sono antipatici i suoceri di Massimo?*

    ....

6. *Lassie è un cane stupido?*

    ....

7. *È giovane Bob Dylan?*

    ....

Exercise 19: From Italian to English

Translate the sentences into English.

1. *Stephen King è un autore molto famoso.*

    ....

2. *La «Divina Commedia» è lunga e interessante.*

    ....

3. *Bill Gates è un uomo generoso.*

    ....

4. *Il dottor Rossi è molto simpatico e ha molti amici.*

    ....

5. *Tutte le università in Italia sono vecchie.*

    ....

Pronunciation Exercise:
The Accented Final Vowel

TRACK 5

TRACK 6

Listen to Track 5 and repeat each word you hear.

casinò, studiò, università, gioventù, città, più, caffè, podestà, tassì, così, parlò, civiltà, inventò, andrà, Perù, rispetterà, autorità

Listen to the following sentences in Track 6. Note the pronunciation of the final accented vowels. Then read aloud the complete sentences.

Non sono mai stato al casinò di Venezia.

Mio cugino studierà all'Università di Napoli.

La gioventù di oggi non è come quella di ieri.

Roma è la città più grande d'Italia.

Ho offerto un caffè al podestà.

Mi hanno chiamato un tassì.

Così parlò Zarathustra.

La civiltà greca inventò la filosofia.

Mio fratello andrà in Perù quest'estate.

Marco non rispetterà l'autorità.

Part 2

Subject Pronouns, Avere and Essere

In this chapter, we will examine subject pronouns and ways of addressing people. We will also study *avere* (to have) and *essere* (to be), two of the most commonly used verbs in Italian, in the present tense and review their use in idiomatic expressions.

Subject Pronouns

The subject pronouns (or personal pronouns) indicate the subject of a verb.

Singular		*Plural*	
io	I	*noi*	we
tu	you (informal)	*voi*	you (informal)
lui, lei	he, she	*loro*	they
Lei	you (formal)	*Loro*	you (formal)

The *tu* and *voi* subject pronouns are used to speak directly to friends, relatives, and children, and in informal situations. The *voi* form is used to address large groups. *Lei* (with a capital *L*) and *Loro* (with a capital *L*) are used in formal situations to show respect to a person you do not know or to people who are older than you, with your boss, or in professional situations.

Exercise 1: The Correct Subject Pronouns

Circle the subject pronoun you would use.

1. You are telling your son and his friend that they have to be careful. *tu, voi, loro*

2. You ask your doctor to refill a prescription. *Lei, lei, lui*

3. You are addressing a group of colleagues at a professional conference. *Voi, Loro, loro*

4. You want to ask your best friend how she/he is doing. *Lei, tu, voi*

The Verb Essere

Essere (to be) is one of the most commonly used verbs in Italian. Learn this verb well—you will see it throughout this book! In the present tense, it is conjugated as follows:

Singular		*Plural*	
io sono	I am	*noi siamo*	we are
tu sei	you (informal) are	*voi siete*	you (informal) are
lui è	he is	*loro sono*	they are
lei è	she is		
Lei è	you (formal) are	*Loro sono*	you (formal) are

It is common, but not required, to omit the subject pronoun in both spoken and written Italian. The subject pronoun can be added for emphasis:

Io sono intelligente. **I am intelligent.**
Sono intelligente. **I am intelligent.**

Essere can be used to indicate geographic origin when followed by the preposition *di* + a place name:

Siamo di Providence. **We are from Providence.**

To find out where someone is from, ask the question, *Di dove sei?* (informal) or *Di dov'è?* (formal).

Essere can also be used to indicate possession when followed by the preposition *di* + a proper name, or a noun:

È la macchina del professore. **It's the professor's car.**
È di Marco. **It's Marco's.**

To find out to whom something belongs, ask the question, *Di chi è?* (Whose is it?) or *Di chi sono?* (Whose are they?)

A sentence can be made negative by placing the word *non* before the conjugated verb:

Gianni e Maria non sono di Roma. **Gianni and Maria are not from Rome.**

TRACK 7

Exercise 2: Massimo è di Quarrata

Listen to Track 7. Write the subjects you hear in the first space. In the second space, rewrite the sentence with each new subject and change the verb conjugation accordingly.

1. ....

2. ....

3. ....

4. ....

5. ....

Exercise 3: D'accordo! (Agreed!)

Read each sentence aloud. If you agree with the statement, move on to the next one. If you do not agree with it, rewrite it, making any necessary corrections.

1. *Tom Cruise è un attore irlandese.*

....

2. *Roma è una città in Francia.*

....

3. *L'italiano è una bella lingua.*

....

4. *Leonardo da Vinci è di Roma.*

   ....

5. *La Ferrari è una macchina italiana.*

   ....

Exercise 4: Singular to Plural and Plural to Singular

Rewrite each of the following sentences, changing singular to plural and plural to singular.

1. *Voi siete intelligenti.*

   ....

2. *Le ragazze italiane sono molto simpatiche.*

   ....

3. *Io sono molto sincero.*

   ....

4. *Le chiese italiane sono vecchie e belle.*

   ....

5. *Gli amici di Stefano sono alti e biondi.*

   ....

The Verb Avere

Avere (to have) is another important and commonly used verb in Italian, as you will see in upcoming chapters!

Avere is conjugated in the present tense as follows:

Singular		**Plural**	
io ho	I have	*noi abbiamo*	we have
tu hai	you (informal) have	*voi avete*	you (informal) have
lui ha	he has	*loro hanno*	they have
lei ha	she has		
Lei ha	you (formal) have	*Loro hanno*	you (formal) have

Hai cugini in California? **Do you have cousins in California?**

Ho tre cugini in California. **I have three cousins in California.**

Exercise 5: Avere

Complete each of the following sentences with the correct form of *avere*.

1. *Lei, signor Buonanno,* .... *una casa al mare?*

2. *Tu e Marcello* .... *dei colleghi simpatici.*

3. *Homer Simpson* .... *tre figli.*

4. *Io* .... *un fratello.*

5. *Marco ed io* .... *degli amici in California.*

Exercise 6: More with Avere

Answer the questions in complete sentences in Italian.

1. *Hai una macchina tedesca?*

   ....

2. *Hai un cane o un gatto? Come si chiama?*

....

3. *Hai i capelli biondi o castani?*

....

4. *Quanti cugini hai?*

....

5. *Hai un condominio in Florida?*

....

Idiomatic Expressions

An idiomatic expression is an expression whose meaning cannot be translated literally from one language into another. For native speakers of English, the figurative meaning of the following expression is quite clear:

It's raining cats and dogs.

For non-native speakers of English, this expression can be puzzling! In order to understand the expression and others like it, one must develop an understanding of the culture in which the idiomatic expression is used.

Avere and *essere* are used with many idiomatic expressions in Italian. The key to understanding these expressions is not to let your knowledge of English get in your way and not to get into the habit of translating the expressions word for word.

Idiomatic expressions with avere:

avere fame	to be hungry
avere sete	to be thirsty
avere sonno	to be sleepy
avere caldo	to be warm (hot)
avere freddo	to be cold

Idiomatic expressions with avere:

avere fretta	to be in a hurry
avere paura (di)	to be afraid (of)
avere bisogno di	to need, have need of
avere voglia di	to want, to feel like
avere ragione	to be right, correct
avere torto	to be wrong, incorrect

Note that in these expressions the structure in English (to be + adjective) differs from the structure in Italian (to have + noun). Since the expressions in Italian include a noun, it logically follows that an adjective can be used to modify that noun:

Io ho sete. **I am thirsty.**
Io ho molta sete. **I am very thirsty.**
Maria ha freddo. **Maria is cold.**
Maria ha molto freddo. **Maria is very cold.**
Mio nipote ha paura del buio. **My nephew is afraid of the dark.**
Mio nipote ha molta paura del buio. **My nephew is very afraid of the dark.**

Avere can also indicate age:

*avere + **number** + anni* **to be... years old**
Quanti anni hai? **How old are you?**
Ho diciotto anni. **I'm eighteen years old.**

Exercise 7: Informal Idiomatic Expressions with Avere

Ask your friend whether…

1. He/she is thirsty.

....

2. He/she is warm.

....

3. He/she is afraid.

....

4. He/she needs a new car.

....

5. He/she feels like talking.

....

Exercise 8: Formal Idiomatic Expressions with Avere

How would you ask an elderly neighbor the same questions?

1. ....

2. ....

3. ....

4. ....

5. ....

Idiomatic Expressions with Essere

Though not as common as idiomatic expressions with *avere*, there are a few useful idiomatic expressions using the verb *essere*:

Essere al verde **to be broke**
Essere in gioco **to be at stake**
Essere nelle nuvole **to daydream, to have one's head in the clouds**

C'è, Ci sono *and* Ecco!

C'è (there is) and *ci sono* (there are) are used to indicate the existence of something. *C'è*, meaning "there is," is singular, and therefore must be used with a singular subject. *Ci sono*, or "there are," is plural, and must be used with a plural subject.

> *C'è un ospedale qui vicino.* **There is a hospital close by.**
> *Ci sono molti ospedali a Boston.* **There are many hospitals in Boston.**

Ecco! is used to point out the existence of something in view. It is invariable and can be used with singular or plural nouns.

> *Non trovo la mia penna!* **I can't find my pen!**
> *Ecco la penna!* **Here's the pen!**
> *Dove sono Marco e Maria?* **Where are Marco and Maria?**
> *Ecco Marco e Maria!* **Here are Marco and Maria!**

Exercise 9: La mia città

Answer the following questions about your city.

1. *C'è un ristorante cinese a* (your city)?

   ....

2. *Quanti abitanti ci sono a* ....?

   ....

3. *C'è un'università a* ....?

   ....

4. *Ci sono ristoranti italiani a* ....?

   ....

5. *C'è una biblioteca pubblica a* ....?

   ....

Exercise 10: On Tour

You're accompanying your friend on a tour of your city. Point out the following buildings and structures using *ecco*.

1. *La chiesa*

....

2. *La sinagoga*

....

3. *Il parco*

....

4. *Il ristorante italiano*

....

5. *La casa del sindaco*

....

Com'è? *and* Come sono?

Com'è? (What is it like?) and *Come sono?* (What are they like?) are used to ask someone to describe what someone or something is like.

> *Io ho una macchina.* **I have a car.**
> *Com'è la macchina?* **What's the car like?**
> *È nuova.* **It's new.**
> *Ho due cugine in Florida.* **I have two cousins in Florida.**
> *Come sono?* **What are they like?**
> *Sono alte e bionde come la loro madre.* **They're tall and blonde like their mother.**

Uses of buono

When paired with a noun, the adjective *buono* (good) has several different endings, most of which are similar in structure to the endings of the indefinite article in the singular, and regular endings in the plural:

un libro	a book	*un buon libro*	a good book
uno studente	a student	*un buono studente*	a good student
un'amica	a (female) friend	*una buon'amica*	a good (female) friend
una studentessa	a (female) student	*una buona studentessa*	a good (female) student
due ragazzi	two boys	*due buoni ragazzi*	two good boys
due ragazze	two girls	*due buone ragazze*	two good girls

When *buono* follows the noun it modifies or the verb *essere*, it has four forms:

È un ragazzo buono. **He's a good boy.**
La pizza è buona. **The pizza is good.**
Ho amici buoni. **I have good friends.**
Le torte sono buone. **The cakes are good.**

In regular usage, certain adjectives—*buono* and *bello* included—normally precede the nouns they modify. These adjectives can be used after a noun for emphasis.

Exercise 11: Buono

Complete with the correct form of *buono*.

1. *Maria e Enza sono due* .... *ragazze.*

2. *Sono* .... *amiche.*

3. *È un* .... *caffè.*

4. _È una_ .... _amica._

5. _È un_ .... _libro._

6. _È un_ .... _albergo._

Uses of bello

The adjective _bello_ (beautiful, handsome, nice) also has several different endings, all of which are similar in structure to the endings of the definite article:

**il** libro	the book	_un be**l** libro_	a beautiful book
**l'**amico	the (male) friend	_un bel**l'**amico_	a handsome (male) friend
**lo** studente	the (male) student	_il bel**lo** studente_	the handsome (male) student
**la** ragazza	the girl	_la bel**la** ragazza_	the beautiful girl
**le** ragazze	the girls	_le bel**le** ragazze_	the beautiful girls
**l'**amica	the (female) friend	_una bel**l'**amica_	a beautiful (female) friend
**i** libri	the books	_i be**i** libri_	the beautiful (or nice) books
**gli** studenti	the students	_i be**gli** studenti_	the beautiful students

Exercise 12: Bello

Replace the adjective _brutto_ with _bello_ in the following sentences.

1. _Che brutta cosa!_ ....

2. _Che brutto giorno!_ ....

3. _Che brutti occhi!_ ....

4. _Che brutto libro!_ ....

5. *Che brutta storia!* ....

6. *Che brutti capelli!* ....

7. *Che brutto edificio!* ....

8. *Che brutti uffici!* ....

Numbers

The cardinal numbers in Italian follow a spelling pattern. Be careful, spelling can be tricky.

1 uno	16 sedici	31 trentuno	500 cinquecento
2 due	17 diciassette	32 trentadue	600 seicento
3 tre	18 diciotto	33 trentatrè	700 settecento
4 quattro	19 diciannove	40 quaranta	800 ottocento
5 cinque	20 venti	50 cinquanta	900 novecento
6 sei	21 ventuno	60 sessanta	1.000 mille
7 sette	22 ventidue	70 settanta	
8 otto	23 ventitrè	80 ottanta	
9 nove	24 ventiquattro	90 novanta	
10 dieci	25 venticinque	100 cento	
11 undici	26 ventisei	101 centouno	
12 dodici	27 ventisette	150 centocinquanta	
13 tredici	28 ventotto	200 duecento	
14 quattordici	29 ventinove	300 trecento	
15 quindici	30 trenta	400 quattrocento	

All of these numbers are invariable except *zero* and *uno*.

The number *uno* has the same forms as the indefinite article. *Un amico* can mean a friend or one friend, depending on the context. The plural of *zero* is *zeri*:

Ci sono due zeri nel numero di telefono. **There are two zeros in the phone number**:

When *–tre* is the last digit of a number larger than 20, the final *–e* is accented:

ventitrè, trentatrè, quarantatrè, etc:

Numbers from *venti* to *novanta* drop their final vowel before adding -*uno* or -*otto:*

ventuno, trentotto, novantuno

The numbers *ventuno, trentuno,* up to *novantuno,* usually drop the final *–o* when followed by a noun:

Mio fratello ha quarantun anni.

When followed by the word *anni,* the numbers *venti, trenta,* up to *novanta,* usually drop the final vowel:

Mio nonno ha ottant'anni.

The function of periods and commas in English is reversed in Italian:

English	Italian
1,000	1.000
1.25%	1,25%

In spoken Italian, the word *virgola* (comma) is used:

English	Italian
1.5% (one point five percent)	1,5% (*uno virgola cinque percento*)

The indefinite article is not used with *cento* (hundred) and *mille* (thousand), as it is in English:

cento dollari **a hundred dollars**
mille dollari **a thousand dollars**

Cento has no plural form. *Mille* has the plural form *mila*:

cento dollari, duecento dollari **one hundred dollars, two hundred dollars**

mille dollari, duemila dollari **one thousand dollars, two thousand dollars**

TRACK 8

Exercise 13: Numbers

Listen to Track 8. Write the numbers in their numerical form, and then go back and spell out each number:

	Number	*Spelling*
1.	....	....
2.	....	....
3.	....	....
4.	....	....
5.	....	....
6.	....	....
7.	....	....
8.	....	....
9.	....	....
10.	....	....

Quanto?

As an adjective, *quanto* (how much or how many) must agree in number and gender with the noun that it modifies. It has four forms: *quanto, quanta, quanti, quante.*

Quanto zucchero metti nel caffè? **How much sugar do you put in your coffee?**

Quanti cugini hai in Italia? **How many cousins do you have in Italy?**

As an adverb, *quanto* (how, how much) is invariable:

Quanto è alta la montagna? **How tall is the mountain?**
Quanto costa una nuova macchina? **How much does a new car cost?**
Quanto costano i dischi? **How much do the records cost?**

Exercise 14: Answering Questions

TRACK 9

Listen to Track 9. Answer the questions in complete sentences in Italian. Spell out all numbers.

1. ....

2. ....

3. ....

4. ....

5. ....

6. ....

7. ....

Days of the Week

In Italian calendars, the week begins with Monday. The days of the week are not capitalized in Italian, except when they are the first word of a sentence.

lunedì	Monday
martedì	Tuesday
mercoledì	Wednesday
giovedì	Thursday
venerdì	Friday
sabato	Saturday
domenica	Sunday

All of the days of the week, except Sunday, are masculine. Since *lunedì, martedì, mercoledì, giovedì,* and *venerdì* end in an accented *–ì*, they do not change from singular to plural.

Io dormirò fino a tardi lunedì mattina. **I will sleep late on Monday morning.**

Io dormo fino a tardi tutti i lunedì. **I sleep late every Monday.**

Sabato and *domenica* have different forms in the plural:

Io dormirò fino a tardi sabato (domenica) mattina. **I will sleep late on Saturday (Sunday) morning.**

Io dormo fino a tardi tutti i sabati (tutte le domeniche). **I sleep late every Satuday (every Sunday).**

A preposition is not needed in Italian to express the equivalent of "on Tuesday" or "on Friday":

Venerdì vado al supermercato. **On Friday I am going to the super-market.**

The singular definite article can be used to indicate a habitual event:

Il sabato vado al supermercato. **I go to the supermarket on Saturdays.**

Vado in biblioteca la domenica. **I go to the library on Sundays.**

Exercise 15: Habitual Actions

The following statements indicate whether the action is happening once or is a habitual action. Indicate which are happening once and which are habitual by circling the correct word.

1. *Mia sorella non lavora il lunedì.* Once or habitual?

2. *Mio fratello va in chiesa ogni domenica.* Once or habitual?

3. *Andiamo al supermercato sabato.* Once or habitual?

4. *Esco con i miei colleghi venerdì sera.* Once or habitual?

5. *Telefono a mia madre tutti i martedì.* Once or habitual?

Exercise 16: Asking and Answering Questions

TRACK 10

Listen to Track 10. Write each question (*domanda*) you hear, then write an answer (*risposta*) to each question in a complete sentence in Italian.

1. *Domanda:* ....

   Risposta: ....

2. *D:* ....

   R: ....

3. *D:* ....

   R: ....

4. *D:* ....

   R: ....

5. *D:* ....

   R: ....

6. *D:* ....

   R: ....

7. *D:* ....

   R: ....

8. *D:* ....

   R: ....

9. *D:* ....

   R: ....

10. *D:* ....

   R: ....

11. *D:* ....

   R: ....

12. *D:* ....

   R: ....

13. *D:* ....

   R: ....

14. *D:* ....

   R: ....

15. *D:* ....

   R: ....

16. *D:* ....

   R: ....

17. *D:* ....

   R: ....

Pronunciation Exercise: The Accented Final Vowel

Native English speakers often have difficulty mastering the pronunciation of double consonants in Italian. Keep in mind that every letter in an Italian word must be pronounced, so it logically follows that double consonants are pronounced longer than single consonants:

Sano **(pronounced sa-no)/***sanno* **(pronounced san-no)**
Lego **(pronounced le-go)/***leggo* **(pronounced leg-go)**
Fata **(pronounced fa-ta)/***fatta* **(pronounced fat-ta)**
Papa **(pronounced pa-pa)/***pappa* **(pronounced pap-pa)**

The double *ss* in Italian has a different pronunciation than the single *s:*

casa **(the *s* is pronounced as in the English word "hose")**
cassa **(the *ss* is pronounced as in the English word "house")**

Exercise 17

Listen to the following words in Track 11, repeating each word that you hear.

single consonant	double consonant
sano	sanno
lego	leggo
pena	penna
fata	fatta
giovane	Giovanni

Listen to each sentence in Track 12, then read aloud the complete sentences. Note the difference in pronunciation between the single and double consonants.

1. *La fata azzurra l'ha fatta.*

2. *Ho dato da mangiare al gatto.*

3. *Sanno che siamo arrivati sani e salvi.*

4. *Mi fa pena che abbia perso la penna.*

5. *Leggo un libro.*

6. *Lego un pacco.*

7. *Mi hanno chiamato due volte quest'anno.*

8. *Pago alla cassa.*

9. *La casa è bella.*

10. *Giovanni è giovane.*

Part 3

First Conjugation Verbs, Prepositions, and Telling Time

We need verbs to form sentences. Expanding our knowledge of verbs enhances our ability to communicate.

–Are Verbs in the Present Tense

There are three categories of verbs in Italian: first conjugation verbs, second conjugation verbs, and third conjugation verbs. First conjugation verbs are verbs whose infinitive forms end in –are. Verbs in this category are the most frequently used. Most –are verbs are regular; that is, they follow a pattern of conjugation.

Some –are verbs in their infinitive form:

aspettare	to wait
lavorare	to work
imparare	to learn
parlare	to speak

To conjugate first conjugation verbs, remove the –are ending and replace it with a different ending for each subject:

Singular	Plural
io parlo	noi parliamo
tu parli	voi parlate
lui parla	loro parlano
lei parla	Loro parlano
Lei parla	

The present tense in Italian can carry different meanings in English, depending on the context:

Io parlo italiano **can mean "I speak Italian," "I am speaking Italian," or "I do speak Italian."**

Io non parlo italiano **can mean "I don't speak Italian," or "I am not speaking Italian."**

The present tense in Italian can also be used to express an action that will take place in the future:

Stasera guardo la televisione. **I will watch TV this evening.**

Exercise 1: Conjugating –Are Verbs

Rewrite the sentences, replacing the subject.

Mario guarda la televisione.

1. *Io* ....

2. *Noi* ....

3. *Voi* ....

4. *Tu* ....

5. *Pietro ed io* ....

6. *Tutti i miei cugini* ....

Io parlo italiano e inglese.

1. *Noi* ....

2. *Mio padre* ....

3. *Tu e Elena* ....

4. *Loro* ....

5. *Ogni studente* ....

6. *I figli del signor Gianni* ....

Tu lavori il venerdì?

1. *Tutti gli studenti* ....

2. *Loro* ....

3. *Mio fratello ed io* ....

4. *Gli avvocati* ....

5. *Gianni* ....

6. *Marcello ed il suo amico* ....

Noi non aspettiamo il treno.

1. *Voi* ....

2. *Marco e Angela* ....

3. *Tu e Marco* ....

4. *Loro* ....

5. *I miei amici ed io* ....

6. *Tutte le ragazze* ....

Exercise 2: Translation Exercise Using –Are Verbs

Translate the following sentences into Italian. Choose from among the –*are* verbs provided. Some idiomatic expressions with *avere* may be needed as well.

pensare (a/di), parlare, mangiare, desiderare, abitare, giocare (a), incominciare, imparare (a), spiegare

1. I am learning to speak Italian.

    ....

2. They are starting to work on Friday.

    ....

3. We are thinking of eating in the new restaurant.

    ....

4. The boys want to explain the situation.

    ....

5. The professor is speaking with a student.

   ....

6. John lives in Boston. He is thinking about working in San Diego.

   ....

7. Do you play tennis? Do you want to play tennis with Marco?

   ....

8. He is afraid of the other children.

   ....

9. We feel like eating the pizza.

   ....

10. You and John do not need the computer today.

    ....

Exercise 3: Listening Comprehension with –Are Verbs

TRACK 13

Listen to the verbs spoken in Track 13. Repeat each verb, then write each infinitive in Italian in the first space provided and the English equivalent in the second space.

1. ....

2. ....

3. ....

4. ....

5. ....

6. ....

7. ....

8. ....

9. ....

10. ....

11. ....

12. ....

13. ....

14. ....

15. ....

16. ....

17. ....

18. ....

19. ....

20. ....

21. ....

22. ....

23. ....

Verbs Ending in –Iare

There are a few commonly used first conjugation verbs that end in –*iare*. To conjugate these verbs, drop the –*i* of the infinitive before adding the –*i* *(tu)* and –*iamo (noi):*

incominciare (to begin)	
io incomincio	noi incominciamo
tu incominci	voi incominciate
lui incomincia	loro incominciano
lei incomincia	Loro incominciano
Lei incomincia	

Verbs Ending in –Care *and* –Gare

There are a few commonly used first conjugation verbs that end in either –*care* or –*gare*. To conjugate these verbs you must add an *h* before the –*i (tu)* and –*iamo (noi):*

giocare (to play)	
io gioco	noi giochiamo
tu giochi	voi giocate
lui gioca	loro giocano
lei gioca	Loro giocano
Lei gioca	

Ascoltare, Aspettare, Guardare

In Italian, the verbs *ascoltare* (to listen or to listen to), *aspettare* (to wait or to wait for), and *guardare* (to watch or to look at) do not take a preposition, as they do in English:

Io ascolto la musica. **I listen to music.**
Noi aspettiamo l'autobus. **We are waiting for the bus.**
Loro guardano le foto. **They are looking at the pictures.**

Pensare a/Pensare di

Pensare is often followed by a preposition. Depending on which preposition is used, the verb takes on a slightly different meaning.
Pensare a + noun = to think about someone or something:

Io penso alla mamma. **I'm thinking about my mom.**

Pensare di + infinitive = to think about doing something:

Io penso di mangiare fuori stasera. **I'm thinking about eating out tonight.**

Double Verb Constructions

In a double verb construction, the first verb is conjugated and the second is left in its infinitive form:

Io desidero mangiare fuori stasera. **I want to eat out this evening.**

Exercise 4: Correct or Incorrect?

Some of the following sentences contain errors. If a sentence is correct, move on to the next one. If it is incorrect, rewrite it, correcting the error.

1. *Noi pensiamo a mangiare in un ristorante.*

....

2. *Alfredo non ha molto pazienza.*

....

3. *Io studio perché desidero imparare.*

....

4. *Dove aspettate per il treno?*

....

5. *Avete fame? Desiderate mangiare la pizza?*

....

6. *Penso a mio fratello. Lui è alla verde.*

....

7. *Io lavori il martedì.*

....

8. *Tu pagi il conto?*

....

9. *Noi giochiamo a tennis ogni giorno.*

....

10. *Hai voglia di studaire l'italiano?*

....

Irregular –Are Verbs: **Andare, Fare, Stare, Dare**

Andare (to go), *fare* (to do), *stare* (to stay, to feel), *dare* (to give) are irregular verbs and do not follow a pattern of conjugation.

andare (to go)	*fare* (to do, to make)	*dare* (to give)	*stare* (to stay)
io vado	*faccio*	*do*	*sto*
tu vai	*fai*	*dai*	*stai*
lui, lei, Lei va	*fa*	*dà*	*sta*
noi andiamo	*facciamo*	*diamo*	*stiamo*
voi andate	*fate*	*date*	*state*
loro, Loro vanno	*fanno*	*danno*	*stanno*

Andate al concerto di Bob Dylan? **Are you going to the Bob Dylan concert?**

Faccio la pizza per cena. **I am making pizza for dinner.**

Come stai? Sto bene, grazie. **How are you? I am fine, thanks.**

Il padre dà le chiavi della macchina al figlio. **The father gives the car keys to his son.**

Exercise 5: Andare, Fare, Dare, *and* Stare

Write the correct form of the verb in parentheses.

1. *Io* .... *a un concerto stasera. (andare)*

2. *Noi* .... *attenzione quando parla. (fare)*

3. *Tu e Mario* .... *a casa oggi? (stare)*

4. *Che cosa desiderate* .... *stasera? (fare)*

5. *Chi* .... *il libro al professore? (dare)*

6. *Dove* .... *noi in vacanza? (andare)*

7. *Marcello, come* .... *tu? (stare)*

8. *Loro* .... *informazioni ai turisti. (dare)*

9. *Mia moglie ed io non desideriamo* .... *gli spaghetti. (fare)*

10. *Lei* .... *colazione alle 8 ogni mattina. (fare)*

Exercise 6: Andare, Fare, Dare, *and* Stare

Complete each sentence with the most appropriate verb.

1. *Come .... Loro oggi?*

2. *Che cosa .... tu?*

3. *Io .... a mangiare al ristorante.*

4. *La madre .... dei soldi a suo figlio.*

Idiomatic Expressions with Fare

There are many commonly used idiomatic expressions using the verb *fare*.

fare attenzione	to pay attention
fare il bagno	to take a bath
fare caldo	to be hot (weather)
fare colazione	to have breakfast
fare la doccia	to take a shower
fare una domanda	to ask a question
fare un errore	to make a mistake
fare una foto(grafia)	to take a picture
fare freddo	to be cold (weather)
fare una gita	to take a short trip
fare un giro	to go for a ride
fare la guerra	to wage war
fare una passeggiata	to take a walk
fare una pausa	to take a break
fare un regalo	to give a gift
fare la spesa	to go food shopping
fare le spese	to go shopping
fare un viaggio	to take a trip

Exercise 7: Idiomatic Expressions with Fare

Translate into Italian.

1. I pay attention when he speaks.

   ....

2. You (*tu*) take a shower.

   ....

3. He is having breakfast.

   ....

4. We don't ask many questions.

   ....

5. You and John are taking a picture.

   ....

6. They take a short trip.

   ....

7. I take a walk every Monday.

   ....

8. He asks too many questions!

   ....

9. We go food shopping on Saturdays.

   ....

10. It's cold outside!

   ....

Interrogative Expressions

Interrogative words and expressions are used to ask questions. Their function and placement are similar to their English counterparts.

Italian	English
Chi?	Who? or Whom?
Che (cosa)?	What?
Come?	How? What?
Dove?	Where?
Quando?	When?
Quale/i?	Which?
Perché?	Why?
Quanto/a/i/e?	How much? How many?

Chi sei? **Who are you?**

Che cosa fai? **What are you doing?**

Come va? **How's it going?**

Dove mangi stasera? **Where are you going to eat this evening?**

Quando comincia il semestre? **When does the semester begin?**

Quale macchina? **Which car?**

Perché non vai al cinema? **Why aren't you going to the movies?**

Quanto costa? **How much does it cost?**

Exercise 8: Question Words

Complete each sentence with the appropriate interrogative word or expression.

1. .... *stai?* (how)

2. .... *vai stasera?* (where)

3. .... *libri desideri comprare?* (how many)

4. .... *fai così?* (why)

5. .... *film desideri vedere questo fine settimana?* (which)

6. .... *pensi di fare per il compleanno di Cristina?* (what)

7. .... *pazienza ha tuo padre?* (how much)

8. .... *costa una nuova BMW?* (how much)

9. .... *fai un viaggio in Italia?* (when)

10. .... *vini sono buoni?* (which)

Prepositions and Their Uses

Prepositions indicate the location, time, position, or direction of an object in relation to the verb. The most commonly used prepositions in Italian are:

a	at, in, to
con	with
da	by, from
di	about, from, of
in	at, in, into
per	for
su	on
tra	between

As you can see, prepositions in Italian don't always have a single equivalent to their English counterparts. Learning proper use of prepositions in Italian requires practice.

When used to indicate a destination or a location, the preposition *a* is used with cities and towns, and the preposition *in* is used with larger geographical areas, including states, large islands, countries, and continents.

I miei amici abitano a Boston. **My friends live in Boston.**

Vado a Boston per vedere una partita dei Red Sox. **I am going to Boston to see a Red Sox game.**

Vado in Italia l'anno prossimo. **I am going to Italy next year.**

L'Italia è in Europa. **Italy is in Europe.**

Exercise 9: Prepositions

Fill in the blank with the correct preposition.

1. *Marcello abita .... Roma.*

2. *Il fratello .... Massimo si chiama Adriano.*

3. *Gli studenti studiano .... biblioteca.*

4. *Telefono .... mia madre ogni domenica.*

5. *Non mi piace la pizza .... le acciughe.*

Articulated Prepositions

The prepositions *a, da, di, in,* and *su* combine with the definite article to form one word. These are called "contractions" or "articulated prepositions."

Vado a + il negozio = Vado al negozio. **I am going to the store.**

Sono i libri di + gli studenti = Sono i libri degli studenti. **They are the students' books.**

	il	**lo**	**l'** (masc.)	**la**	**l'** (fem.)	**i**	**gli**	**le**
a	*al*	*allo*	*all'*	*alla*	*all'*	*ai*	*agli*	*alle*
di	*del*	*dello*	*dell'*	*della*	*dell'*	*dei*	*degli*	*delle*
da	*dal*	*dallo*	*dall'*	*dalla*	*dall'*	*dai*	*dagli*	*dalle*
su	*sul*	*sullo*	*sull'*	*sulla*	*sull'*	*sui*	*sugli*	*sulle*
in	*nel*	*nello*	*nell'*	*nella*	*nell'*	*nei*	*negli*	*nelle*

The prepositions *con, per,* and *tra,* when followed by a definite article, do not form a contraction.

Mio padre parla con il mio amico. **My father is speaking with my friend.**

Il libro d'italiano è tra il dizionario e il calendario. **The Italian book is between the dictionary and the calendar.**

Exercise 10: **Un Viaggio in Italia**

TRACK 14

Listen to Track 14 and answer the questions in complete sentences in Italian.

1. *Dove va John quest'estate?*

....

2. *Con chi viaggia?*

....

3. *Dov'è 'La creazione dell'uomo'?*

....

4. *Dov'è 'La nascita di Venere'?*

....

5. *Prima di tornare a Chicago, dove vanno?*

....

Exercise 11: Articulated Prepositions

Translate the prepositional phrases into Italian. Some will require articulated prepositions, others will not.

1. (of Mr. Romeo) *Dove sono i figli* ....?

2. (in a building) *L'ufficio del professore è* ....

3. (in the center of town) *C'è un buon ristorante* ....

4. (of the computer) *Hai bisogno* ....

5. (in Denver) *I miei amici abitano* ....

6. (Franco's books) *Ecco* ....

7. (in the churches) *Ci sono molte persone* ....

8. (in the library) *Oggi studiamo* ....

9. (from the other girl) *È un regalo* ....

10. (in the classrooms) *Gli studenti sono* ....

11. (of the election) *Oggi è il giorno* ....

12. (between two books) *Il quaderno è* ....

13. (with sugar) *Il cameriere porta il caffè* ....

14. (in a new restaurant) *Pietro lavora* ....

15. (with a friend) *Giovanni mangia* ....

Exercise 12: Translation

Translate the following into Italian.

1. I live in a small house.

....

2. The professor explains the lesson to the students.

....

3. The conference is in the hotel downtown.

....

4. Today John is at home.

....

5. Francesco's books are on the bed.

....

6. The childrens' toys are in the living room.

....

7. Whose pen is this?

....

8. It is the lawyer's pen.

....

9. Here are John's friends.

....

10. The gift is from John's friend.

....

11. There are many flowers on the trees.

....

12. Peter works in a restaurant in the center of town.

....

13. The calendar is between two books on the desk.

....

14. He is a good friend from Boston.

....

15. The children bring many gifts for the teacher.

....

16. They work in the United States.

....

17. They are arriving on the train from New York.

....

18. The train arrives at the station tonight.

....

19. I listen to music when I work.

....

20. Are you buying many clothes in the new stores on Newbury Street?

....

The preposition *a* is also used after a conjugated verb that is followed by an infinitive:

andare a	to go to...
aiutare a	to help to...
cominciare a	to start/begin to...
imparare a	to learn to...
incoraggiare a	to encourage to...
insegnare a	to teach to...
provare a	to try to...
riuscire a	to manage to...

Andiamo [a mangiare] al ristorante stasera. **We are going to [eat in a] restaurant this evening.**

Imparo a parlare italiano. **I am learning to speak Italian.**

Giovanni prova a sciare. **Giovanni is trying to ski.**

Che ora è? Che ore sono?: *Telling Time in Italian*

The questions *Che ora è?* and *Che ore sono?* both mean "What time is it?" and can be used interchangeably.

> *Che ora è? Sono le due e trenta.* **What time is it? It's 2:30.**
> *Che ore sono? Sono le due e trenta.* **What time is it? It's 2:30.**

The expression *Sono le…* is used to express all times from 2:00 on:

> *Sono le due.* **It's 2:00.**
> *Sono le quattro e quindici.* **It's 4:15.**
> *Sono le otto meno due.* **It's 7:58. (literally, "It's 8:00 minus 2.")**
> *Sono le dodici e venti.* **It's 12:20.**

The expression *È l'…* is used to express all times using the 1:00 hour.

> *È l'una.* **It's 1:00.**
> *È l'una e dieci.* **It's 1:10.**
> *È l'una meno cinque.* **It's 12:55. (literally, "It's 1:00 minus 5.")**
> *È l'una e quarantacinque.* **It's 1:45.**

It is common in Italy to see the 24-hour clock used for scheduling purposes (train or plane schedules, conference schedules, television programming, etc.).

> *Il treno per Bari parte dal binario sei alle diciannove e venti.* **The train for Bari leaves from Track 6 at 7:20.**

È… is used with the following time expressions:
È mezzogiorno. **It's noon.**
È mezzanotte. **It's midnight.**

The expression *A che ora…?* is used to ask "(At) what time…?":

> *A che ora vai alla festa?* **(At) what time are you going to the party?**
> *A che ora torni stasera?* **(At) what time are you returning this evening?**

Exercise 13: Telling Time

State the times in Italian, spelling out all numbers.

1. It's 5:17.

....

2. It's 3:08.

....

3. It's 14:24.

....

4. It's 8:30.

....

5. It's 12:45.

....

6. It's 18:44.

....

7. It's 1:15.

....

8. It's midnight.

....

9. It's 6:09.

....

10. It's 1:55.

....

Exercise 14: At What Time?

Answer the questions in full sentences in Italian.

1. *Che ore sono?*

   ....

2. *A che ora mangi stasera?*

   ....

3. *A che ora vai a letto?*

   ....

4. *A che ora vai al lavoro domani mattina?*

   ....

5. *A che ora sei a casa domani pomeriggio?*

   ....

Exercise 15: Verb Conjugations

Conjugate the following verbs in the present tense.

	Mangiare	**Pagare**	**Parlare**
io	....	....	....
tu	....	....	....
lui/lei	....	....	....
noi	....	....	....
voi	....	....	....
loro	....	....	....

	Dare	*Fare*	*Andare*
io	....	....	....
tu	....	....	....
lui/lei	....	....	....
noi	....	....	....
voi	....	....	....
loro	....	....	....

	Stare	*Incominciare*	*Giocare*
io	....	....	....
tu	....	....	....
lui/lei	....	....	....
noi	....	....	....
voi	....	....	....
loro	....	....	....

Exercise 16: Articulated Prepositions

Fill in the following chart with the correct articulated prepositions.

	Il	Lo	L'	La	L'	I	Gli	Le
a	....	....	....	....	....	....	....	....
da	....	....	....	....	....	....	....	....
di	....	....	....	....	....	....	....	....

	Il	Lo	L'	La	L'	I	Gli	Le
in	....	....	....	....	....	....	....	....
su	....	....	....	....	....	....	....	....

Exercise 17: Present Tense Verbs

Complete the sentences using the correct present tense conjugation of the verb in parentheses. You may refer to the glossary for assistance.

1. (to wait for) *Noi* .... *il treno?*

2. (to learn) *Luca e Mario* .... *l'italiano.*

3. (to eat) *Tu* .... *la pizza.*

4. (to watch) *Tu e Maria* .... *la televisione.*

5. (to play) *Noi* .... *a tennis oggi.*

6. (to explain) *Gli altri professori ed io* .... *le lezioni agli studenti.*

7. (to think about) *Io sono di Providence. Io* .... *gli amici a Providence.*

8. (to buy) *Marco* .... *molti CD.*

9. (to study) *Tu non* .... *perché non hai molto tempo libero.*

10. (to begin) *La lezione d'italiano* .... *alle 4.*

11. *Oggi noi* (to listen to) .... *una conferenza.*

12. *Gli studenti* (to attend/to frequent) .... *l'università.*

13. *Io* (to teach) .... *l'italiano.*

14. *Io e Elena* (to pay) .... *i biglietti per il concerto.*

15. *Giovanni e Michelle* (to want) .... *mangiare gli spaghetti alla carbonara.*

Exercise 18: Answering Questions

Answer the questions in full sentences in Italian.

1. *Quando sei al verde, a chi chiedi i soldi?*

....

2. *Quanti e quali sono i giorni della settimana?*

....

3. *Che cosa fai stasera quando finisci di fare gli esercizi d'italiano?*

....

4. *Quanti cugini hai? Come si chiamano? Dove abitano?*

....

Pronunciation Exercise: The Letters L and GL

The letter *L* in Italian is pronounced like the *L* in "like."

Exercise 19: Listening Exercise

TRACK 15

Listen to the following words from Track 15, and then repeat.

lago	lake
lento	slow
libro	book
locale	place
lungo	long

The *GL* in Italian is pronounced like the "–lli–" in the English "million." Practice saying the word "million," focusing on the position of the tongue as you're saying the "–lli–" combination.

TRACK 16

Exercise 20: Listening Exercise

Listen to the following words from Track 16, and then repeat them.

famiglia	family
moglie	wife
figli	sons
aglio	garlic

TRACK 17

Exercise 21: Listening Exercise

Listen to Track 17 and read along. Then try to pronounce each sentence.

1. *Gli studenti l'hanno letto.* The students read it.

2. *I figli fanno gli spaghetti all'aglio e olio.* The sons are making spaghetti with garlic and oil.

3. *Vogliamo leggere il libro.* We want to read the book.

4. *La Sicilia è un'isola con un clima caldo.* Sicily is an island with a warm climate.

5. *Quella bella ragazza è la figlia del signor Luigi Miglia.* That beautiful girl is Mr. Luigi Miglia's daughter.

Part 4

Second and Third Conjugation Verbs and Adverbs

Let's continue to expand your knowledge of verbs. You will see similarities with verbs that you've already learned, but be careful not to confuse *–are*, *–ere*, and *–ire* verbs.

–Ere and –Ire Verbs in the Present Tense

Second and third conjugation verbs are verbs whose infinitive forms end in –*ere* and –*ire*, respectively. Notice that –*ere* and –*ire* verbs differ from each other only in the *voi* forms.

scrivere *(to write)*

Io scrivo	noi scriviamo
tu scrivi	voi scrivete
lui scrive	loro scrivono
lei scrive	Loro scrivono
Lei scrive	

dormire *(to sleep)*

io dormo	noi dormiamo
tu dormi	voi dormite
lui dorme	loro dormono
lei dorme	Loro dormono
Lei dorme	

There are more irregular second and third conjugation verbs than first conjugation verbs. Irregular second and third conjugation verbs will be presented later in Part 4.

Some regular –*ere* verbs:	
assistere	to attend
chiedere	to ask
chiudere	to close
conoscere	to know
correre	to run
credere	to believe
decidere (di)	to decide (to do something)
discutere (di)	to discuss (something)
leggere	to read
mettere	to put

Some regular *–ere* verbs:	
perdere	to lose
prendere	to take
ricevere	to receive
ripetere	to repeat
rispondere	to answer
scrivere	to write
spendere	to spend
vedere	to see
vendere	to sell
vivere	to live

Exercise 1: Conjugating –Ere Verbs

Complete each sentence with the correct form of the verb in parentheses.

1. *Noi non* .... *una lettera ai nonni.* (to write)

2. *Voi* .... *negli UFO?* (to believe)

3. *Io* .... *un caffè a colazione ogni mattina.* (to take)

4. *Lui desidera* .... *la sua macchina.* (to sell)

5. *Mio padre* .... *sempre le chiavi della macchina.* (to lose)

6. *Tu e Marisa* .... *di politica dopo l'elezione.* (to discuss)

7. *Io e mia moglie non* .... *tuo fratello.* (to know)

8. *I rappresentanti della ditta non* .... *alla conferenza.* (to attend)

9. *Io non* .... *lo zucchero nel caffè.* (to put)

10. *Angela* .... *la finestra perché ha freddo.* (to close)

Exercise 2: Reading Comprehension

Complete the paragraph with the correct form of the verb. Choose from the verbs listed below. Each verb may be used only once.

chiedere, discutere, leggere, prendere, vedere

Ogni mattina .... un caffè al bar vicino a casa mia. Quando sono al bar .... i miei vicini di casa; di solito noi .... di politica, di musica, o delle notizie del giorno. Quando non partecipo alla conversazione, ... il giornale. .... il conto, pago, e vado in ufficio.

Exercise 3: Working with –Ere Verbs

Complete each sentence with a verb from the list of *–ere* verbs presented at the beginning of Part 4. Not every verb will be used; some may be used more than once.

1. *Mia moglie ed io .... un gelato dopo cena.*

2. *Il cameriere .... la mancia dai clienti.*

3. *Tu e Elena .... alle mie lettere.*

4. *Noi .... di andare in macchina.*

5. *Giovanni e Mario .... di sport nel bar.*

6. *Sì, è vero. Io .... la mia macchina.*

7. *Mia sorella .... sempre le chiavi di casa.*

8. *Mariella, perché non .... alla signora che ore sono?*

9. *Lui .... la porta perché tira vento.*

10. *I miei cugini .... nell'astrologia.*

Some useful –ire verbs:

aprire	to open
dormire	to sleep
offrire	to offer
partire (da)	to leave (from)
seguire	to follow
sentire	to hear
servire	to serve

Exercise 4: Answering Questions

Answer the questions in full sentences in Italian.

1. *Fino a che ora dormi il sabato mattina?*

   ....

2. *Quando ricevi un'email da un collega, rispondi subito?*

   ....

3. *A che ora esci dall'ufficio il venerdì pomeriggio?*

   ....

4. *Tu segui la politica? Discuti di politica con la tua famiglia?*

   ....

5. *Tu ascolti la musica classica?*

   ....

Irregular –Ere Verbs

Here are some commonly used irregular –ere (second conjugation) verbs. They do not follow a pattern of conjugation in the present tense, so they must be memorized.

bere	to drink
rimanere	to remain, to stay
scegliere	to choose
tenere	to keep

Bere (to drink)

io bevo	*noi beviamo*
tu bevi	*voi bevete*
lui beve	*loro bevono*
lei beve	*Loro bevono*
Lei beve	

Rimanere (to stay, to remain)

io rimango	*noi rimaniamo*
tu rimani	*voi rimanete*
lui rimane	*loro rimangono*
lei rimane	*Loro rimangono*
Lei rimane	

Scegliere (to choose)

io scelgo	*noi scegliamo*
tu scegli	*voi scegliete*
lui sceglie	*loro scelgono*
lei sceglie	*Loro scelgono*
Lei sceglie	

Tenere (to keep)

io tengo	*noi teniamo*
tu tieni	*voi tenete*
lui tiene	*loro tengono*
lei tiene	*Loro tengono*
Lei tiene	

Exercise 5: Change the Subject

TRACK 18

Listen to Track 18. Listen to the sentence and repeat it aloud. Then rewrite it, changing the subject to those listed below.

1. *Marco*

   ....

2. *Tutti i miei amici*

   ....

3. *Tu e Marta*

   ....

4. *Io*

   ....

Irregular –Ire Verbs

There are many third conjugation verbs that add an *–isc–* between the stem and ending in all forms except the *noi* and *voi* forms. There is no foolproof method to distinguish the *–isc–* verbs from the regular *–ire* verbs. To memorize them is to learn them.

Some common verbs that follow this pattern of conjugation:	
capire	to understand
costruire	to build
finire	to finish
preferire	to prefer
pulire	to clean
restituire	to give back
riferire	to report, to relate
spedire	to send
suggerire	to suggest, to recommend
ubbidire	to obey

Here's a sample conjugation:

Capire (to understand)	
io capisco	noi capiamo
tu capisci	voi capite
lui capisce	loro capiscono
lei capisce	Loro capiscono
Lei capisce	

Exercise 6: Questions and Answers

Answer the questions in complete sentences in Italian.

1. *Quale ristorante preferisci: il ristorante italiano o il ristorante cinese?*

   ....

2. *Quando finisci di mangiare, prendi un caffè?*

   ....

3. *Tu capisci l'italiano?*

   ....

4. *Puoi suggerire un film italiano?*

   ....

5. *A che ora finisci di lavorare il venerdì pomeriggio?*

   ....

More Irregular –Ire Verbs

Dire, uscire, and *venire* are three commonly used third conjugation verbs that are irregular in the present tense.

Dire (to say/to tell)	
Io dico	noi diciamo
tu dici	voi dite
lui dice	loro dicono
lei dice	Loro dicono
Lei dice	

Uscire (to go out)	
io esco	noi usciamo
tu esci	voi uscite
lui esce	loro escono
lei esce	Loro escono
Lei esce	

Venire (to come)	
io vengo	noi veniamo
tu vieni	voi venite
lui viene	loro vengono
lei viene	Loro vengono
Lei viene	

Exercise 7: Listening Comprehension

TRACK 19

Listen to the sentences in Track 19. Repeat each sentence, and then rewrite it with the new subject provided.

1. *Elena e Caterina*

    ....

2. *Tu e Mario*

    ....

3. *Io*

....

4. *Gli altri ragazzi ed io*

....

5. *Il signor Giovanni*

....

Modal Verbs: Dovere, Potere, *and* Volere

Modal verbs express possibility, ability, need, or intention. The modal verbs *dovere* (must, to have to), *potere* (can, to be able to), and *volere* (to want to) are irregular in the present tense. They are often followed by an infinitive. In limited instances, *dovere* and *volere* may be followed by a noun.

Volere (to want to)	
io voglio	*noi vogliamo*
tu vuoi	*voi volete*
lui vuole	*loro vogliono*
lei vuole	*Loro vogliono*
Lei vuole	

Potere (can, to be able to)	
io posso	*noi possiamo*
tu puoi	*voi potete*
lui può	*loro possono*
lei può	*Loro possono*
Lei può	

Dovere (must, to have to)	
io devo	*noi dobbiamo*
tu devi	*voi dovete*
lui deve	*loro devono*
lei deve	*Loro devono*
Lei deve	

Some examples:

Io voglio andare in vacanza in Messico. **I want to go on vacation in Mexico.**

Non posso andare in vacanza in Messico perché devo lavorare tutta l'estate. **I can't go on vacation in Mexico because I have to work all summer.**

Io non posso andare a teatro stasera, perché devo studiare. **I can't go to the theater tonight, because I have to study.**

Io devo cinque dollari a Stefano. **(when followed by a noun,** *dovere* **means to owe). I owe Stefano five dollars.**

Io voglio un caffè. **I want a coffee.**

Io voglio bere un caffè. **I want to drink a coffee.**

Exercise 8: **Dovere, Potere,** *and* **Volere**

The following people want to do certain things. Say that they are unable to do them, and why, using the verbs *potere* and *dovere*, as in the example.

Marco vuole fare una passeggiata. Non può fare una passeggiata perché deve studiare. **Marco wants to take a walk. He can't take a walk because he has to study.**

1. *Tu vuoi comprare una nuova Mercedes.*

   ....

2. *Davide e Maria vogliono fare un viaggio in Inghilterra.*

   ....

3. *I miei amici vogliono andare al cinema.*

   ....

4. *Lui vuole ascoltare la musica.*

   ....

5. *Elena ed io vogliamo visitare Venezia.*

   ....

"To Know": Sapere *and* Conoscere

Both *sapere* and *conoscere* correspond to the verb "to know" in English.

Sapere **is irregular in the present tense:**	
io so	*noi sappiamo*
tu sai	*voi sapete*
lui sa	*loro sanno*
lei sa	*Loro sanno*
Lei sa	

Sapere means "to know a fact" or "to know how" to do something:

Io so che Giovanni è intelligente. **I know that John is intelligent.**
Loro sanno che il museo chiude alle nove. **They know that the museum closes at nine.**
Voi non sapete sciare? È facilissimo! **You don't know how to ski? It's easy!**

Exercise 9: Conoscere

Conoscere is a regular second conjugation verb. It means "to know or to be familiar with" a person, a place, or a thing, or it can mean "to meet" someone for the first time. Can you conjugate it?

io		*noi*	
tu		*voi*	
lui		*loro*	
lei		*Loro*	
Lei			

Exercise 10: Sapere or Conoscere?

Write the correct form of *sapere* or *conoscere*, according to the context of the sentence.

1. *Giovanni non* .... *che io vengo alla festa.*

2. *Marcello e Marta* .... *bene la città di Boston.*

3. *Tu e Maria* .... *chi è Marcello Mastroianni?*

4. *Sì, noi* .... *che è un famoso attore italiano.*

5. *Massimo vuole* .... *la mia amica.*

6. *Tu* .... *dov'è il museo?*

7. *Io* .... *sciare ma non* .... *giocare a tennis.*

8. *Lei* .... *il ristorante I Tre Colori?*

9. *Tutti gli studenti* .... *parlare inglese.*

10. *Volete* .... *quanti anni ha lo zio?*

Time Expressions

We will now take a look at some useful words that will help us to express events that happen(ed) rarely, often, now, later, or at some point in the past.

puntuale	punctual
in anticipo	early
in ritardo	late
ogni volta	each (every) time
una volta…	once…
…al giorno	…a day
…alla settimana	…a week
…al mese	…a month

…all'anno	…a year
due volte…	twice…
ogni tanto	every now and then
ogni giorno, settimana, mese, anno	every day, week, month, year
a volte	sometimes
qualche volta	sometimes
di quando in quando	every now and then
di rado	rarely
di solito	usually
di tanto in tanto	every now and then
tutti i giorni	every day
tutte le sere	every evening

Exercise 11: Time Expressions

Rewrite the sentences incorporating the time expression in parentheses.

1. *Gli aeroplani partono dall'aeroporto di Boston.* (late)

   ....

2. *Mangio fuori in un ristorante con la mia famiglia.* (often)

   ....

3. *Telefono a mia madre.* (once a week)

   ....

4. *Leggo un libro.* (every now and then)

   ....

5. *Guardo la televisione.* (every evening)

   ....

6. *Vado al cinema.* (rarely)

   ....

7. *Vado in vacanza in Europa.* (every year)

   ....

8. *I politici dicono la verità.* (every now and then)

....

9. *Esco con i miei amici.* (often)

....

10. *Vado a teatro.* (every evening)

....

Adverbs

An adverb modifies a verb or an adjective. We have already seen a few adverbs (*molto, tanto, troppo, poco*) in Italian in Part 1:

Tu parli molto. **You talk a lot.**
Lui beve troppo. **He drinks too much.**
I ragazzi sono tanto intelligenti. **The boys are so intelligent.**
È poco furbo. **He isn't so astute.**

In English, adverbs often end in "–ly": "quickly," "easily," "particularly."

In Italian, the suffix *–mente* corresponds to the English "–ly" suffix. To form an adverb in Italian, the *–mente* suffix is added to the feminine singular form of the adjective.

Adjective	*Feminine Singular Form*	*Adverb*
libero	*libera*	*liberamente*
tranquillo	*tranquilla*	*tranquillamente*
attento	*attenta*	*attentamente*
rapido	*rapida*	*rapidamente*

Adjectives whose singular forms end in *–e* add the suffix *–mente* without changing the final vowel:

Adjective	*Adverb*
intelligente	*intelligentemente*
triste	*tristemente*

Adjectives whose singular forms end in *–le* or *–re* drop the final *–e* before adding the suffix *–mente*:

Adjective	Adverb
probabile	probabilmente
particolare	particolarmente

Exercise 12: From Adjective to Adverb

Rewrite the following adjectives as adverbs.

1. *facile* ....

2. *raro* ....

3. *disperato* ....

4. *recente* ....

5. *magnifico* ....

6. *difficile* ....

7. *diligente* ....

8. *doloroso* ....

9. *tranquillo* ....

10. *economico* ....

There are several commonly used adverbs that do not derive from adjectives:

bene	well
male	badly
presto	early
sempre	always

Exercise 13: More with Adverbs

Fill in the blank with the correct form of the adverb. The first sentence contains a clue as to which adverb you should use.

1. *Andrea Boccelli è un buon cantante. Lui canta* ....

2. *Sto attento quando lui parla. Io ascolto* ....

3. *L'italiano per me è facile. Parlo italiano* ....

4. *Il signor Ferragamo ha molti vestiti eleganti. Lui si veste*

    ....

5. *Giovanni è disperato perché non trova le chiavi della macchina. Cerca le chiavi* ....

Practice: Conjugation and Translation

It's time to test your new knowledge. Try the following exercises, and then check your answers in Appendix D.

Exercise 14: Conjugation

Complete each sentence with the correct form of the verb in parentheses. Try not to refer to the text, but feel free to use the glossary to look up a verb or two.

1. *Tu* .... *molte lettere agli amici?* (to write)

2. *Io* .... *al telefono in casa mia.* (to answer)

3. *I camerieri* .... *il caffè ai clienti.* (to serve)

4. *Voi* .... *da casa.* (to leave)

5. *Noi* .... *la finestra.* (to close)

6. *Gli studenti* .... *il libro d'italiano.* (to read)

7. *Tu e Maria* .... *molti messaggi elettronici.* (to receive)

8. *Gianni* .... *un caffè al professore.* (to offer)

9. *Tu* .... *negli UFO?* (to believe)

10. *Tutti gli studenti* .... *in biblioteca?* (to sleep)

11. *Che cosa* .... *tu nel caffè?* (to put)

12. *Tu e gli altri ragazzi* .... *la domanda.* (to repeat)

13. *La mia amica* .... *la finestra.* (to open)

14. *Gli studenti* .... *dei messaggi elettronici.* (to send)

15. *Noi* .... *ogni mattina.* (to have breakfast)

16. *Gina e Lorenzo* .... *della statua.* (to take a picture)

17. *Voi* .... *il libro al professore.* (to return/to give back)

18. *Loro non* .... *la spiegazione del professore.* (to understand)

19. *La Boston University* .... *un nuovo dormitorio.* (to build)

20. *Gli studenti* .... *in classe.* (to ask a question)

21. *Io* .... *bere il caffè espresso.* (to prefer)

22. *I compagni di stanza non* .... *spesso.* (to clean)

23. *Tu e Mario* .... (to take a short trip)

24. *Preferisco* .... *dopo la lezione.* (to take a break)

25. *Giovanna* .... (to be broke)

Exercise 15: Translation

Translate the following sentences into Italian.

1. I want to go out tonight.

   ....

2. Do you know John?

   ....

3. We go out with your son's friends (hint: the friends of your son).

   ....

4. We don't want to go to the party.

   ....

5. Do you know that John studies Italian?

   ....

6. You can't watch TV now. You must do the Italian exercises!

   ....

7. Why aren't John and Michael coming tonight?

   ....

8. You must be hungry. Do you want some pizza?

   ....

9. I can't study because I have to return the book to the library.

   ....

10. I can't understand. Can you repeat the question?

    ....

Pronunciation Exercises: S and Z

In Italian, the letter *s* has two distinct sounds. The difference is similar to the difference present in the two English words "rice" (here there is a distinct "s" sound) and "rise" (here there is more of a "z" sound).

When the letter *s* appears at the beginning of a word, it has the same sound as the "s" sound in "rice," "house," "snake," and "sip."

Exercise 16: The Letter S

TRACK 20

Listen to Track 20. Repeat each word you hear.

salame	*salute*	*salve*
secolo	*secondo*	*seguire*
sicuro	*signore*	*simpatico*
soldi	*sole*	*sotto*
subito	*sufficiente*	*suonare*

When the letter *s* is followed by *ca, co, cu, che, chi, f, p, qu,* or *t,* it has the same sound as the *s* sound in "rice," "house," "snake," and "sip."

Exercise 17: The Letter S

TRACK 21

Listen to Track 21. Repeat each word you hear.

scaffale	*schiavo*	*stadio*
sconsigliare	*scarpa*	*sfilata*
scultore	*scorso*	*specchio*
scheda	*scusa*	*squarcio*
schiacciare	*scherzo*	*stampare*
scale	*schiuma*	*sfortuna*
scoprire	*sfidare*	*spedire*
scuola	*spagnolo*	*squillare*
schema	*squadra*	*stendere*

When the letter *s* is doubled (*ss*), it has the same sound as the "s" sound in "rice," "house," "snake," and "sip."

Exercise 18: The Letter S

TRACK 22

Listen to Track 22. Repeat each word you hear.

aggressivo	*nessuno*	*pessimo*
cassa	*ortodosso*	*sassofono*
messa	*passa*	*stesso*

When the letter *s* is followed by the consonants *b, d, g, l, m, n, r,* or *v,* it has the same sound as the "z" sound in "rise," "wise," "lies," and "pies."

Exercise 19: The Letter S

TRACK 23

Listen to Track 23. Repeat each word you hear.

sbadigliare	*sbagliato*	*snodare*
sdegno	*sdraiato*	*sregolato*
sgarbato	*sgretolarsi*	*svizzera*
slogarsi	*slegare*	*snello*
smettere	*smalto*	*sviluppare*

When the letter *s* occurs between two vowels, it has the same sound as the "z" sound in "rise," "wise," "lies," and "pies."

Exercise 20: The Letter S

TRACK 24

Listen to Track 24. Repeat each word you hear.

casa	*misi*	*visito*
vaso	*peso*	*base*

When followed by –*ce*, –*ci*, –*cia*, –*cie*, –*cio*, or –*ciu*, the *s* is pronounced as the "sh" in the English words "ship," "shine," and "harsh."

TRACK 25

Exercise 21: The Letter S

Listen to Track 25. Repeat each word you hear.

pesce	*scelta*	*scena*
pesci	*scimmia*	*scintillare*
sciare	*sciarpa*	*scialle*
scienza	*scientifico*	*scienziato*
sciopero	*sciocco*	*sciogliersi*
sciupare	*prosciutto*	*asciugare*

The Letter Z

In Italian, the letter *z* has two sounds: like the "ts" in "cats," "bits," and "rots," and like the "ds" in "cards," "bids," and "rods."

The difference in pronunciation is mostly regional, but most Italians seem to prefer the "ds" sound.

TRACK 26

Exercise 22: The Letter Z

Listen to Track 26. Repeat each word you hear.

zaino	*zucchini*	*azzurro*
zucchero	*zuppa*	*gazzetta*
zero	*mezzogiorno*	

However, there are some exceptions. The words in the following exercise are invariably pronounced using the "ts" sound of "cats," "hats," and "mats."

Exercise 23: The Letter Z

Listen to Track 27. Repeat each word you hear.

pizza
mozzarella
pezzi
bellezza

Distinguishing between these two sounds can be difficult. In the meantime, try to be aware of the sounds whenever you hear Italian being spoken.

Exercise 24: The Letters S and Z

Listen to Track 28. Listen to the sentences, and then read them aloud, paying close attention to the pronunciation of the "s" and "z" sounds.

1. *Se non mi sbaglio, il prosciutto costa sessanta dollari al chilo.*

2. *Il pizzaiolo fa la pizza a mezzogiorno.*

3. *Ha scelto la sciarpa azzurra.*

4. *Le scarpe sono sullo scaffale.*

5. *Ha smesso di aspettare.*

6. *Ha messo lo zucchero nel caffè a colazione.*

7. *Legge La Gazzetta dello Sport per leggere le ultime notizie sulla sua squadra.*

8. *Sai se Stefano si è sposato con Isella?*

9. *Mi sono sbagliato.*

10. *La stazione di Salerno è sempre stata nello stesso posto.*

Part 5

Reflexive and Reciprocal Verbs, Possessives, and the Present Progressive

In Part 5 you will expand your knowledge of verbs in the present tense. Reflexive and reciprocal verbs are commonly used in Italian. Forming them isn't that tricky, and once you learn them you will see just how useful they are. You will study the present progressive and the possessive adjectives and pronouns.

Reflexive Verbs

Reflexive verbs are verbs whose action falls back on the subject. Reflexive verbs can be found in the *–are*, *–ere*, and *–ire* categories, so there is no difference in the endings of the conjugations. The only difference is in the addition of a reflexive pronoun, which is placed before the conjugated verb.

> *Io chiamo Giovanni.* **I call Giovanni. (non-reflexive)**

> *Io mi chiamo Giovanni.* **I call myself Giovanni. (My name is Giovanni.) (reflexive)**

You can recognize a reflexive verb by the reflexive pronoun (*si*) attached to the end of the infinitive.

Exercise 1: Reflexive or Not?

In the blank space, indicate whether the verb is reflexive or not.

1. *dormire* ....
2. *chiamarsi* ....
3. *mettere* ....
4. *parlare* ....
5. *vestirsi* ....
6. *mettersi* ....
7. *perdersi* ....
8. *addormentarsi* ....
9. *chiamare* ....
10. *perdere* ....

Conjugating reflexive verbs isn't tricky; the only difference between a reflexive and non-reflexive verb is the addition of the reflexive pronoun.

The reflexive pronoun must correspond with the subject of the verb and is placed immediately before the conjugated verb.

Subject Pronoun	Reflexive Pronoun
io	mi
tu	ti
lui	si
lei	si
Lei	si
noi	ci
voi	vi
loro	si
Loro	si

Exercise 2: Listening for Reflexive Verbs

TRACK 29

Listen to Track 29 and repeat the present-tense conjugations of three reflexive verbs: *alzarsi* (to get up), *mettersi* (to put on), and *divertirsi* (to have fun). Some useful reflexive verbs:

Italian	English
addormentarsi	to fall asleep
arrabbiarsi	to get angry
alzarsi	to get up
annoiarsi	to get bored
chiamarsi	to be called, to call oneself
divertirsi	to enjoy oneself
farsi la barba	to shave
fermarsi	to stop
innamorarsi	to fall in love
laurearsi	to graduate
lavarsi	to wash

Italian	English
mettersi	to put on
preoccuparsi	to worry
prepararsi	to prepare oneself
riposarsi	to rest
scusarsi	to apologize
sedersi	to sit down
sentirsi	to feel
sposarsi	to get married
svegliarsi	to wake up
vestirsi	to get dressed

Exercise 3: Picking Out the Reflexive Pronouns

Circle the reflexive pronouns in the following sentences. Be careful: Not all of the sentences have a reflexive verb.

1. *Giovanni si alza molto presto.*

2. *Elena ed io vogliamo svegliarci alle otto.*

3. *Io chiamo i miei amici quando voglio andare al cinema.*

4. *È importante divertirsi.*

5. *Vi fermate al bar a prendere un caffè?*

Exercise 4: Listening Comprehension

TRACK 30

Listen to the sentences in Track 30, repeating each one, and then listen again, writing each sentence you hear.

1. ....

2. ....

3. ....

4. ....

5. ....

Exercise 5: Conjugating Reflexive Verbs

Conjugate the reflexive verbs in the present tense.

	Svegliarsi	**Mettersi**	**Sentirsi**
io	....	....	....
tu	....	....	....
lui	....	....	....
lei	....	....	....
Lei	....	....	....
noi	....	....	....
voi	....	....	....
loro	....	....	....
Loro	....	....	....

Exercise 6: Change the Subject

Change the subject from *tu* to *Gianni e Teresa*.

1. *Quando vai ad una festa ti diverti molto.*

   ....

2. *Devi svegliarti presto perché dobbiamo partire prima delle nove.*

   ....

3. *Tu sei contento perché ti sposi l'anno prossimo.*

   ....

4. *Tu non ti senti molto bene.*

....

5. *Ti fermi al bar a bere qualcosa.*

....

Exercise 7: Reflexive or Not?

Choose the correct verb in the following sentences.

1. *Io (mi sveglio/sveglio) i bambini perché devono andare a scuola.*

2. *Noi (ci divertiamo/divertiamo) alla festa.*

3. *Tu (ti lavi/lavi) la macchina perché è sporca.*

4. *Giovanni (si mette/mette) una cravatta perché ha una riunione importante.*

5. *(Vi fermate/fermate) al bar a prendere un caffè?*

Reciprocal Construction Verbs

Reciprocal verbs express a reciprocal action. By definition, they must have a plural subject.

Noi ci vediamo ogni giorno. **We see each other every day.**

The action of the verb in the sentence above is reciprocal: "I see you every day, and you see me every day." = "We see each other every day."

The expression *ci vediamo* could have two possible meanings: "we see ourselves" (reflexive) or "we see each other" (reciprocal). The context of the conversation will help to clear up any misunderstandings.

Exercise 8: Reflexive or Reciprocal?

Are the following verbs reflexive or reciprocal? Or both? Circle your answer and check Appendix D to see if you're right.

1. *Mi sveglio alle otto ogni mattina.*   reflexive, reciprocal, both

2. *Io e Marco ci scriviamo ogni giorno.*   reflexive, reciprocal, both

3. *Mario e Angela si salutano.*   reflexive, reciprocal, both

4. *Non mi sento molto bene.*   reflexive, reciprocal, both

5. *Ci vediamo.*   reflexive, reciprocal, both

Exercise 9: Forming Reciprocal Verbs

Combine the two sentences to form a reciprocal construction.

1. *Io vedo Marco. Marco vede me.*

   ....

2. *Tu scrivi a tuo nonno. Tuo nonno scrive a te.*

   ....

3. *Massimo saluta Monica. Monica saluta Massimo.*

   ....

4. *Io mi sposo con Elena. Elena si sposa con me.*

   ....

5. *Tu vedi i tuoi amici ogni sabato sera. I tuoi amici ti vedono ogni sabato sera.*

   ....

Possessive Adjectives

Possessive adjectives express ownership or relationship with family members. As adjectives, they must agree in number and gender with the noun that they modify. Note the use of the definite article in the formation of the possessive adjective in Italian.

Subject	Possessor	Masculine Singular	Feminine Singular	Masculine Plural	Feminine Plural
io	my	*il mio*	*la mia*	*i miei*	*le mie*
tu	your (informal, singular)	*il tuo*	*la tua*	*i tuoi*	*le tue*
lui	his	*il suo*	*la sua*	*i suoi*	*le sue*
lei	her	*il suo*	*la sua*	*i suoi*	*le sue*
Lei	your (formal, singular)	*il Suo*	*la Sua*	*i Suoi*	*le Sue*
noi	our	*il nostro*	*la nostra*	*i nostri*	*le nostre*
voi	your (informal, plural)	*il vostro*	*la vostra*	*i vostri*	*le vostre*
loro	their	*il loro*	*la loro*	*i loro*	*le loro*
Loro	your (formal, plural)	*il Loro*	*la Loro*	*i Loro*	*le Loro*

Exercise 10: Using Possessive Adjectives

Translate the expressions into Italian. Don't forget the definite article!

1. my book ....

2. our car ....

3. your (plural, formal) friends ....

4. your (plural, informal) anniversary ....

5. his house ....

6. her computer ....

7. their family ....

8. your (singular, informal) friend ....

9. your (singular, formal) dog ....

10. his girlfriend ....

When used to express relationship to a family member, the definite article is omitted, except with the *loro* possessive form.

Mio fratello non viene alla festa. **My brother isn't coming to the party.**
Il loro fratello non viene alla festa. **Their brother isn't coming to the party.**
I miei fratelli non vengono alla festa. **My brothers are not coming to the party.**

Exercise 11: Article or No Article?

Choose the correct way of expressing possession.

1. *il mio libro/mio libro*

2. *la loro sorella/loro sorella*

3. *i nostri amici/nostri amici*

4. *il mio padre/mio padre*

5. *la Sua casa/Sua casa*

6. *i miei fratelli/miei fratelli*

7. *la vostra famiglia/vostra famiglia*

8. *la mia cugina/mia cugina*

9. *i nostri cugini/nostri cugini*

10. *il suo ragazzo/suo ragazzo*

Exercise 12: Number and Gender of Possessive Adjectives

Rewrite the sentence, substituting for the nouns that follow. Make all necessary changes to the possessive adjective.

1. *Io vedo mio fratello ogni giorno.*

    sorella ....

    amici ....

    cugini ....

    madre ....

    nonni ....

2. *I Loro amici non possono venire alla festa.*

    padre ....

    fratello ....

    sorelle ....

    amica ....

    zio ....

3. *La tua casa non è troppo grande.*

    macchina ....

    albero di Natale ....

    tavolo ....

    uffici ....

    case ....

4. *Sua zia fa le spese il sabato.*

    nipoti ....

    fidanzato ....

    figlie ....

    fratello ....

    amici ....

Exercise 13: Express in Italian

Translate the following sentences into Italian.

1. My brothers and his sister are good friends.

   ....

2. You can call my father this evening.

   ....

3. His uncle's name is Pietro.

   ....

4. My wife and I are going out with his friends on Saturday.

   ....

5. Do you know my cousins?

   ....

Exercise 14: Correct Use of Possessive Adjectives

Complete the sentences with the correct possessive pronoun.

1. *Noi invitiamo* (your brothers) .... *alla festa.*

2. (Your books) .... *sono nella stanza* (of your brother)

   ....

3. *Linda e Mario parlano* (to their dear aunt) ....

4. (His little brother) .... *è in Italia e* (his cousins)

   .... *sono in Francia.*

5. (Their uncle) .... *è molto ricco.* (Mine) .... *è povero.*

6. (Our Japanese car) .... *è dal meccanico.*

7. (Her daughters) .... *fanno un viaggio in Italia.*

8. (Your boyfriend) .... *non lavora il sabato e la domenica.*

9. *Oggi c'è una festa a casa* (of my relatives) ....

10. *Tu vedi* (all your cousins) ....

Possessive Pronouns

As you know, a pronoun takes the place of a noun. While possessive adjectives are always followed by a noun, possessive pronouns stand alone. Possessive pronouns are always preceded by the definite article, even when referring to a singular family member.

Possessive Pronoun	English Equivalent
il mio/la mia/i miei/le mie	mine
il tuo/la tua/i tuoi/le tue	yours (singular, informal)
il suo/la sua/i suoi/le sue	his or hers
il Suo/la Sua/i Suoi/le Sue	yours (singular, formal)
il nostro/la nostra/i nostri/le nostre	ours
il vostro/la vostra/i vostri/le vostre	yours (plural, informal)
il loro/la loro/i loro/le loro	theirs
il Loro/la Loro/i Loro/le Loro	yours (plural, formal)

Exercise 15: Identifying the Pronoun

Choose the correct translation for each pronoun.
1. *il suo* (mine, yours, his, theirs)
2. *i nostri* (hers, yours, mine, ours)
3. *la Loro* (theirs, his, ours, yours)
4. *il loro* (mine, yours, his, theirs)
5. *i tuoi* (his, ours, yours, theirs)
6. *le vostre* (ours, yours, mine, theirs)
7. *la Sua* (yours, his, hers, ours)
8. *le mie* (hers, yours, mine, ours)
9. *la nostra* (mine, ours, his, theirs)
10. *i loro* (theirs, hers, ours, yours)

Exercise 16: From Noun to Pronoun

Respond to the following sentences with a logical statement containing a possessive pronoun. For example, *Mio fratello ha ventidue anni. Il suo ha diciotto anni.* Answers will vary.

1. *I nostri amici escono ogni venerdì sera.*

   ....

2. *Le Loro sorelle non vanno in piscine sabato mattina.*

   ....

3. *La Loro macchina è una BMW.*

   ....

4. *Non so se il loro zio viene con noi.*

   ....

5. *I tuoi cugini non sono molto simpatici.*

   ....

6. *Le vostre amiche vogliono divertirsi.*

   ....

7. *Signora Savastano, c'è Sua figlia per favore?*

   ....

8. *Le mie penne sono sul tavolo.*

   ....

9. *Nostra zia è molto generosa.*

   ....

10. *Il mio cane non è molto intelligente.*

   ....

Exercise 17: Making a Sentence Negative

Rewrite each sentence as a negative statement. Pay close attention to the placement of *non* in relation to the reflexive pronoun.

1. *Ti diverti quando esci con i tuoi amici.*

   ....

2. *Ci siamo annoiati alla conferenza.*

   ....

3. *Mio padre si sente molto bene.*

   ....

4. *Mio fratello vuole sposarsi l'anno prossimo.*

   ....

5. *I miei amici si arrabbiano quando non voglio uscire.*

   ....

6. *Le tue sorelle si salutano dopo la festa.*

   ....

7. *Il loro zio vuole svegliarsi presto domani mattina.*

   ....

8. *Ci vediamo la settimana prossima.*

   ....

9. *Tu e Marianna vi preparate per il viaggio.*

   ....

10. *Mi addormento quando lui parla.*

    ....

Exercise 18: Working with Reflexive Verbs

Circle the words or letters that make the verb reflexive.

1. *I miei amici non vogliono svegliarsi presto.*

2. *Noi non riusciamo ad addormentarci perché c'è troppo rumore.*

3. *Ti alzi presto domani mattina?*

4. *Come si chiama suo fratello?*

5. *Mio padre si arrabbia quando lascio la porta aperta.*

6. *Ci divertiamo molto quando andiamo a casa sua.*

7. *Mi devo preparare per il viaggio.*

8. *Giovanni si innamora facilmente.*

9. *I ragazzi si annoiano a scuola.*

10. *Tu e Gabriella vi vedete spesso?*

Noun and Adjective Suffixes

A suffix is a group of letters attached to the end of a word to form a new word. In English, common suffixes are "–ly," used to change an adjective into an adverb ("happy" becomes "happily"), or "–ed," used to express the past tense of a verb ("like" becomes "liked"). In Italian, suffixes are commonly used at the ends of nouns and adjectives. There is no set of rules that tells you which suffixes can be used. The best way to learn them is to listen for them when native speakers are talking to.

Italian Noun	English Noun	Suffix	New Word	New Meaning
casa	house	–etta	casetta	little house
naso	nose	–one	nasone	big nose
sorella	sister	–ina	sorellina	little sister
tempo	weather	–accio	tempaccio	bad weather
parola	word	–accia	parolaccia	bad word
ragazzo	boy	–ino	ragazzino	little boy
cavallo	horse	–uccio	cavalluccio	toy horse

Exercise 19: Guess the Meaning

Circle the correct meaning of the noun.

1. *cavallino*   (young horse/big horse)
2. *pezzetto*   (big piece/small piece)
3. *doloretto*   (big pain/small pain)
4. *vestituccio*   (humble, cheap dress/elegant dress)
5. *chiesetta*   (cathedral/small church)

The Present Progressive

The present progressive is used to express an action in progress. Though the regular present tense could be used to express an action in progress, the use of the present tense to express a progressive action could lead to misunderstandings. As we know, *Io canto* could mean "I sing," "I do sing," or "I am singing" (progressive). To clear up any ambiguity, the progressive tense can be used.

The present progressive tense is formed by combining the present tense of the verb *stare* with the gerund form of the verb.

Exercise 20: Stare

Conjugate *stare* in the present tense.

io		*noi*	
tu		*voi*	
lui		*loro*	
lei		*Loro*	
Lei			

The gerund, which corresponds to verb + "–ing" in English (walking, talking, studying, etc.), is easy to form:

Verb	Gerund Ending	Gerund
parlare	–ando	*parlando*
mettere	–endo	*mettendo*
dormire	–endo	*dormendo*

Sto mangiando. **I am eating (at this very moment).**

Mio padre sta dormendo. **My father is sleeping (at this very moment).**

Exercise 21: Forming the Gerund

Transform the following infinitives into gerunds.

1. *cantare* ....
2. *perdere* ....
3. *telefonare* ....
4. *giocare* ....
5. *partire* ....

6. *vedere* ....
7. *aprire* ....
8. *scrivere* ....
9. *leggere* ....
10. *mangiare* ....

Exercise 22: From Present to Progressive

Transform the following sentences from the regular present tense to the present progressive tense.

1. *Guardo un film.*

    ....

2. *Mio fratello apre la finestra.*

    ....

3. *Telefoniamo ai nostri amici.*

    ....

4. *I tuoi amici giocano a tennis.*

    ....

5. *Il treno parte dalla stazione.*

    ....

6. *Che cosa scrivi?*

    ....

7. *Marco legge il giornale.*

    ....

8. *Tu e Lisa mangiate la pizza.*

    ....

9. *Noi corriamo.*

    ....

10. *Ascoltate la musica?*

    ....

TRACK 31

Exercise 23: Listening Comprehension

Listen to each sentence in Track 31 and repeat. Then indicate whether each sentence is in the regular present or the progressive tense.

1. present or progressive?
2. present or progressive?
3. present or progressive?
4. present or progressive?
5. present or progressive?
6. present or progressive?
7. present or progressive?
8. present or progressive?
9. present or progressive?
10. present or progressive?

Let's Practice

Test yourself. Try not to refer back to the grammatical explanations.

Exercise 24: Answering Questions

Answer the questions in complete sentences in Italian. Your answers will vary.

1. *A che ora ti svegli quando devi andare al lavoro?*

   ....

2. *A che ora ti alzi il sabato?*

   ....

3. *Che cosa ti metti quando hai freddo?*

   ....

4. *Ti diverti quando esci con i tuoi amici?*

....

5. *Ti annoi quando fai gli esercizi d'italiano?*

....

6. *Ti innamori facilmente?*

....

7. *Ti arrabbi quando i tuoi amici non telefonano?*

....

8. *A che ora ti addormenti la sera?*

....

9. *Come ti prepari per un lungo viaggio?*

....

10. *Vuoi riposarti questo weekend?*

....

11. *Prima di andare in ufficio, ti fermi a Starbucks per comprare un caffè?*

....

12. *Ti arrabbi facilmente?*

....

13. *Ti vesti in fretta ogni mattina?*

....

14. *Tu e i tuoi amici vi mandate molti messaggi elettronici?*

    ....

15. *Tu e i tuoi genitori vi parlate spesso?*

    ....

Exercise 25: Translation

Choose the correct translation.

1. *mi annoio* (she gets bored, we get bored, they get bored, I get bored)

2. *si sposano* (they are getting married, he is getting married, we are getting married, I am getting married)

3. *ti alzi* (I get up, he gets up, you get up, we get up)

4. *vi arrabbiate* (I get angry, you get angry, we get angry, they get angry)

5. *ci prepariamo* (they get ready, we get ready, I get ready, you get ready)

6. *mi scuso* (they apologize, we apologize, I apologize, she apologizes)

7. *vi vedete* (you see yourselves, you see each other, they see themselves, they see each other)

8. *si lava* (they wash up, we wash up, he washes up, I wash up)

9. *ci addormentiamo* (they fall asleep, you fall asleep, she falls asleep, we fall asleep)

10. *ti senti* (you feel, they feel, we feel, he feels)

Exercise 26: Changing the Subject

Rewrite the paragraph, changing the subjects accordingly.

Ogni giorno io mi alzo alle sette. Mi lavo e mi vesto velocemente: mi metto i jeans e una t-shirt e mi preparo per uscire. Torno a casa alle quattro e mi metto a studiare. La sera guardo la TV. Vado a letto alle dieci e mi addormento subito.

1. *tu*

   ....

   ....

   ....

   ....

2. *Marco*

   ....

   ....

   ....

   ....

3. *mio fratello ed io*

   ....

   ....

   ....

   ....

4. *tu e tua sorella*

   ....

   ....

   ....

   ....

5. *Giovanni e suo fratello*

   ....

   ....

   ....

Exercise 27: Translation Practice

Translate the questions into Italian, and then answer them in complete sentences in Italian.

1. What time do you wake up when you have to go to work?
   Domanda: ....

   ....

   Risposta: ....

   ....

2. What time do you get up on Saturdays?
   Domanda: ....

   ....

   Risposta: ....

   ....

3. What do you put on when you are cold?
   Domanda: ....

   ....

   Risposta: ....

   ....

4. How do you prepare yourself for a trip?
   Domanda: ....

   ....

   Risposta: ....

   ....

5. Do you have fun when you go out with your friends?
   Domanda: ....

   ....

Risposta: ....

....

6. Do you stop at a coffee shop before (*prima di*) going to your office?

Domanda: ....

....

Risposta: ....

....

7. Do you get angry when your friends don't call?

Domanda: ....

....

Risposta: ....

....

8. Do you fall in love easily?

Domanda: ....

....

Risposta: ....

....

9. Do you want to get married?

Domanda: ....

....

Risposta: ....

....

10. What time do you fall asleep at night?

Domanda: ....

....

Risposta: ....

....

11. Do you have lunch with your friends every now and then?

    Domanda: ....

    ....

    Risposta: ....

    ....

12. What do you do when you want to enjoy yourself on a Friday evening?

    Domanda: ....

    ....

    Risposta: ....

    ....

13. What do you put on when you have to go to an elegant restaurant?

    Domanda: ....

    ....

    Risposta: ....

    ....

14. How many times a week do you speak to your parents?

    Domanda: ....

    ....

    Risposta: ....

    ....

15. How many times a month do you eat in an elegant restaurant?

    Domanda: ....

    ....

    Risposta: ....

    ....

Exercise 28: Conjugation Practice

Conjugate the following infinitives in the present tense.

1. *arrabbiarsi*

   ....

   ....

   ....

2. *innamorarsi*

   ....

   ....

   ....

3. *mettersi*

   ....

   ....

   ....

Exercise 29: A Day in the Life

Write ten sentences describing your daily routine, using as many reflexive verbs as possible.

1. ....

2. ....

3. ....

4. ....

5. ....

6. ....

7. ....

8. ....

9. ....

10. ....

Exercise 30: The Present Progressive

Fill in the blank with the present progressive form of the verb in parentheses.

1. *Maria* ....(to wake up)

2. *I miei amici* .... *al ristorante in centro.* (to eat)

3. *Noi* .... *a tennis.* (to play)

4. *Mio fratello* .... *in bicicletta.* (to go)

5. *Io e mia sorella* .... *un caffè.* (to take)

6. *Tu e Massimo* .... *la porta del garage.* (to open)

7. *Simone e Alessio* .... *nella camera da letto?* (to study)

8. *Che cosa* .... *tu?* (to read)

9. *Il cameriere* .... *la minestra.* (to serve)

10. *Tutti i suoi amici* .... *la musica.* (to listen)

Pronunciation Exercise: The Letters C and G

In Italian, the letter *c* has two distinct sounds: like the hard "k" sound in the English word "key," and like the softer "ch" sound in "child." The letter *g* also has two distinct sounds: like the hard "g" sound of "garden," and like the softer "j" sound of the English word "jar."

TRACK 32

Exercise 31: The Letter C

Listen to Track 32. Repeat each word you hear.

1. *cameriere*
2. *amico*
3. *cura*
4. *che*
5. *chi*

The Italian *c* is pronounced as a hard "k" sound when it is followed by *a, o, u, he, hi.*

TRACK 33

Exercise 32: The Letter C

Listen to Track 33. Repeat each word you hear.

1. *cucinare*
2. *amici*
3. *cento*
4. *celebrare*
5. *ciao*

The Italian *c* is pronounced like the "ch" in "child" when it is followed by an *e* or *i.*

TRACK 34

Exercise 33: The Letter G

Listen to Track 34. Repeat each word you hear.

1. *gatto*
2. *gonfiare*
3. *guscio*
4. *ghetto*
5. *ghiaccio*
6. *grasso*

The Italian *g* is pronounced as a hard "g" sound when it is followed by *a, o, u, he, hi,* or *r*.

TRACK 35

Exercise 34: The Letter G

Listen to Track 35. Repeat each word you hear.

1. *gettare*
2. *genio*
3. *Gino*
4. *pagina*
5. *cugino*

The Italian *g* is pronounced like the "j" in "jar" when it is followed by an *e* or *i*.

Exercise 35: The Letters C and G

TRACK 36

Listen to the sentences on Track 36, and then read them aloud, paying close attention to the pronunciation of the *s* and *z* sounds.

1. *Gino mangia il formaggio.*

2. *Cento gatti giocano nel parco.*

3. *Come canta bene la zia Catia!*

4. *La cugina della mia amica non sa cucinare.*

5. *"Ecco il carpaccio!," dice il cameriere.*

6. *Ha messo lo zucchero nel caffè a colazione.*

7. *Chi mangia il gelato al cioccolato?*

8. *La città di Parigi è in Francia.*

9. *Si dice che si mangi bene in Germania.*

10. *Vai al cinema con Carlo?*

Part 6

Indirect and Direct Object Pronouns, Demonstrative Adjectives

In this section, you will look at indirect and direct objects, as well as some useful demonstrative adjectives. Many (not all) of the verbs that we have seen can take either a direct or indirect object. As with any noun, objects can be substituted with pronouns.

Direct Objects and Direct Object Pronouns

A direct object answers the question "Whom?" or "What?" in relation to the action of the verb. Take for example the sentence "John reads a book." The direct object in this sentence—a book—answers the question "What?" in relation to the action of the verb. In the sentence "I see John," the direct object—John—answers the question "Whom?" in relation to the action of the verb. Bear in mind that not all verbs take a direct object; only those that can perform an action on someone or something. These verbs are commonly referred to as transitive verbs. Intransitive verbs, on the other hand, cannot be followed by a direct object.

Exercise 1: Transitive or Intransitive?

Identify the following verbs as transitive (can take a direct object) or intransitive (cannot take a direct object).

1. *leggere* ....

2. *arrivare* ....

3. *restituire* ....

4. *mangiare* ....

5. *andare* ....

6. *bere* ....

7. *prendere* ....

8. *venire* ....

9. *offrire* ....

10. *partire* ....

Exercise 2: Identifying the Direct Object

Underline the direct objects in the following sentences. Be careful: Some of the sentences may not contain a direct object.

1. *Marco sta scrivendo una lettera ai suoi nonni.*

2. *Oggi a pranzo voglio mangiare un panino.*

3. *Il treno arriva alle otto alla stazione di Firenze.*

4. *Telefono all'agenzia di viaggi.*

5. *La mia amica parla italiano, francese, e russo.*

6. *Io e mia moglie abbiamo molti amici.*

7. *Tu conosci John?*

8. *I miei cugini non vogliono venire a cena domani sera.*

Exercise 3: Circling the Object

Circle the direct object in each sentence.

1. *Non voglio prendere il caffè dopo cena.*

2. *I ragazzi stanno ascoltando la musica.*

3. *Il postino porta la posta ogni giorno alle ore tredici.*

4. *I miei zii portano una torta a casa nostra stasera.*

5. *Tutti i miei amici sanno cantare le canzoni napoletane.*

6. *Tu suoni la chitarra.*

7. *Non so fare gli spaghetti alla carbonara.*

8. *Sto leggendo La Divina Commedia.*

9. *Io preferisco l'estate.*

10. *A che ora finisci i tuoi compiti?*

Exercise 4: Something's Not Right

Read the following paragraphs. You will notice a repetition of the direct object. Underline all of the direct objects in each paragraph.

1. *A colazione bevo il caffè con un po' di latte. Quando vado in ufficio bevo il caffè. Quando finisco di mangiare, bevo il caffè senza zucchero. Ogni tanto io bevo il caffè con un po' di anisetta. Il sabato sera vado con mia moglie a mangiare in un ristorante. Quando finiamo di mangiare beviamo il caffè.*

2. *Ogni giorno a pranzo mangio la pizza. A volte mangio la pizza con i funghi. A volte mangio la pizza con il salamino piccante. Mi piace mangiare la pizza quando esco con i miei amici, ma di solito loro non vogliono mangiare la pizza. Quando mangio la pizza bevo la birra.*

3. *Io leggo molti libri. Leggo i libri quando finisco di lavorare. Leggo i libri quando finisco di mangiare. Il sabato vado in una libreria e compro due o tre libri. A casa tengo i libri sugli scaffali. Mi piace leggere i libri.*

4. *Io scrivo molte lettere. Scrivo molte lettere agli amici in Italia. Scrivo poche lettere ai cugini a Londra. Scrivo lettere ogni giorno. Scrivo le lettere mentre bevo il caffè. Mando molte lettere ma non ricevo molte lettere. Non ricevo lettere perché gli amici non scrivono lettere.*

To avoid repeating the same word, we can use a direct object pronoun in the place of the direct object. There are two groups of direct object pronouns in Italian—those that precede the conjugated verb, and those that follow the conjugated verb (disjunctive pronouns). The following chart outlines the direct object pronouns that are placed before the conjugated verb in Italian.

Singular	*Plural*
mi (me)	*ci* (us)
ti (you)	*vi* (you)
lo (him, it)	*li* (them)
la (her, it)	*le* (them)
La (you [formal])	*Li, Le* (you [formal])

The second group of pronouns—the disjunctive pronouns—add emphasis. These pronouns are placed after the conjugated verb, or after a preposition.

Singular	Plural
me (me)	*noi* (us)
te (you)	*voi* (you)
lui (him)	*loro* (them)
lei (her)	*loro* (them)
Lei (you [formal])	*Loro* (you [formal])

Io lo vedo ogni giorno. **I see him (or it) every day.**
Io vedo lui ogni giorno. **I see him every day.**
Marco e Stefano non ci portano all'aeroporto. **Marco and Stefano aren't bringing us to the airport.**
Marco e Stefano non portano noi all'aeroporto. **Marco and Stefano aren't bringing us to the airport.**

When the sentence is negative (using the word *non*), the direct object pronoun is placed between the *non* and the conjugated verb.

Exercise 5: Picking Out the Direct Object Pronoun

Circle the direct object pronouns in the following sentences.

1. *Inviti i tuoi zii a cena.*

2. *Mi metto una cravatta quando vado a mangiare fuori.*

3. *Mio fratello ha una BMW.*

4. *Penso di comprare una casa in campagna.*

5. *Ricevo molte email dai miei amici.*

6. *Faccio un viaggio in Italia quest'estate.*

7. *Vado a trovare mio cugino in Italia.*

8. *Mio cugino studia storia dell'arte all'Università di Napoli.*

9. *Non frequenta tutte le lezioni.*

10. *Prendo il caffè a colazione tutte le mattine.*

Exercise 6: From Noun to Pronoun

Rewrite the sentences, substituting the direct object pronoun for the direct object.

1. *Io bevo la grappa.*

   ....

2. *Prendi il caffè con lo zucchero.*

   ....

3. *Vedo Marco ogni giorno.*

   ....

4. *Voglio conoscere Maria e Elena.*

   ....

5. *Gli studenti capiscono le lezioni.*

   ....

6. *Io leggo il libro.*

   ....

7. *Lui vuole vedere me e mia moglie.*

   ....

8. *Noi aspettiamo l'autobus.*

   ....

9. *Volete ascoltare la musica.*

   ....

10. *Maria conosce le studentesse.*

    ....

Exercise 7: Using Direct Object Pronouns

Rewrite each sentence, substituting a direct object pronoun for the direct object.

1. *Vado a prendere un caffè.*

   ....

2. *Sta scrivendo una lettera.*

   ....

3. *Marco non mangia la carne.*

   ....

4. *Tu e Luisa capite l'italiano.*

   ....

5. *Non voglio lasciare un messaggio.*

   ....

6. *Compro i biglietti domani mattina.*

   ....

7. *Mio padre beve il Chianti.*

   ....

8. *Vedo te e Maria.*

   ....

9. *Marco parla a me e a Giuseppe.*

   ....

10. *Porto Massimo e Simone alla festa.*

    ....

Exercise 8: Something's Not Right

Rewrite the following paragraphs, substituting a direct object pronoun for the direct objects where appropriate.

1. *A colazione bevo il caffè con un po' di latte. Quando vado in ufficio bevo il caffè. Quando finisco di mangiare, bevo il caffè senza zucchero. Ogni tanto bevo il caffè con un po' di anisetta. Il sabato sera vado con mia moglie a mangiare in un ristorante. Quando finiamo di mangiare beviamo il caffè.*

   ....

   ....

   ....

   ....

2. *Ogni giorno a pranzo mangio la pizza. A volte mangio la pizza con i funghi. A volte mangio la pizza con il salamino piccante. Mi piace mangiare la pizza quando esco con i miei amici, ma di solito loro non vogliono mangiare la pizza. Quando mangio la pizza bevo la birra.*

   ....

   ....

   ....

   ....

3. *Io leggo molti libri. Leggo i libri dopo il lavoro. Leggo i libri dopo cena. Il sabato vado in una libreria e compro due o tre libri. A casa tengo i libri sugli scaffali. Mi piace leggere i libri.*

   ....

   ....

   ....

   ....

4. *Io scrivo molte lettere. Scrivo lettere ai miei amici in Italia. Scrivo lettere ai cugini a Londra. Scrivo lettere ogni giorno. Scrivo lettere mentre bevo il caffè. Mando molte lettere, ma non ricevo molte lettere. Non ricevo lettere perché i miei amici non scrivono lettere.*

....

....

....

....

Indirect Objects and Indirect Object Pronouns

An indirect object answers the question "To what or whom?" or "For what or whom?" in relation to the action of the verb. Take, for example, the sentence "John gives the book to me." We've already seen the direct object in this sentence—a book. The indirect object—to me—answers the question "To whom?" in relation to the action of the verb.

Exercise 9: Finding the Indirect Object

Circle the indirect object in the following sentences.

1. *Do il libro al mio amico.*

2. *Puoi telefonare a mio padre stasera.*

3. *Non vuole chiedere soldi a suo padre.*

4. *Penso di regalare un orologio a mio fratello per il suo compleanno.*

5. *Mando molte email ai miei cugini in Italia.*

6. *Il pizzaiolo fa una pizza per il cliente.*

7. *Mando una lettera a lui.*

8. *Restituisco la penna a Lei.*

9. *Compro dei fiori per te e Maria.*

10. *Tommaso dice bugie a noi.*

The following chart outlines the indirect object pronouns in Italian.

Singular	Plural
mi (to/for me)	*ci* (to/for us)
ti (to/for you)	*vi* (to/for you)
gli (to/for him)	
le (to/for her)	*loro/gli* (to/for them)
Le (to/for you [formal])	*Loro* (to/for you [formal])

Like the direct object pronoun, the indirect object pronoun comes before the conjugated verb, except *loro/Loro,* which always follow the conjugated verb. Disjunctive pronouns can also be used in indirect object pronoun constructions. When used in an indirect object construction, the disjunctive pronoun is preceded by a preposition.

When the sentence is negative (using the word *non*), the indirect object pronoun is placed between *non* and the conjugated verb.

Gli parlo ogni giorno. **I speak to him every day.**

Parlo a lui ogni giorno. **I speak to him every day.**

Non le parlo mai. **I never speak to her.**

Non parlo mai a lei. **I never speak to her.**

Dico loro la verità. **I am telling them the truth.**

Dico la verità a loro. **I am telling them the truth.**

The following verbs require an indirect object in order to specify the recipient of the action of the verb. Note that the English equivalents of these verbs do not all require an indirect object:

Italian	English
chiedere/domandare	to ask
consigliare	to advise
dare	to give
dire	to say, to tell
insegnare	to teach
mandare	to send

Italian	English
mostrare	to show
offrire	to offer
portare	to bring
prestare	to lend
regalare	to give as a gift
restituire	to return (something to someone)
rispondere	to reply
scrivere	to write
spedire	to send
spiegare	to explain
telefonare	to telephone

Exercise 10: Use of Pronouns

Rewrite the sentences substituting an indirect object pronoun for the indirect object.

1. *Telefono a mia madre stasera.* ....

2. *Mando una lettera a mio fratello.* ....

3. *Non chiedo dei soldi a mio padre.* ....

4. *Tu e Maria restituite il libro a tuo zio.* ....

5. *Il professore spiega la regola agli studenti.* ....

6. *Non offriamo un caffè ai nostri amici.* ....

7. *Il bambino chiede aiuto a suo padre.* ....

8. *Giuseppe e Patrizia consigliano un film a noi.* ....

9. *Non presto la macchina a te.* ....

10. *Marcello dice le bugie ai suoi amici.* ....

Exercise 11: Using Indirect Object Pronouns

Rewrite each sentence, substituting an indirect object pronoun for the indirect object.

1. *Do consigli ai miei amici.*

   ....

2. *Presto la macchina a te.*

   ....

3. *Porto dei fiori a voi.*

   ....

4. *Martina dice le bugie a sua madre.*

   ....

5. *Telefono a Davide e Maria stasera.*

   ....

6. *Compro un regalo per mio fratello.*

   ....

7. *Voglio parlare a te e a Sara.*

   ....

8. *Signora Baldini, posso parlare con Lei?*

   ....

9. *Gli spaghetti al pomodoro piacciono a me.*

   ....

10. *A noi piace la pizzai.*

    ....

Double Verb Constructions with Object Pronouns

You have already seen some double verb constructions with the verbs *dovere*, *potere*, and *volere*. The sentence *Io voglio andare al cinema* (I want to go to the movies) is considered a double verb construction because two verbs are being used. The first verb (*voglio*, in this case) is conjugated, while the second is used in its infinitive form. When a double verb construction is used with either a direct object pronoun or an indirect object pronoun, the object pronoun can either precede the conjugated verb or attach to the end of the infinitive.

Noi vogliamo vederli stasera. **We want to see them this evening.**
Non li possiamo vedere stasera. **We can't see them this evening.**

Exercise 12: Double Verb Constructions with Pronouns

Answer the following questions in complete sentences in Italian. Substitute either a direct object pronoun or an indirect object pronoun for the direct or indirect object.

1. *Quando vuoi vedere le tue amiche?*

   ....

2. *Mi puoi telefonare stasera?*

   ....

3. *Vuoi bere la grappa quando finisci di mangiare?*

   ....

4. *Vuoi ascoltare la musica?*

   ....

5. *Ti piace ascoltare la musica classica?*

   ....

6. *A Stefano piace mangiare gli spaghetti alla carbonara?*

....

7. *Tu sai fare gli spaghetti alla carbonara?*

....

8. *Vuoi studiare i pronomi?*

....

9. *Quando vuoi fare gli esercizi sui pronomi?*

....

10. *Vuoi fare la colazione a casa mia?*

....

Exercise 13: Double Verb Constructions

Rewrite each sentence in the space provided using a double verb construction with *dovere*, *potere*, or *volere*, as in the example: *Ti telefono stasera* to *Devo telefonarti stasera.*

1. Faccio gli spaghetti stasera.

....

2. Marco chiede il conto.

....

3. Chi paga il conto?

....

4. Porti tuo fratello stasera.

....

5. Guardiamo la partita alle otto.

....

6. Parlo alla mia amica.

....

7. Vediamo i nostri amici stasera.

....

8. Tu e Marisa non mangiate la pizza?

....

9. Marco non ascolta suo padre.

....

10. Massimo telefona a Monica.

....

Double Object Pronouns

Up to now we have substituted a pronoun for either the direct or indirect object. As in English, in Italian it is possible to substitute for both pronouns. Take, for example, the sentence "I give the book to John." In English, we can substitute both a direct object pronoun and an indirect object pronoun for the objects in this sentence so that it becomes "I gave it to him." When both pronouns are used in a sentence in Italian, the indirect object pronoun always precedes the direct object pronoun, except when the indirect object pronoun *loro/Loro* is used. The following chart outlines the indirect/direct double object pronoun combinations.

Indirect Object Pronoun		*Direct Object Pronoun*		
	+*lo*	+*la*	+*li*	+*le*
mi	*me lo*	*me la*	*me li*	*me le*
ti	*te lo*	*te la*	*te li*	*te le*
gli/le	*glielo*	*gliela*	*glieli*	*gliele*
ci	*ce lo*	*ce la*	*ce li*	*ce le*

Indirect Object Pronoun		Direct Object Pronoun		
vi	ve lo	ve la	ve li	ve le
loro	lo…loro	la…loro	li…loro	le…loro
gli/le	glielo	gliela	glieli	gliele

(the indirect object pronoun *gli* can also be used to mean "to them")

It is possible to use a direct object with a reflexive verb as well. Take, for example, the sentence *Mi metto una cravatta*. This sentence is reflexive, since I am putting something on myself, and it also has a direct object—*una cravatta* (necktie). It is possible to use both a reflexive pronoun and a direct object pronoun in the same sentence. If we were to substitute a direct object pronoun for this sentence, we would have *Me la metto* (I put it on). The following chart outlines the reflexive/direct double object pronoun combinations.

Reflexive Pronoun		Direct Object Pronoun		
	+lo	+la	+li	+le
mi	me lo	me la	me li	me le
ti	te lo	te la	te li	te le
si	se lo	se la	se li	se le
ci	ce lo	ce la	ce li	ce le
vi	ve lo	ve la	ve li	ve le
si	se lo	se la	se li	se le

Exercise 14: Double Object Pronouns

Rewrite the following sentences, incorporating a double object pronoun.

1. *Do il libro agli studenti.*

    ....

2. *Io mi lavo la faccia ogni mattina.*

    ....

3. *Mandiamo molte e-mail a lei.*

    ....

4. *Mi presti la tua macchina?*

....

5. *Ti regaliamo una nuova penna.*

....

6. *Porto un regalo per i tuoi fratelli.*

....

7. *Noi ci mettiamo una nuova cravatta.*

....

8. *Preparano i dolci per me e per Lucia.*

....

9. *Mio padre dà la mancia al cameriere.*

....

10. *Ti scrivo le poesie.*

....

When using double construction verbs, you can either put the double object pronouns before the conjugated verb or attach them to the end of the infinitive. When attached to the end of the infinitive, the pronouns combine to form one word.

> *Te li do domani.* **I will give them to you tomorrow.**
> *Posso darteli domani.* **I can give them to you tomorrow.**

Exercise 15: Double Object Constructions

Rewrite the sentence in the space provided using a double verb construction with *dovere, potere,* or *volere,* and a double object pronoun, as in the example: *Ti do il libro stasera* to *Devo dartelo stasera.*

1. Resituisco la penna a te.

....

2. Do la ricetta al farmacista.

....

3. Mostro i libri ai clienti.

....

4. Pietro offre un caffè a me e a Tommaso.

....

5. Loro portano la torta a mia madre.

....

6. Io e Gabriella spediamo i pacchi a te e a tuo fratello.

....

7. Ti consiglio un buon film.

....

8. Eugenio regala l'orologio a suo nipote.

....

9. Non chiedo soldi a mio padre.

....

10. Marcello chiede aiuto a te e a Michele.

....

Demonstrative Adjectives

A demonstrative adjectives indicates a particular person or object. In English, the demonstrative adjectives are "this," "these," "that," and "those." "This" and "these" are used when the person or object is in close proximity to the speaker. "That" and "those" are used to point to a person or an object distant from the speaker. Think about the meaning of the sentence "I like this car, but I don't like that one." You are probably standing closer to "this" car than you are to "that" car. Like all adjectives in Italian, the demonstrative adjectives *quello* ("that") and *questo* ("this") must agree in number and gender with the nouns they modify. Remember that as adjectives, *quello* and *questo* always precede the nouns that they modify.

The adjective *quello*, like the adjective *bello,* has seven possible endings, all of which are similar in structure to the endings of the definite article:

il libro	the book
*que**l** libro*	that book
l'amico	the (male) friend
quell'amico	that (male) friend
***lo** studente*	the (male) student
*quel**lo** studente*	that (male) student
***la** ragazza*	the girl
*quel**la** ragazza*	that girl
***le** ragazze*	the girls
*quel**le** ragazze*	those girls
l'amica	the (female) friend
quell'amica	that (female) friend
***i** libri*	the books
*que**i** libri*	those books
***gli** studenti*	the students
*que**gli** studenti*	those students

Exercise 16: Practicing with Quello

Provide the correct form of *quello*.

1. .... *uomini stanno chiaccherando un po' troppo.*

2. *Quando penso a* .... *anni, mi viene la nostalgia.*

3. *Mi piace tantissimo* .... *nuova macchina.*

4. *Vuole comprare* .... *studio in via Panzani.*

5. *Non ho ancora visto* .... *film.*

6. .... *pizze sono buone.*

7. *A mia moglie piacciono* .... *fiori.*

8. *Luigino sta parlando con* .... *suo amico.*

9. *Tu conosci* .... *ragazze?*

10. .... *autobus si ferma davanti alla biblioteca?*

The adjective *questo* has five forms: *questo, questa, quest', questi, queste:*

Questo ragazzo è simpatico. **This boy is nice.**
Questa ragazza è simpatica. **This girl is nice.**
Vado in Italia quest'anno. **I am going to Italy this year.**
Questi ragazzi fanno troppo rumore. **These boys are making too much noise.**
Queste ragazze si annoiano facilmente. **These girls get bored easily.**

Exercise 17: Practicing with Questo

Provide the correct form of *questo*.

1. .... *ragazzi sono antipatici.*

2. *Pensiamo di andare a Venezia* .... *estate.*

3. *Mi piace tantissimo* .... *nuova macchina.*

4. *Non voglio leggere* .... *libro.*

5. *Ho già visto* .... *film.*

6. *Non posso mangiare* .... *lasagne.*

7. *A mia moglie piacciono* .... *fiori.*

8. *Non facciamo un viaggio* .... *anno.*

9. *Tu conosci* .... *ragazza?*

10. .... *autobus si ferma davanti alla biblioteca?*

Exercise 18: Translation Exercise

Translate the following sentences into Italian.

1. He is buying those beautiful flowers for his wife.

   ....

2. He wants to go to Rome this summer.

   ....

3. These books are too heavy.

   ....

4. I have too many appointments this week.

   ....

5. Those Italian movies are very interesting.

   ....

6. I can't drink this beer because it is too warm.

   ....

7. Those men are talking about politics.

   ....

8. I want to see that movie with my father.

   ....

9. These children get bored too easily.

   ....

10. That idea is very interesting.

    ....

Questo and *quello* can also be used as pronouns. As pronouns, they must agree in number and in gender with the nouns they replace. As pronouns, *questo* and *quello* each have four forms: *questo, questa, questi, queste* and *quello, quella, quelli, quelle*. Following are some examples of *questo* and *quello* used as pronouns.

*Queste **(adjective)** scarpe sono troppo strette ma quelle **(pronoun)** mi stanno benissimo.*
*Quei **(adjective)** ragazzi sono buoni ma quelli **(pronoun)** sono cattivi.*

Exercise 19: This and That

Finish the sentences with the correct form of the pronoun *questo* or *quello*, following the example.

Questo ragazzo è alto ma quello è basso.

1. *Queste signore sono italiane, ma* ....

2. *Quell'uomo è ricco, ma* ....

3. *Questi ragazzi studiano l'italiano, ma* ....

4. *Queste idee sono poco chiare, ma* ....

5. *Quei film sono noiosi, ma* ....

6. *Quegli studenti sono pigri, ma* ....

7. *Questa pizza è calda, ma* ....

8. *Quelli grigi sono brutti, ma* ....

9. *Questo ragazzo legge il giornale, ma* ....

10. *Quel libro è interessante, ma* ....

Months and Days

The months of the year are presented here as a vocabulary exercise. You will certainly notice some similarities between the Italian words and their English counterparts (*marzo* = March). Remember that in Italian the months of the year are not capitalized.

I mesi	The months
gennaio	January
febbraio	February
marzo	March
aprile	April
maggio	May
giugno	June
luglio	July
agosto	August
settembre	September
ottobre	October
novembre	November
dicembre	December

In English, when we want to express the date, we use ordinal numbers—February 21st, March 23rd, October 25th, etc. In Italian, only the first day of the month is expressed with an ordinal number (*il primo luglio* = July 1st); otherwise, use cardinal numbers preceded by the definite article. Do you notice a pattern in the following year expressions?

milleottocento	**1800**
millenovecento	**1900**
millenovecentosettantacinque	**1975**
millenovecentottanta	**1980**
duemila	**2000**

Exercise 20: Days and Dates

Fill in dates for the following holidays.

1. *Il giorno di San Valentino è* ....
2. *Il giorno di Natale è* ....
3. *Il mio compleanno è* ....
4. *Il giorno della Festa della mamma è* ....
5. *Il giorno dell'indipendenza americana è* ....

Exercise 21: Answering Questions

Answer the questions in complete sentences in Italian.

1. Qual'è la data di oggi?

   ....

2. Quand'è il tuo compleanno?

   ....

3. Quand'è il primo giorno d'estate?

   ....

4. Quand'è il Giorno del ringraziamento?

....

5. Quand'è Capodanno?

....

Seasons and Weather

Here is some useful vocabulary for talking about the weather and the seasons. Bear in mind that many of these expressions are idiomatic and do not translate literally from Italian to English.

Useful Weather Expressions

Che tempo fa?	How is the weather?
Fa bel tempo.	The weather is nice.
Fa brutto tempo.	The weather is bad.
Fa caldo.	It is hot.
Fa freddo.	It is cold.
Fa fresco.	It is cool.
Piove.	It is raining.
Nevica.	It is snowing.
Tira vento.	It is windy.
C'è sole	It is sunny.
C'è nebbia.	It is foggy.
È nuvoloso.	It is cloudy.
È sereno.	It is clear.
la pioggia	the rain
la neve	the snow
il vento	the wind
primavera	Spring
estate	Summer
inverno	Winter
autunno	Fall

Exercise 22: The Weather and the Seasons

Listen to Track 37. Repeat each question aloud. Listen to the track again, and then write each question down. After you have written each question, answer them in complete sentences in Italian.

1. *Domanda:* ....
   ....

   Risposta: ....
   ....

2. *Domanda:* ....
   ....

   Risposta: ....
   ....

3. *Domanda:* ....
   ....

   Risposta: ....
   ....

4. *Domanda:* ....
   ....

   Risposta: ....
   ....

5. *Domanda:* ....
   ....

   Risposta: ....
   ....

Let's Practice

Exercise 23: More Practice with Double Object Pronouns

Rewrite the following sentences, incorporating a double object pronoun.

1. *Do il libro agli studenti.*

   ....

2. *Mandiamo un'email a lei.*

   ....

3. *Ti regaliamo una nuova penna.*

   ....

4. *Noi ci mettiamo una cravatta.*

   ....

5. *Luigino sta portando la mancia al cameriere.*

   ....

Exercise 24: Indirect Object or Direct Object?

Substitute either the indirect or direct object pronoun.

1. *Noi leggiamo il libro.*

   ....

2. *Voi parlate ai vostri amici.*

   ....

3. *La ragazza compra una pizza.*

   ....

4. *Gino telefona a sua madre.*

   ....

Exercise 25: The Months

Without looking back, give the equivalent in Italian.

1. January ....

2. February ....

3. March ....

4. April ....

5. May ....

6. June ....

7. July ....

8. August ....

9. September ....

10. October ....

11. November ....

12. December ....

Exercise 26: More on the Adjective Quello

Give the correct form of the adjective *quello*.

1. .... *libro è interessante.*

2. .... *libri sono interessanti.*

3. .... *studente è intelligente.*

4. .... *studenti sono intelligenti.*

5. .... *amica è studiosa.*

6. .... *amiche sono studiose.*

7. .... *ragazza è simpatica.*

8. .... *ragazze sono simpatiche.*

Exercise 27: More on the Adjective Questo

Give the correct form of the adjective *questo.*

1. .... *libro è interessante.*

2. .... *libri sono interessanti.*

3. .... *amico è studioso.*

4. .... *amica è studiosa.*

5. .... *ragazza è simpatica.*

6. .... *ragazze sono simpatiche.*

Exercise 28: Answering Questions

Answer the questions in complete sentences in Italian.

1. *Qual è la data di oggi?*

....

2. *Che giorno è oggi?*

....

3. *Qual è la data di domani?*

....

4. *In che mese siamo?*

....

5. *In che mese è il tuo compleanno?*

....

6. *Che tempo fa oggi?*

....

7. *Quand'è il giorno dell'indipendenza?*

....

8. *Quand'è Halloween?*

....

9. *Qual è l'ultimo giorno dell'anno?*

....

10. *Quale stagione preferisci? Perché?*

....

Exercise 29: Translation Exercise

Translate the following sentences into Italian.

1. Today is April first.

....

2. It is July 14th, 2007.

....

3. I have been living here since March 3, 2000.

....

4. Next Tuesday is the first day of spring.

    ....

5. It rains a lot in Boston in April.

    ....

Pronunciation Exercise: The Letters N and GN

In Italian, the letter *n* is pronounced like the "n" in the English word "nose." When the *n* is doubled—as in *penna,* for example—the "n" sound is slightly lengthened.

Exercise 30: Pronunciation of the Letter N

TRACK 38

Listen to Track 38. Repeat each word.

naso	*niente*	*nubile*
Natale	*nipote*	*numero*
nevicare	*notturno*	
nebbia	*notte*	

Exercise 31: Pronunciation of the Letter N

TRACK 39

Listen the Track 39 and repeat each word.

pena	*sano*	*noni*
penna	*sanno*	*nonni*
pagano	*mano*	
pagheranno	*fanno*	

The combination *gn* in Italian is similar to the "ny"/"ni" sounds in the English words "canyon" and "onion." Practice saying these two words aloud, focusing on the position of the tongue when vocalizing the "ny"/"ni" sounds.

TRACK 40

Exercise 32: Pronunciation of the Letters GN

Listen to Track 40 and repeat each word.

gnocchi	campagna	bisogno
Spagna	ognuno	montagna
signora	magnifico	
compagno	sogno	

TRACK 41

Exercise 33: Pronunciation of the Letters N and GN

Listen to Track 41. Repeat each sentence.

1. *Mangio gli gnocchi alla panna.*

2. *Sanno che sono sani e che hanno nove anni.*

3. *John è del Montana. Abita in cima a una montagna.*

4. *Fanno compagnia ai nonni.*

5. *Ognuno ha bisogno di una nuova macchina.*

Part 7

The Impersonal *Si*, *Piacere*, Commands

Part 7 examines some grammatical points essential to developing fluency in the language.

The Impersonal Si Construction

While in English impersonal statements are often preceded by the impersonal subjects "one", "they", or "people", Italian uses the pronoun *si* followed by the third-person singular form of the verb. The impersonal subject is represented by the particle *si*:

Si mangia bene in quel ristorante. **One eats well in that restaurant.**

If the sentence contains a direct object, Italian uses the pronoun *si* followed by the third-person singular form of the verb (when the sentence has a singular direct object) or the third-person plural form of the verb (when the sentence has a plural direct object). This construction implies the passive voice:

Si parlano italiano e francese in Svizzera. **Italian and French are spoken in Switzerland.**

Exercise 1: Impersonal or Passive Voice

Indicate whether the sentences imply an impersonal subject (one, you, they) or the passive voice.

1. *In Italia si parla italiano.* ....

2. *Si deve fare attenzione!* ....

3. *Si dice che pioverà domani.* ....

4. *Non si può fumare nei luoghi pubblici.* ....

5. *Si bevono le birre inglesi in quel locale.* ....

6. *Si parlano quattro lingue in Svizzera.* ....

7. *Si spende poco e si mangia bene in quel ristorante.* ....

8. *Si prevede un'estate calda.* ....

9. *Si studia l'italiano all'università.* ....

10. *Si comprano oggetti usati in quel negozio.* ....

Exercise 2: Translation Exercise

Translate the sentences in Exercise 1 from Italian to English. Remember that the impersonal subjects—one, you, or they—can be used for those sentences in which an impersonal subject is implied.

1. ....

2. ....

3. ....

4. ....

5. ....

6. ....

7. ....

8. ....

9. ....

10. ....

Exercise 3: From Personal to Impersonal

Restate the sentences using the impersonal *si* construction.

1. *Se studi molto, impari molto.*

   ....

2. *Dicono che nevicherà stasera.*

   ....

3. *Andiamo a teatro stasera?*

   ....

4. *Spendiamo poco in quel ristorante.*

   ....

5. *Dicono che Roma sia caotica.*

....

6. *Devi fare attenzione!*

....

7. *Non potete fare così.*

....

8. *Scusi, non può fumare qui.*

....

9. *Mangiamo molto bene in quel ristorante.*

....

10. *Partono alle otto.*

....

Exercise 4: From Active to Passive Voice

Restate the sentences in the passive voice.

1. *Vendiamo la macchina.*

....

2. *Beviamo i vini italiani.*

....

3. *Dici la verità.*

....

4. *Spendiamo tutti i soldi.*

....

5. *Dicono le bugie.*

....

6. *Fanno la pizza in quel ristorante.*

....

7. *Non dovete mangiare gli spinaci.*

   ....

8. *Spiegano le regole del gioco.*

   ....

9. *Mangi gli spaghetti alla carbonara.*

   ....

10. *Vendono libri usati.*

   ....

Exercise 5: Impersonal or Passive?

Circle either the impersonal or passive voice construction.

1. *Si dice che sia vero.*

   ....

2. *Si legge il giornale.*

   ....

3. *Si vendono macchine usate.*

   ....

4. *Si spendono tanti soldi.*

   ....

5. *Si dicono le bugie.*

   ....

6. *Si accetta la carta di credito.*

   ....

7. *Non si ha più pazienza.*

   ....

8. *Non si può lasciare la macchina davanti alla stazione.*

   ....

9. *Se si vuole imparare, si deve studiare.*

....

10. *Si affittano camere.*

....

When the impersonal *si* construction is followed by an adjective, the adjective must have a masculine plural ending, as in the following example:

Quando si è stanchi, non si deve guidare. **When you're tired, you shouldn't drive.**

Exercise 6: The Impersonal Si with Adjectives

Rewrite the sentences using the impersonal *si* construction with an adjective and making all other necessary changes.

1. *Quando sei giovane non hai molte preoccupazioni.*

....

2. *Quando sei ricco non sei sempre felice.*

....

3. *Quando sei stanco non puoi lavorare.*

....

4. *Quando sei triste non ragioni.*

....

5. *Quando sei onesto dici la verità.*

....

Reflexive verbs can be used in both impersonal and passive constructions. When a reflexive verb is used in an impersonal or passive construction, it must be prededed by *ci si*, as opposed to simply *si* for non reflexive verbs.

Ci si veste in fretta. **One dresses in a hurry.**

TRACK 42

Exercise 7: Identifying and Transforming Reflexive Verbs

Listen to each sentence in Track 42 and repeat. Then listen again, write each sentence, and circle the reflexive verb. After identifying each reflexive verb, write the sentence in either the impersonal or passive voice.

1. ....

   ....

2. ....

   ....

3. ....

   ....

4. ....

   ....

5. ....

   ....

6. ....

   ....

7. ....

   ....

8. ....

   ....

9. ....

   ....

10. ....

   ....

The Verb Piacere

Piacere ("to please," often mistakenly translated as "to like") is irregular. Keep in mind that English and Italian have different ways of expressing the notion of liking and not liking. In English, we say "I like pizza." In Italian, we say, *Mi piace la pizza,* literally "Pizza pleases me." Notice that the direct object in the English sentence—pizza—becomes the subject in Italian, and that the subject of the English sentence—I—becomes the indirect object (to me) in Italian. *Piacere* is most often used in its third-person singular (*piace*) and plural (*piacciono*) forms; a singular subject requires the singular form of the verb, and a plural subject requires a plural form of the verb.

Exercise 8: Identifying the Subject

Circle the subject in each sentence.

1. *Mi piace Michele.*

2. *Ti piacciono le birre irlandesi?*

3. *A Mario piace la pizza.*

4. *A Giovanni e Angela piace cucinare.*

5. *Vi piacciono i film di Roberto Benigni.*

6. *A Maria piacciono loro.*

7. *A loro piace Maria.*

8. *Gli piacciono i miei amici.*

9. *Al gatto piace giocare con lo spago.*

10. *A voi piacciono i biscotti della nonna.*

Exercise 9: **Piace or Piacciono?**

Choose the correct form of the verb *piacere*—*piace* or *piacciono*—in the following sentences.

1. *Mi (piace/piacciono) gli spaghetti al pomodoro.*
2. *Ti (piace/piacciono) leggere?*
3. *A Mario (piace/piacciono) i racconti di Alberto Moravia.*
4. *Ai miei genitori (piace/piacciono) andare a teatro.*
5. *Non mi (piace/piacciono) il tuo atteggiamento.*
6. *Ai nostri amici (piace/piacciono) i vostri amici.*
7. *Ti (piace/piacciono) i vini italiani?*
8. *Mi (piace/piacciono) l'arrosto di vitello.*
9. *Non le (piace/piacciono) la tua fidanzata.*
10. *Ci (piace/piacciono) le lasagne della nonna.*

Exercise 10: **Sentence Building**

In English, rearrange the sentences from subject + verb + direct object to subject + verb + indirect object. Doing so will make translating the sentences in Exercise 11 much easier. Here's an example:

I like you. > You are pleasing to me.

1. We like pasta.

   ....

2. You and John like the movie.

   ....

3. We like to go out on Friday nights.

   ....

4. He likes her.

   ....

5. But she doesn't like him.

   ....

6. I like all of Bob Dylan's songs.

   ....

7. They like their professor.

   ....

8. My grandparents like to take walks.

   ....

9. Their uncle does not like to work.

   ....

10. My brother's kids like ice cream.

    ....

11. We like your friends.

    ....

Exercise 11: Translation Exercise

Translate the restructured sentences from Exercise 10 into Italian.

1. ....

2. ....

3. ....

4. ....

5. ....

6. ....

7. ....

8. ....

9. ....

10. ....

11. ....

Exercise 12: Logical Endings

Provide a logical ending to each statement using the verb *piacere*, as in the example:

Mio fratello non va al concerto, perché non gli piace la musica classica.
My brother isn't going to the concert because he doesn't like classical music.

1. *Mia madre non va alla festa, perché…*

   ....

2. *I miei genitori non vengono a cena, perché…*

   ....

3. *Telefoni a Gabriella, perché…*

   ....

4. *Mangi al ristorante stasera, perché…*

   ....

5. *Michele e Maria vanno in treno, perché…*

   ....

6. *Non voglio parlare con Alberto, perché…*

   ....

7. *Non abbiamo voglia di studiare, perché…*

   ....

8. *Pietro vuole comprare una nuova cravatta, perché...*

....

9. *Tu e Bruno non preparate la cena, perché...*

....

10. *Non mangiamo al ristorante cinese, perché...*

....

Exercise 13: Likes and Dislikes—Informal

How would you ask whether your friend likes the following things?

1. *le lasagne*

....

2. *sciare*

....

3. *il tiramisù*

....

4. *i film di Roberto Rossellini*

....

5. *il vino rosso*

....

Exercise 14: Likes and Dislikes—Formal

How would you ask your elderly neighbor if he or she likes the following things?

1. *le lasagne*

....

2. *sciare*

....

3. *il tiramisù*

....

4. *i film di Roberto Rossellini*

....

5. *il vino rosso*

....

The Verb Mancare

Mancare (literally "to be lacking," but figuratively translates as "to miss" in English) has a structure similar to that of the verb *piacere*. In English, we say, "I miss my brother." In Italian, this sentiment is expressed by saying "My brother is lacking to me." It sounds awkward, but that's the way it's done. The verb *mancare* is conjugated like any other first conjugation verb that ends in *–care*. Try to remember the present tense conjugation as you complete Exercise 15.

Exercise 15: Conjugating Mancare

Conjugate the verb *mancare* in the present tense.

io   ....

tu   ....

lui/lei/Lei   ....

noi   ....

voi   ....

loro/Loro   ....

Exercise 16: Sentence Building

In English, rearrange the sentences from subject + verb + direct object to subject + verb + indirect object. Doing so will make translating the sentences in Exercise 17 much easier. For example:

I miss John. > John is lacking to me.

1. We miss our friends.

....

2. You and John miss your uncle.

....

3. I miss my father.

....

4. He misses her.

....

5. But she doesn't miss him.

....

6. They miss us.

....

7. I miss you and Michele.

....

8. My grandparents miss us.

....

9. They miss their uncle.

....

10. My brother misses my sister.

....

Exercise 17: Translation Exercise

Translate the restructured sentences from Exercise 16 into Italian.

1. ....

2. ....

3. ....

4. ....

5. ....

6. ....

7. ....

8. ....

9. ....

10. ....

Commands with Regular Verbs

Commands, or imperatives, are used to give orders or advice and, when written, are usually followed by an exclamation point. Command forms are limited mostly to the second-person subjects, and can be both formal and informal, though commands can also work with the *noi* form in Italian, as in *Mangiamo!* (Let's eat!). Look at the table below. What similarities and differences do you notice?

Present tense of mangiare	*Command of* mangiare
(io) mangio	---
(tu) mangi	*Mangia!*
(Lei) mangia	*Mangi!*
(noi) mangiamo	*Mangiamo!*
(voi) mangiate	*Mangiate!*
(Loro) mangiano	*Mangino!*

Forming commands can be tricky, because in some cases the command form of a verb looks very similar to its present tense. In some cases, affirmative commands differ from negative commands. There are many possible combinations.

Affirmative *tu* (you, singular, informal)	Negative *tu* (you, singular, informal)
Affirmative *Lei* (you, singular, formal)	Negative *Lei* (you, singular, formal)
Affirmative *noi* (us)	Negative *noi* (us)
Affirmative *voi* (you, plural, informal)	Negative *voi* (you, plural, informal)
Affirmative *Loro* (you, plural, formal)	Negative *Loro* (you, plural, formal)

We will work first with the affirmative *tu, noi,* and *voi* forms of regular verbs.

parlare	ripetere	partire	pulire
(tu)Parla!	Ripeti!	Parti!	Pulisci!
(noi)Parliamo!	Ripetiamo!	Partiamo!	Puliamo!
(voi)Parlate!	Ripetete!	Partite!	Pulite!

Exercise 18: Forming Informal Commands

Give the *tu, noi,* and *voi* forms of the following regular verbs.

ascoltare

(tu) ....

(noi) ....

(voi) ....

prendere

(tu) ....

(noi) ....

(voi) ....

dormire

(tu) ....

(noi) ....

(voi) ....

finire

(tu) ....

(noi) ....

(voi) ....

Exercise 19: Your New Coworker

TRACK 43

Listen to Track 43. Your new coworker asks for your advice to help him get acclimated to his new surroundings. Once you've listened to each question, listen again and write each question down. Then respond to his questions with an affirmative *tu* command, as in the example:

Dove posso mangiare? Mangia al ristorante Culinary Affair!

1. ....

2. ....

3. ....

4. ....

5. ....

Exercise 20: Now in the Plural

Give the same commands to two new coworkers. You will use the affirmative *voi* form.

1. ....

2. ....

3. ....

4. ....

5. ....

The following table shows the forms of the affirmative *Lei* (you, singular, formal) and *Loro* (you, plural, formal) commands:

parlare	ripetere	partire	pulire
(Lei)Parli!	Ripeta!	Parta!	Pulisca!
(Loro)Parlino!	Ripetano!	Partano!	Puliscano!

Exercise 21: Forming Formal Commands

Give the *Lei* and *Loro* forms of the following regular verbs.

ascoltare

(Lei) ....

(Loro) ....

prendere

(Lei) ....

(Loro) ....

dormire

(Lei) ....

(Loro) ....

finire

(Lei) ....

(Loro) ....

Exercise 22: Your New Neighbor

Listen to Track 44. Your new neighbor asks for your advice to help her get acclimated to her new surroundings. Once you've listened to each question, listen again and write each question down. Then respond to her questions with an affirmative *Lei* command, as in the example:

Dove posso comprare un giornale? Compri il giornale all'edicola!

1. ....

2. ....

3. ....

4. ....

5. ....

Exercise 23: Now in the Plural

Give the same commands to two new neighbors. You will use the affirmative *Loro* form.

1. ....

2. ....

3. ....

4. ....

5. ....

The negative *tu* command is formed by the negative word *non* + infinitive, as in the following example:

Affirmative tu Command   **Negative tu command**

Mangia!   *Non mangiare!*

All other forms (*Lei, noi, voi, Loro*) are made by placing the negative word *non* before the regular command forms, as in the following chart:

Affirmative	*Negative*
(tu)Mangia!	Non mangiare!
(Lei)Mangi!	Non mangi!
(noi)Mangiamo!	Non mangiamo!
(voi)Mangiate!	Non mangiate!
(Loro)Mangino!	Non mangino!

Exercise 24: From Affirmative to Negative

TRACK 45

Listen to the commands as spoken by the speaker in Track 45. Repeat each command, then listen again and write each command. Rewrite the commands in the second space, changing them from the affirmative *tu* commands to the negative *tu* commands.

1. *Compra il giornale!*

   ....

   ....

2. *Metti le chiavi sul tavolo!*

   ....

   ....

3. *Porta tuo fratello a scuola!*

   ....

   ....

4. *Finisci i tuoi compiti!*

   ....

   ....

5. *Dormi!*

   ....

   ....

6. *Bevi il caffè!*

   ....

   ....

7. *Presta la macchina a tuo fratello!*

   ....

   ....

8. *Sveglia i bambini alle otto!*

   ....

   ....

9. *Prendi quel libro!*

   ....

   ....

Exercise 25: Forming Commands

How would you give the following commands?

1. Negative *tu* command of the verb *pulire*

   ....

2. Affirmative *noi* command of the verb *leggere*

   ....

3. Negative *Loro* command of the verb *parcheggiare*

   ....

4. Negative *voi* command of the verb *lasciare*

   ....

5. Affirmative *tu* command of the verb *ascoltare*

   ....

6. Negative *noi* command of the verb *aspettare*

   ....

7. Affirmative *Loro* command of the verb *sentire*

    ....

8. Affirmative *Lei* command of the verb *prendere*

    ....

9. Negative *Lei* command of the verb *parlare*

    ....

Commands with Irregular Verbs

Irregular verbs follow no set pattern. Below are the command forms of some common verbs.

avere	essere	stare	andare	dare	fare	dire	venire
(tu) abbi	sii	sta' (stai)	va' (vai)	da' (dai)	fa' (fai)	di'	vieni
(Lei) abbia	sia	stia	vada	dia	faccia	dica	venga
(noi) abbiamo	siamo	stiamo	andiamo	diamo	facciamo	diciamo	veniamo
(voi) abbiate	siate	state	andate	date	fate	dite	venite
(Loro) abbiano	siano	stiano	vadano	diano	facciano	dicano	vengano

Exercise 26: Commands with Irregular Verbs

Tell a friend to do the following things, using the *tu* command of the verbs indicated.

1. *essere generoso/a*

    ....

2. *andare a sciare*

    ....

3. *stare zitto/a*

....

4. *dare dei soldi ad un amico*

....

5. *avere pazienza*

....

6. *andare a giocare*

....

7. *fare colazione*

....

8. *dire qualcosa in italiano*

....

Exercise 27: Commands with Irregular Verbs

Now tell a friend not to do the following things, using the negative *tu* command of the verbs indicated.

1. *essere generoso/a*

....

2. *andare a sciare*

....

3. *stare zitto/a*

....

4. *dare dei soldi ad un amico*

....

5. *avere pazienza*

....

6. *andare a giocare*

   ....

7. *fare colazione*

   ....

8. *dire qualcosa in italiano*

   ....

Exercise 28: Commands with Irregular Verbs

How would you tell your elderly neighbor to do the following things? Use the affirmative *Lei* command.

1. *essere ragionevole*

   ....

2. *andare a fare le spese*

   ....

3. *fare attenzione*

   ....

4. *stare attento/a*

   ....

5. *avere pazienza*

   ....

6. *dire "Buon giorno!"*

   ....

7. *fare colazione*

   ....

8. *dire qualcosa in italiano*

   ....

Commands with Object and Reflexive Pronouns

Object and reflexive pronouns, except the indirect object pronoun *loro*, attach to the end of both affirmative and negative *tu, noi,* and *voi* imperative forms and precede the *Lei* and *Loro* imperative forms. The indirect object pronoun *loro* always follows the *tu, noi, voi, Lei,* and *Loro* forms. When a pronoun (either direct or indirect) attaches to a single syllable command (*da', di', fa', sta', va'*), the first letter of the pronoun is doubled, except in the case of *gli*. With the negative *tu, noi,* and *voi* commands, the pronouns may either precede or follow the imperative form of the verb.

> *Non mi dica!* **Don't tell me! (formal)**
> *Non farlo!* **Don't do it!**
> *Non lo fare!* **Don't do it!**
> *Si sveglino!* **Wake up! (formal)**

Exercise 29: Imperatives with Pronouns

Respond using the *tu* or *voi* form of the imperative, as in the example. Use an object or reflexive pronoun in your answer.

Possiamo prendere la macchina? Sì, prendetela!

1. *Devo dire la verità?*
   Sì........................!

2. *Posso telefonarti stasera?*
   No, non ....!

3. *Dobbiamo fare colazione?*
   Sì, ...!

4. *Dobbiamo divertirci?*
   Sì, ...!

5. *Devo svegliare i bambini presto?*
   Sì, ...!

Exercise 30: Imperatives with Pronouns

Respond using the *Lei* or *Loro* form of the imperative, as in the example. Use an object or reflexive pronoun in your answer.

Posso leggere il giornale? Sì, lo legga!

1. *Posso preparare il tiramisù?*
   Sì, ...!

2. *Devo dare la mancia al cameriere?*
   No, non ....!

3. *Possiamo portare dei fiori?*
   Sì, ...!

4. *Faccio un dolce per la festa?*
   Sì, ...!

5. *A che ora devo alzarmi?*
   ..!

Let's Practice

Try the following exercise without referring back in the text.

Exercise 31: I Command You!

Translate each command into English.

1. *Non parlare!* ....

2. *Andiamo alla festa!* ....

3. *Non mi dire una bugia!* ....

4. *Per favore, chiuda la porta!* ....

5. *Ehi, ragazzi, non fate chiasso!* ....

6. *Svegliati!* ....

7. *Prestagli la macchina!* ....

8. *Non si arrabbi!* ....

Exercise 32: Make It Positive

Make each of the following negative commands positive.

1. *Non me lo dire!* ....

2. *Non fate così!* ....

3. *Non leggete quel libro!* ....

4. *Non ascoltarlo!* ....

5. *Non rispondere loro!* ....

Exercise 33: A Suggestion, a Command

TRACK 46

Listen to Track 46. The sentences you will hear illustrate the commands. Write down each sentence, then translate it into English.

1. ....

   ....

2. ....

   ....

3. ....

   ....

4. ....

....

5. ....

....

6. ....

....

7. ....

....

8. ....

....

9. ....

....

10. ....

....

Exercise 34: Imperative Forms of Irregular Verbs

Try to give the imperative (command) forms for the following verbs without referring back in the book.

andare
(tu)
(Lei)
(noi)
(voi)
(Loro)

dare

(tu) ....

(Lei) ....

(noi) ....

(voi) ....

(Loro) ....

fare

(tu) ....

(Lei) ....

(noi) ....

(voi) ....

(Loro) ....

stare

(tu) ....

(Lei) ....

(noi) ....

(voi) ....

(Loro) ....

dire

(tu) ....

(Lei) ....

(noi) ....

(voi) ....

(Loro) ....

avere

(tu) ....

(Lei) ....

(noi) ....

(voi) ....

(Loro) ....

essere

(tu) ....

(Lei) ....

(noi) ....

(voi) ....

(Loro) ....

venire

(tu) ....

(Lei) ....

(noi) ....

(voi) ....

(Loro) ....

Exercise 35: To Like or Not To Like

Choose the correct form of *piacere*.

1. *Mi (piace/piacciono) la pasta.*
2. *Ti (piace/piacciono) gli spaghetti al pomodoro?*
3. *Gli (piace/piacciono) le lasagne.*
4. *Le (piace/piacciono) il caffè.*
5. *Gli (piace/piacciono) la torta.*
6. *A voi (piace/piacciono) i ravioli.*
7. *A me (piace/piacciono) l'insalata verde.*
8. *A noi (piace/piacciono) le mele.*
9. *A Maria (piace/piacciono) i romanzi di Alberto Moravia.*
10. *A Giacomo (piace/piacciono) il prosciutto crudo.*

Pronunciation Exercise: Diphthongs

A general rule of pronunciation in Italian is that one letter produces one sound. In the name *Maria*, for example, the *i* is stressed. When one of the two vowels of a two-vowel combination is stressed (*Maria, leone, trattoria*), we articulate both vowel sounds, except in the case of diphthongs. A diphthong is a combination of two vowels that produce a single vowel sound. In Italian, diphthongs occur when an unstressed *i* or *u* is either preceded by or followed by *a, e,* or *o.*

TRACK 47

Exercise 36: Two Vowels, Two Sounds

Listen to the following words in Track 47 and repeat each one to practice your pronunciation. Note that the one-letter, one-sound rule applies to these words because one of the vowels of the two-vowel combination carries the stress of the word.

osteria	*psicologia*	*idea*
bugia	*farmacia*	*Gabriella*
leone	*eroe*	*io*

TRACK 48

Exercise 37: Two Vowels, One Sound

Listen to the following words in Track 48 and repeat each one. Note that the diphthong rule applies to these words.

lei	*vigliacco*	*quello*
più	*hai*	*autobus*
uomo	*vorrei*	*tabaccaio*
biondo	*piano*	

Part 8

The *Passato Prossimo* and the *Imperfetto*

Mastering the *passato prossimo* (present perfect) and the *imperfetto* (imperfect) will allow you to talk about events that took place (*passato prossimo*) or that were taking place (*imperfetto*) in the past. In addition, this part presents the pluperfect tense and some useful time expressions.

The Passato Prossimo *with* Avere *and* Essere

In English, the present perfect is a compound tense formed with the auxiliary verb "to have" with the past participle of the verb, as in "I have eaten." In Italian, the *passato prossimo* is also a compound tense made up of two parts: an auxiliary verb (either *avere* or *essere*) and the past participle of the verb. The *passato prossimo* can have a few different meanings: *Io ho mangiato* could translate as "I have eaten," "I ate," or "I did eat," depending on the context.

Io ho mangiato gli spaghetti. **I ate the spaghetti.**

Noi siamo andati al concerto ieri sera. **We went to the concert last night.**

In order to form the *passato prossimo*, it is important to have mastered the auxiliary verbs *avere* and *essere*. Can you recall their present tense conjugations?

Exercise 1: Avere *and* Essere *in the Present Tense*

Conjugate the verbs *avere* and *essere* in the present tense.

	avere	essere
io	....	....
tu	....	....
lui/lei/Lei	....	....
noi	....	....
voi	....	....
loro/Loro	....	....

The second component of the *passato prossimo* conjugation is the past participle. In Italian, the past participle is formed by replacing the *–are*, *–ere*, and *–ire* of the infinitive with *–ato*, *–uto*, and *–ito*, respectively.

mangiare	*mangiato*
vedere	*veduto*
partire	*partito*

There are many irregular past participles, especially with second conjugation (*–ere*) verbs:

Infinitive	*Irregular Past Participle*
accendere	acceso
aprire	aperto
bere	bevuto
chiedere	chiesto
chiudere	chiuso
conoscere	conosciuto
cuocere	cotto
dire	detto
essere	stato
fare	fatto
leggere	letto
mettere	messo
morire	morto
nascere	nato
offrire	offerto
perdere	perduto or perso
prendere	preso
rendere	reso
rispondere	risposto
scegliere	scelto
scendere	sceso
scrivere	scritto
spendere	speso
vedere	veduto or visto
vincere	vinto

Exercise 2: Past Participles—Regular or Irregular?

Provide the past participles of the verbs listed. Some are regular, some are irregular.

1. *spendere* ....

2. *scrivere* ....

3. *rispondere* ....

4. *prendere* ....

5. *perdere* ....

6. *mettere* ....

7. *leggere* ....

8. *conoscere* ....

9. *chiudere* ....

10. *chiedere* ....

11. *bere* ....

12. *fare* ....

13. *andare* ....

14. *venire* ....

15. *diventare* ....

16. *restare* ....

17. *stare* ....

18. *essere* ....

19. *morire* ....

20. *arrivare* ....

21. *partire* ....

22. *ritornare* ....

23. *entrare* ....

24. *uscire* ....

25. *salire* ....

26. *scendere* ....

27. *cadere* ....

28. *nascere* ....

29. *offrire* ....

30. *dire* ....

31. *aprire* ....

32. *vedere* ....

For most Italian verbs (including transitive verbs—those that can take a direct object), the *passato prossimo* is formed with the auxiliary verb *avere* plus the past participle of the main verb. The auxiliary verb *essere* is used with most intransitive verbs (verbs that cannot take a direct object). When the auxiliary verb *essere* is used, the last letter of the past participle must agree in number and gender with the subject of the verb. Below are some examples of the *passato prossimo* with the auxiliary verbs *avere* and *essere*.

Noi abbiamo letto il libro. **We read the book.**

Loro sono andati al supermercato. **They went to the supermarket.**

Maria ha guardato il film. **Maria watched the movie.**

Laura e Anna sono arrivate in ritardo. **Laura and Anna arrived late.**

TRACK 49

Exercise 3: Sentence Analysis

Listen to Track 49. Repeat each sentence to practice your pronunciation. Then listen to the track again, writing down each sentence in the first space. Next, write the infinitive of the verb used in the sentence in the second space, the past participle of the verb in the third space, and whether that verb takes *avere* or *essere* as an auxiliary verb in the *passato prossimo* in the fourth space.

1. Sentence ....

    Infinitive .... Past Participle .... *Avere/Essere* ....

2. Sentence ....

    Infinitive .... Past Participle .... *Avere/Essere* ....

3. Sentence ....

    Infinitive .... Past Participle .... *Avere/Essere* ....

4. Sentence ....

    Infinitive .... Past Participle .... *Avere/Essere* ....

5. Sentence ....

    Infinitive .... Past Participle .... *Avere/Essere* ....

6. Sentence ....

    Infinitive .... Past Participle .... *Avere/Essere* ....

7. Sentence ....

    Infinitive .... Past Participle .... *Avere/Essere* ....

8. Sentence ....

    Infinitive .... Past Participle .... *Avere/Essere* ....

9. Sentence ....

    Infinitive .... Past Participle .... *Avere/Essere* ....

10. Sentence ....

    Infinitive .... Past Participle .... *Avere/Essere* ....

11. Sentence ....

    Infinitive .... Past Participle .... *Avere/Essere* ....

12. Sentence ....

    Infinitive .... Past Participle .... *Avere/Essere* ....

13. Sentence ....

    Infinitive .... Past Participle .... *Avere/Essere* ....

14. Sentence ....

    Infinitive .... Past Participle .... *Avere/Essere* ....

Exercise 4: From Present to Past

Transform the sentences in Exercise 3 from the present to the past tense.

1. ....

2. ....

3. ....

4. ....

5. ....

6. ....

7. ....

8. ....

9. ....

10. ....

11. ....

12. ....

13. ....

14. ....

Exercise 5: From Present to Past

Change from the present to the past tense.

1. *Io mangio la pizza.*

   ....

2. *Maria va all'università venerdì scorso.*

   ....

3. *Noi usciamo sabato sera.*

   ....

4. *Bevo il caffè a colazione.*

   ....

5. *Gli studenti arrivano in classe alle 4.15.*

   ....

6. *Le sue amiche restano a casa stasera.*

   ....

7. *Non ho tempo.*

   ....

8. *Loro dicono sempre la verità.*

    ....

9. *Voi fate attenzione in classe.*

    ....

10. *Lei legge molti libri.*

    ....

11. *Maria e Marco partono alle 8.*

    ....

12. *Tu dormi molto.*

    ....

13. *Noi siamo dei bravi studenti.*

    ....

Exercise 6: Questions about Your Past

Answer the questions in complete sentences in Italian. Your answers will vary.

1. *Che cosa hai fatto sabato scorso? Hai fatto le spese?*

    ....

    ....

2. *Racconta di un viaggio che hai fatto. Dove sei andato? Con chi? Hai visitato un museo? Hai visto dei monumenti? Hai mangiato in un ristorante straordinario? Hai viaggiato in treno, in macchina, o in aereo?*

    ....

    ....

3. *Hai mai fatto un viaggio in Italia? Inghilterra? Germania? Spagna? Quali città hai visitato? Che cosa hai visto?*

    ....

    ....

4. *Hai mai visto un film italiano? Quale film hai visto?*

    ....

    ....

5. *Hai mai mangiato in un ristorante lussuoso? Che cosa hai mangiato? Che cosa hai bevuto? Quanto hai speso?*

   ....

   ....

6. *Hai mai conosciuto una persona famosa? Chi? Quando l'hai conosciuta?*

   ....

   ....

7. *Che cosa hai fatto l'estate scorsa? Hai fatto un viaggio? Dove? Hai letto molto? Hai dormito molto?*

   ....

   ....

Exercise 7: Translation Exercise

Translate the sentences into Italian.

1. I am very tired because I didn't sleep last night.

   ....

2. Why? Did you go out?

   ....

3. No, I worked until 8:00.

   ....

4. What time did you get home?

   ....

5. I have to go to work at 7:00 tomorrow morning.

   ....

6. Do you know that I went to the theater Friday night?

   ....

7. We saw a play by Carlo Goldoni.

   ....

8. Do you like to travel? Did you go on vacation last year? Did you go by car, by train, or by plane?

....

The Passato Prossimo *with Reflexive and* Reciprocal Verbs

Reflexive and reciprocal verbs are conjugated with the auxiliary verb *essere* in the *passato prossimo*. Since they are conjugated with *essere,* the last letter of the past participle must agree in number and gender with the subject of the sentence. The reflexive and reciprocal pronouns should precede the auxiliary verb *essere.*

> *Maria si sveglia alle otto.* **Maria wakes up at 8:00. (present)**
>
> *Maria si è svegliata alle otto.* **Maria woke up at 8:00. (past)**

Exercise 8: Reflexive Verbs in the Past Tense

Change the following sentences from the present to the past tense.

1. *Noi ci svegliamo molto presto.*

....

2. *Vittoria si prepara per il viaggio.*

....

3. *Luisa e Francesca si annoiano alla festa.*

....

4. *Fabio e Giuseppe si divertono molto.*

....

5. *Tu e Luisella vi arrabbiate.*

....

6. *I ragazzi non si sentono bene oggi.*

   ....

7. *Le bambine si lavano le mani.*

   ....

8. *Sara si innamora di Filippo.*

   ....

9. *Ti riposi questo weekend?*

   ....

10. *Mi fermo al bar a prendere un caffè.*

   ....

Exercise 9: Reciprocal Constructions in the Past Tense

Answer each question in the past tense using the reciprocal construction, as in the example.

Marco ha visto i suoi cugini? Sì, Marco e i suoi cugini si sono visti.

1. *Tu hai visto la tua ragazza?*

   ....

2. *Angela ha scritto a suo cugino?*

   ....

3. *Hai parlato a tua madre?*

   ....

4. *Marco ha telefonato a Angela?*

   ....

5. *Giuseppe ha chiamato i suoi amici?*

   ....

The Passato Prossimo *with Object Pronouns*

The past participle of a verb conjugated with *avere* must agree in number and gender with the direct object pronoun (*mi, ti, lo, la, La, ci, vi, li, le, Li, Le*) that precedes the verb.

Io ho letto il libro. **becomes** *Io l'ho letto.*
Noi abbiamo mangiato la pizza. **becomes** *Noi l'abbiamo mangiata.*
Ho visto te e Marianna. **becomes** *Vi ho visti.*
Maria ha conosciuto noi. **becomes** *Maria ci ha conosciuti.*

Exercise 10: *Working with Object Pronouns in the Past Tense*

Change from the present to the past tense. Then replace the direct objects with the direct object pronouns, as in the example.

Io mangio gli spaghetti. Io li ho mangiati.
Io bevo l'acqua. Io l'ho bevuta.

1. *Io leggo i libri.*

   ....

2. *Noi mangiamo la pasta.*

   ....

3. *Loro guardano la televisione.*

   ....

4. *Tu dai gli esami.*

   ....

5. *Tu leggi il libro.*

   ....

6. *Noi mangiamo le lasagne.*

   ....

7. *Loro cercano le chiavi.*

   ....

8. *Maria vede me e mia sorella.*

   ....

9. *Lei compra le riviste.*

   ....

10. *Voi volete vedere il film.*

    ....

11. *Lui non capisce la lezione.*

    ....

12. *Noi facciamo la pizza domenica sera.*

    ....

13. *Non potete ascoltare i dischi.*

    ....

14. *Cerchiamo te e tua sorella.*

    ....

The Imperfetto

The *imperfetto* (imperfect) is used to express a habitual or ongoing action in the past. Here are some examples of the imperfect tense in English:

I used to go to the movies on Saturday evenings.
My brother was watching television while I was talking on the phone.

In both instances, the action is clearly happening in the past. However, the action in both sentences is incomplete (or imperfect); we know that the action described used to happen, or was happening, but we don't know when the actions were brought to an end. Following are the conjugations of –*are*, –*ere*, and –*ire* verbs in the *imperfetto*:

parlare	vedere	dormire
io parlavo	*vedevo*	*dormivo*
tu parlavi	*vedevi*	*dormivi*
lui/lei/Lei parlava	*vedeva*	*dormiva*
noi parlavamo	*vedevamo*	*dormivamo*
voi parlavate	*vedevate*	*dormivate*
loro/Loro parlavano	*vedevano*	*dormivano*

TRACK 50

Exercise 11: From Present to Imperfetto

Listen to Track 50. Repeat each sentence, then listen again, writing down each sentence you hear. Finally, rewrite the sentences, changing from the present tense to the *imperfetto*.

1. ....

....

2. ....

....

3. ....

....

4. ....

....

5. ....

....

6. ....

....

7. ....

   ....

8. ....

   ....

9. ....

   ....

Exercise 12: Conjugating the Imperfetto

Conjugate each verb in the *imperfetto*.

andare (to go):

....

....

....

ricevere (to receive):

....

....

....

costruire (to build):

....

....

....

Exercise 13: Translating Exercise with the Imperfetto

Translate the sentences into Italian using the *imperfetto*.

1. I was speaking with your friends.

    ....

    ....

2. You used to play baseball with your grandfather.

   ....

   ....

3. He was sleeping while his boss was speaking.

   ....

   ....

4. When I was ten years old, I used to drink a lot of orange soda.

   ....

   ....

5. He was not telling a lie.

   ....

   ....

6. They were beautiful.

   ....

   ....

7. While I was reading the newspaper, my wife was talking with her brother.

   ....

   ....

8. I used to go shopping on Saturdays.

   ....

   ....

Comparison of Passato Prossimo and Imperfetto

The *passato prossimo* expresses an action that is over and done (I ate the pizza), and the *imperfetto* expresses an ongoing action in the past (I was eating the pizza). Examine the following sentences, paying close attention to the use of the *imperfetto* and *passato prossimo*:

Mentre guardavo la televisione, il telefono ha squillato. **While I was watching television, the phone rang.**

Mentre io guardavo la televisione, mia moglie leggeva un libro. **While I was watching television, my wife was reading a book.**

In the first instance, the second action (the phone rang) interrupted an ongoing action (I was studying). In the second instance, the two actions (I was watching, my wife was reading) happen simultaneously in the past.

Exercise 14: Passato Prossimo or Imperfetto?

Complete each sentence with either the *passato prossimo* or the *imperfetto*, according to the context.

1. *Ieri pomeriggio, mentre io* (to read) ...., *mio fratello,* (to listen to) .... *la musica.*

2. *"Marcello, con chi* (to speak) .... *quando io* (to arrive) ....?" *"Io* (to speak) .... *con Martina."*

3. *La settimana scorsa io e mia moglie* (to go) .... *nel Vermont perché* (to be beautiful weather) .... *e noi* (to want) .... *vedere le foglie che* (to change) .... *colore.*

4. *Quando Michele* (to be 12 years old) .... (to attend) .... *la scuola media.*

5. *L'anno scorso mio fratello* (to sell) .... *la casa perché* (to find) .... *un nuovo lavoro a Boston.*

6. *Il weekend scorso io* (to have to) .... *andare a Philadelphia perché il mio capo non* (to feel well) ....

7. *Il volo* (to leave) .... *alle 8 e noi* (to arrive) .... *all'aeroporto alle 8 e 15.*

8. *Non* (to be able) .... *andare alla festa ieri sera perché* (to have to) .... *vedere mio padre.*

9. *Ieri sera Federico* (to meet) .... *mio fratello.*

10. *Mentre noi* (to watch) .... *il film, loro* (to talk) .... *al telefono.*

The Trapassato Prossimo

The *trapassato prossimo* is equivalent to the past perfect in English. It is used to express an action in the past that took place before another past action expressed by the *passato prossimo* or the *imperfetto*. Examine the following sentence:

Non sono andato al cinema venerdì sera perché avevo già visto il film.
I did not go to the movies on Friday night because I had already seen the movie.

It is clear that the second action of this sentence took place before the first. In Italian, the *trapassato prossimo* is formed with the *imperfetto* of the auxiliary verbs *avere* or *essere*, plus the past participle of the main verb. The imperfect forms of *avere* and *essere* are as follows:

avere	**essere**
io avevo	*ero*
tu avevi	*eri*
lui/lei/Lei aveva	*era*
noi avevamo	*eravamo*
voi avevate	*eravate*
loro/Loro avevano	*erano*

Exercise 15: The **Trapassato Prossimo**

Transform the sentences from the *passato prossimo* to the *trapassato prossimo.*

1. *Ho mangiato la pasta.*

   ....

2. *Siamo andati in spiaggia.*

   ....

3. *Vi siete visti l'anno scorso.*

   ....

4. *Il signor Gianni ha chiamato la polizia.*

   ....

5. *Tu hai saputo la verità.*

   ....

6. *Non ha visto il film.*

   ....

7. *Mi sono svegliato presto.*

   ....

8. *Hai già letto quel libro.*

   ....

9. *Abbiamo ascoltato musica tutta la sera.*

   ....

10. *Si sono innamorati.*

    ....

Da quanto tempo? *and* Da quando?

Da quanto tempo? and *Da quando?* are expressions used to indicate actions that began in the past and continue into the present. In English we say, "I have been reading since six o'clock" or "I have been living here since 1994." Italian uses the present tense of the verb + *da* + the time expression to convey these same ideas.

> *Io suono la chitarra da nove anni.* **I have been playing the guitar for nine years.**

> *Noi studiamo l'italiano da un anno.* **We have been studying Italian for a year.**

> *Da quanto tempo…?* (How long have you been…) and *Da quando…?* (Since when…?) can be used to introduce a question:

> *Da quanto tempo giochi a tennis?* **How long have you been playing tennis?**

> *Da quando abiti in questa città?* **Since when have you been living in this city?**

Exercise 16: Listening Comprehension

TRACK 51

Listen to Track 51 and repeat each question. Then listen again, writing down each question you hear. Finally, answer the questions in complete sentences in Italian.

1. *Domanda:*

....

Risposta:

....

2. *Domanda:*

....

Risposta:

....

3. *Domanda:*

....

Risposta:

....

4. *Domanda:*

....

Risposta:

....

5. *Domanda:*

....

Risposta:

....

6. *Domanda:*

....

Risposta:

....

7. *Domanda:*

....

Risposta:

....

8. *Domanda:*

....

Risposta:

....

9. *Domanda:*

....

Risposta:

....

10. *Domanda:*

....

Risposta:

....

Let's Practice

Try to complete the following exercises without referring back to the text.

Exercise 17: Past or Present?

Conjugate the verb in parentheses in Italian in the present or past tense, according to the time references indicated.

1. *Ieri mattina Marco* (to wake up) .... *alle 7 e* (to get up) .... *alle 7. 30. Lui* (to prepare) .... *la colazi-one per suo figlio e* (to go) .... *in ufficio dove* (to work) .... *tutto il giorno.*

2. *Stasera io* (to want) .... *andare al cinema con il mio ami-co. Il mio amico* (to be called) .... *Giovanni. Normal-mente lui* (to get bored) .... *al cinema. Questa volta io e Giovanni* (to have fun) .... *sicuramente perché* (to go) .... *andiamo a vedere un film divertentissimo. Dopo il film* (to stop) .... *al bar a prendere un caffè.*

3. *Due giorni fa io* (to get up) .... *molto tardi, poi* (to wash) .... *e* (to dress) .... *velocemente per-ché io non* (to want) .... *arrivare tardi al mio lavoro. Il mio capo* (to be) .... *molto simpatico ma io non* (to be able) .... *arrivare tardi al lavoro perché lui* (to get angry) .... *facilmente!*

Exercise 18: Answering Questions in Italian

Answer the questions in complete sentences in Italian.

1. *A che ora ti sei svegliato/a stamattina?*

....

2. *Che cosa hai fatto ieri pomeriggio?*

....

3. *A che ora ti sei addormentato/a la notte scorsa?*

....

4. *Sei mai stato/a in Florida? Quanto tempo fa?*

....

5. *Hai mai visto un film italiano? Come si chiama?*

....

Exercise 19: Time Expressions in the Past

Answer each question using the expression of time in parentheses.

1. *Quando sei andato a studiare in biblioteca?* (last night)

....

....

2. *Quando hai veduto i tuoi genitori?* (last week)

....

....

3. *Quando hai letto «la Divina Commedia»?* (nine years ago)

....

....

4. *Quando hai lavato la macchina?* (last Tuesday)

....

....

5. *Quando hai conosciuto mia sorella?* (yesterday)

....

....

Exercise 20: Translation Exercise

Translate the sentences into Italian.

1. Marco and Angela got married.

   ....

   ....

2. John got mad because his friend did not call.

   ....

   ....

3. I have not yet had breakfast.

   ....

   ....

4. My friends and I never see each other.

   ....

   ....

5. Last night I fell asleep at 11:00.

   ....

   ....

6. They watched television all evening.

   ....

   ....

7. I worked every Saturday for three months because I wanted to earn a lot of money.

   ....

   ....

8. He paid for our coffee because we didn't have money.

   ....

   ....

9. The conference starts at 8:00 in the morning.

....

....

Exercise 21: From Present to Past

Change the sentences from the present to the past tense. Replace the direct objects with the direct object pronouns.

1. *Marcello compra le sigarette.*

    ....

2. *Tu e Vincenzo fumate un sigaro.*

    ....

3. *Io e Simone compriamo una maglietta.*

    ....

4. *Io vedo Carlo e i suoi amici al ristorante.*

    ....

5. *Federico e i suoi amici ordinano la grappa.*

    ....

6. *Tu bevi il caffè.*

    ....

7. *Simone non ascolta i suoi genitori.*

    ....

8. *Il signor Gianni chiama la sua amica.*

    ....

9. *La polizia cerca i ragazzi.*

    ....

Exercise 22: A Love Story

Fill in the blank with the correct form of the *passato prossimo* or the *imperfetto*, according to the context. Then write a few sentences to complete the story.

Il mese scorso, Mary, una ragazza canadese, (to take a trip) .... *in Sicilia. Mary* (to take) .... *il volo dall'aeroporto di Toronto ed* (to arrive) .... *a Palermo. Mary* (to take a walk) .... *e* (to buy) .... *dei vestiti nei negozi di Palermo. Mary* (to see) .... *il Palazzo dei Normanni e le catacombe dei Cappuccini. Il giorno dopo* (to be bad weather) .... *così Mary* (to pass) .... *la giornata in albergo. Quella sera Mary* (to eat) .... *in una piccola trattoria. Alla trattoria Mary* (to meet) .... *un bel cameriere siciliano. Il cameriere* (to be called) .... *Piero. Quella sera, Mary e Piero* (to go) .... *al cinema a vedere un film di Roberto Benigni e a ballare per tre ore in discoteca. Il giorno dopo Mary* (to return) .... *in Canada. Piero* (to stay) .... *a Palermo, ma* (to write) .... *una lettera d'amore a Mary. Quando Mary* (to arrive) .... *a casa,* (to find) .... *la lettera di Piero. Lei* (to read) .... *la lettera di Piero e gli* (to phone) .... *per invitarlo a Toronto...*

....

....

....

....

Exercise 23: Further into the Past

Complete each sentence by providing the correct form of the verb in either the *passato prossimo* or *trapassato prossimo,* according to the context.

1. *La settimana scorsa mia moglie* (to read) .... *il libro che io le* (to gift) .... *l'anno scorso.*

2. *Luisella non* (to go) .... *in Germania, perché* (to visit) .... *Amburgo l'anno scorso.*

3. *Marcello non* (to eat) .... *con noi, perché* (to have breakfast) .... *dai suoi nonni.*

4. *Quando io* (to call) .... *mio fratello, lui* (to leave) .... *già.*

5. *Alessio non* (to come) .... *al cinema perché* (to see) .... *il film la settimana scorsa.*

Exercise 24: Translation

Translate the sentences into Italian.

1. When Dante wrote the *Divine Comedy,* Charles Dickens had not yet written *David Copperfield.*

   ....
   ....

2. I had already fallen asleep when he arrived.

   ....
   ....

3. I didn't buy the flour today because my wife had bought it yesterday.

   ....
   ....

4. We made dinner for the friends that we had met in Italy.

....

....

5. I didn't read the book last night because I had read it last month.

....

....

Exercise 25: When I Was a Child

Complete each sentence with a logical statement, as in the example. To express a habitual action, use the *imperfetto*. To say that you did something once, or a limited number of times, use the *passato prossimo*.

Quando ero piccolo giocavo a baseball con i miei amici. **When I was young, I used to play baseball with my friends.**

1. *Quando ero piccolo…*

....

2. *Quando ero piccolo…andavo a scuola tutti i giorni.*

....

3. *Quando ero piccolo…*

....

4. *Quando ero piccolo…*

....

5. *Mia madre aveva paura quando…*

....

6. *Quando avevo quindici anni…*

....

7. *Quando avevo sedici anni…*

....

8. *Quando avevo diciotto anni…*

....

Pronunciation Exercise: The Letters F and V

Exercise 26: Pronunciation of the Letter F

Listen to Track 52 and repeat each word.

famiglia	*ferie*	*forno*
fanno	*difficile*	*fontina*
fabbrica	*fila*	*furbo*
caffè	*finale*	*futuro*
felice	*fondo*	*fuoco*

In Italian the letter *f* is pronounced like the "f" in the English word "fan." When the *f* is doubled—*caffè*, for example—the "f" sound is slightly lengthened.

Exercise 27: Pronunciation of the Letter V

Listen to Track 53 and repeat each word.

vario	*piove*	*voce*
vaso	*piovve*	*voglia*
vapore	*viaggio*	*volta*
vecchia	*vicino*	*vulcano*
vedere	*via*	*vuoto*

In Italian the letter *v* is pronounced like the "v" in the English word "van." When the *v* is doubled—*piovve*, for example—the "v" sound is slightly lengthened.

Exercise 28: Pronunciation of the Letters F and V

TRACK 54

Listen to Track 54 and repeat each sentence.

1. *Per favore, fate i compiti.*

2. *Piovve quel giorno che prendemmo il caffè insieme.*

3. *Filippo e Federico bevvero tanto vino.*

4. *Fidatevi!*

5. *Offro una fettina di fontina a voi.*

Part 9

The Future Tense, the Conditional Mood, and the Subjunctive

Part 9 introduces the future tense and the conditional mood. The future tense will help you to express events that will take place in the future. The conditional mood is used to express what "would" happen and corresponds to the English "would + verb," as in "I would go" or "They would come." In Part 9 we will also examine the subjunctive mood, which is used to express personal feelings, possibility, or doubt.

Future Tense (Simple)

The simple future expresses an action that will take place in the future. In Italian, the simple future is formed by adding the following endings to *–are*, *–ere*, and *–ire* verbs:

parlare (to speak)

io parlerò	*noi parleremo*
tu parlerai	*voi parlerete*
lui/lei/Lei parlerà	*loro/Loro parleranno*

rispondere (to respond)

io risponderò	*noi risponderemo*
tu risponderai	*voi risponderete*
lui/lei/Lei risponderà	*loro/Loro risponderanno*

dormire (to sleep)

io dormirò	*noi dormiremo*
tu dormirai	*voi dormirete*
lui/lei/Lei dormirà	*loro/Loro dormiranno*

There are several irregular simple future endings for common verbs:

giocare	*io giocherò, tu giocherai, etc.*
pagare	*io pagherò, tu pagherai, etc.*
incominciare	*io incomincerò, tu incomincerai, etc.*
bere	*io berrò, tu berrai, etc.*
dare	*io darò, tu darai, etc.*
essere	*io sarò, tu sarai, etc.*
fare	*io farò, tu farai, etc.*
stare	*io starò, tu starai, etc.*
andare	*io andrò, tu andrai, etc.*
avere	*io avrò, tu avrai, etc.*
dovere	*io dovrò, tu dovrai, etc.*
potere	*io potrò, tu potrai, etc.*

vedere	io vedrò, tu vedrai, etc.
venire	io verrò, tu verrai, etc.
volere	io vorrò, to vorrai, etc.

L'estate prossima andrò in Italia e vedrò i miei cugini. **Next summer I will go to Italy and I will see my cousins.**

The simple future tense may also be used to express probability, or something that is probably true. In English, we express probability with the construction "must be + verb." So, depending on the context, *pioverà* can mean "It will rain" or "It must be raining."

Exercise 1: Recognizing the Simple Future Tense

Underline the verb conjugation in the simple future tense.

1. *loro dormivano, noi dormiamo, tu dormirai*

2. *voi bevete, loro berranno, noi bevevamo*

3. *lui vuole, io vorrò, noi volevamo*

4. *io parlavo, loro parlano, noi parleremo*

5. *tu studierai, loro studiano, lui studiava*

6. *noi siamo, loro saranno, io ero*

7. *lui pagherà, voi pagavate, tu paghi*

8. *io avevo, loro hanno, tu avrai*

9. *tu dici, lei diceva, io dirò*

10. *loro facevano, io faccio, voi farete*

Exercise 2: From Present to Future

Rewrite each sentence, changing the verb from the present to the future tense.

1. *I ragazzi non vanno in Italia.*

   ....

2. *Tu bevi il vino a cena.*

   ....

3. *Domani sera io sto a casa.*

   ....

4. *To ricevi molte email.*

   ....

5. *Mio figlio diventa famoso.*

   ....

6. *Non veniamo a casa tua domani sera.*

   ....

7. *Voglio fare un viaggio in Italia.*

   ....

8. *Tu e Anna potete dormire da noi.*

   ....

9. *Balliamo tutta la sera.*

   ....

10. *Preferisco andare a Roma.*

    ....

Exercise 3: In the Future

Conjugate the verb in parentheses in the future tense.

1. *Io e Marianna* .... *in un ristorante cinese.* (to eat)

2. *I miei fratelli* .... *a fare le spese.* (to go)

3. *Lei* .... *la TV stasera.* (to watch)

4. *Tutti i ragazzi* .... *i libri sul tavolo.* (to put)

5. *Mio nipote* .... *del cane.* (to be afraid)

6. *Io* .... *la prossima settimana.* (to be broke)

7. *I medici* .... *della diagnosi.* (to be certain)

8. *Tu e Marta* .... *il vino al ristorante stasera.* (to drink)

9. *Anna* .... *la verità a suo padre.* (to say)

10. *Tutti i miei amici* .... *andare in macchina.* (to prefer)

Exercise 4: Talking about Your Future

TRACK 55

Listen to Track 55 and repeat each question. Then listen again, writing each question after you hear it. Finally, go back and write your answers.

1. *Domanda:*

   ....

   Risposta:

   ....

2. *Domanda:*

   ....

   Risposta:

   ....

3. *Domanda:*

   ....

   Risposta:

   ....

4. *Domanda:*

....

Risposta:

....

5. *Domanda:*

....

Risposta:

....

6. *Domanda:*

....

Risposta:

....

7. *Domanda:*

....

Risposta:

....

8. *Domanda:*

....

Risposta:

....

9. *Domanda:*

....

Risposta:

....

10. *Domanda:*

....

Risposta:

....

The Future Perfect

The future perfect is a compound tense used to express an event that will have happened before something else happens. It can also be used to express probability—something that must have already happened. The future perfect is formed by pairing the future tense of the verbs *avere* or *essere* with the past participle of the main verb. Let's review the future tense of the verbs *avere* and *essere:*

avere	essere
io avrò	*sarò*
tu avrai	*sarai*
lui/lei/Lei avrà	*sarà*
noi avremo	*saremo*
voi avrete	*sarete*
loro/Loro avranno	*saranno*

Tu sarai già partito quando io arrivo. **You will have already left when I arrive.**

Loro avranno mangiato. **They must have eaten.**

Exercise 5: Recognizing the Future Perfect

TRACK 56

Listen to each future perfect verb conjugation in Track 56. Then listen again, writing each verb conjugation in the space provided and underlining the correct translation for each verb.

1. ....
   (you will have left, they will have left, she will have left)

2. ....
   (we will have eaten, she will have eaten, I will have eaten)

3. ....
   (we will have gone, you will have gone, he will have gone)

4. ....

    (she will have drunk, you will have drunk, they will have drunk)

5. ....

    (he will have become, they will have become, I will have become)

6. ....

    (it will have slept, they will have slept, we will have slept)

7. ....

    (we will have believed, I will have believed, they will have believed)

8. ....

    (I will have been able to return, she will have been able to return, we will have been able to return)

9. ....

    (you will have listened, she will have listened, we will have listened)

10. ....

    (he will have made, you will have made)

Exercise 6: Will Have

Fill in the blank with the correct future perfect form of the verb.

1. *Il mio amico* .... *una bella cena.* (to prepare)

2. *Tutti i miei cugini* .... *il caffè al bar.* (to take)

3. *Tu ed io* .... *da Firenze a Roma.* (to drive)

4. *Tu e Larissa* .... *per due ore.* (to wait)

5. *Giorgio e Lorenzo* .... *il rumore.* (to hear)

6. *Tutti gli studenti* .... *l'esame.* (to finish)

7. *Mia nonna* .... *il regalo che le abbiamo mandato.* (to receive)

8. *Tu* .... *al supermercato.* (to go)

9. *I ragazzi* .... *a casa.* (to return)

10. *Voi* .... *molto presto stamattina.* (to wake up)

Conditional Mood

The conditional mood expresses something that "might" happen. It corresponds to the English "would + verb," as in "I would go" or "They would come." The present tense of the conditional mood, like the simple future tense in the indicative, is one word (verb stem + conditional ending). Verbs that have an irregular stem in the simple future tense have the same irregular stem in the present conditional:

parlare (to speak)	
io parlerei	*noi parleremmo*
tu parlersti	*voi parlereste*
lui/lei/Lei parlerebbe	*loro/Loro parlerebbero*

rispondere (to respond)	
io risponderei	*noi risponderemmo*
tu risponderesti	*voi rispondereste*
lui/lei/Lei risponderebbe	*loro/Loro risponderebbero*

dormire (to sleep)	
io dormirei	*noi dormiremmo*
tu dormiresti	*voi dormireste*
lui/lei/Lei dormirebbe	*loro/Loro dormirebbero*

Verbs that have an irregular stem in the simple future tense have the same irregular stem in the present conditional:

giocare	*io giocherei, tu giocheresti,* etc.
pagare	*io pagherei, tu pagheresti,* etc.
incominciare	*io incomincerei, tu incominceresti,* etc.
bere	*io berrei, tu berresti,* etc.
dare	*io darei, tu daresti,* etc.
essere	*io sarei, tu saresti,* etc.

fare	io farei, tu faresti, etc.
stare	io starei, tu staresti, etc.
andare	io andrei, tu andresti, etc.
avere	io avrei, tu avresti, etc.
dovere	io dovrei, tu dovresti, etc.
potere	io potrei, tu potresti, etc.
vedere	io vedrei, tu vedresti, etc.
venire	io verrei, tu verresti, etc.
volere	io vorrei, to vorresti, etc.

The present conditional is used to express the potential of something that would happen if something else happens first:

Parlerei con il mio capo. ***I would speak to my boss.***
Andrei in Italia. ***I would go to Italy.***

Exercise 7: Recognizing the Conditional

Underline the verb conjugation in the present conditional.

1. *io partirò, tu partiresti, loro partivano*

2. *noi beviamo, loro berranno, io berrei*

3. *lui mangia, io mangerò, tu mangeresti*

4. *io abiterei, loro abitano, noi abiteremo*

5. *lui farà, loro fanno, loro farebbero*

6. *noi saremo, noi saremmo, io ero*

7. *voi davate, tu darai, io darei*

8. *lei stava, tu starai, loro starebbero*

9. *tu dirai, lei diceva, io direi*

10. *loro puliscono, tu puliresti, voi pulirete*

Exercise 8: Correct Translation

TRACK 57

Listen to each conditional verb conjugation in Track 57, then listen again, writing each verb conjugation in the space provided and underlining the correct translation for each verb.

1. ....
   (I would like, we would like, they would like)

2. ....
   (I would dream, she would dream, we would dream)

3. ....
   (you would arrive, they would arrive, he would arrive)

4. ....
   (I would sleep, he would sleep, we would sleep)

5. ....
   (she would finish, they would finish, I would finish)

6. ....
   (I would be, he would be, she would be)

7. ....
   (he would bring, they would bring, you would bring)

8. ....
   (we would go, you would go, he would go)

9. ....
   (I would give, we would give, you would give)

10. ....
    (I would write, you would write, we would write)

Exercise 9: Conditional Situations

Fill in the blanks with the correct form of the verb in the present conditional.

1. *Io* .... *a casa tua, ma non ho tempo.* (to eat)

2. *I miei cugini* .... *da noi, ma devono partire stasera.* (to sleep)

3. *Marco* .... *la mancia al cameriere, ma è al verde.* (to give)

4. *Mia madre mi* .... *un orologio.* (to give a gift)

5. *Io* .... *la finestra, ma non ho caldo.* (to open)

6. *Che cosa* .... *tuo padre?* (to think)

7. *Noi* .... *un arrosto di vitello.* (to want)

8. *Loro* .... *alle otto, se avessero i biglietti.* (to leave)

9. *Mio figlio* .... *presto.* (to wake up)

10. *Tu e Giorgio* .... *l'autobus.* (to wait for)

Conditional Perfect

The conditional perfect describes an action that would have taken place, but did not. The conditional perfect is a compound tense formed by pairing the present conditional of *avere* or *essere* with the past participle of the main verb. Let's review the present conditional of *avere* and *essere*:

avere	essere
io avrei	*sarei*
tu avresti	*saresti*
lui/lei/Lei avrebbe	*sarebbe*
noi avremmo	*saremmo*
voi avreste	*sareste*
loro/Loro avrebbero	*sarebbero*

Loro sarebbero andati in Italia, ma non avevano i soldi. **They would have gone to Italy, but they didn't have money.**

Io avrei mangiato il gelato, ma non ce n'era più. **I would have eaten ice cream, but there wasn't any.**

Exercise 10: The Conditional Perfect

Rewrite each sentence, changing the verb from the present tense to the conditional perfect.

1. *Compro una macchina.*

   ....

2. *Leggiamo il libro.*

   ....

3. *Voi non dovete mangiare prima delle otto.*

   ....

4. *Anna e Carlo aiutano il figlio.*

   ....

5. *Fai le lasagne per cena.*

   ....

6. *Dice sempre la verità.*

   ....

7. *Non ho tempo.*

   ....

8. *Mi vesto in fretta.*

   ....

9. *Gaetano mangia gli spaghetti.*

....

10. *Tu e Marcello tornate presto.*

....

Exercise 11: Recognizing the Conditional Perfect

TRACK 58

Listen to each conditional perfect verb conjugation in Track 58, then listen again, writing each verb conjugation in the space provided. Underline the correct translation for each verb.

1. ....
   (we would have left, they would have left, she would have left)

2. ....
   (she would have bought, they would have bought, we would have bought)

3. ....
   (I would have apologized, he would have apologized, she would have apologized)

4. ....
   (they would have preferred, you would have preferred, she would have preferred)

5. ....
   (you would have come, they would have come, we would have come)

6. ....
   (she would have brought, you would have brought, it would have brought)

7. ....
   (we would have called, you would have called, I would have called)

8. ....
   (they would have earned, we would have earned, you would have earned)

9. ....
   (you would have been, he would have been, we would have been)

10. ....
    (I would have left, they would have left, she would have left)

The Subjunctive

We have seen verbs in the indicative (the mood that expresses or indicates matters of fact), the imperative (the mood that allows speakers to impart commands or exhortations), and the conditional (the mood that allows speakers to convey hypothetical situations). The subjunctive mood expresses a belief, feeling, uncertainty, or opinion, and is often used when the dependent clause is introduced by the declarative conjunction *che* and the subject of the two clauses is different (if the subject is the same, the subjunctive is not used). Compare these two examples:

> *Io penso che lui sia un bravo ragazzo.* **I think he is a nice guy.**
> *Giovanni pensa di stare a casa.* **Giovanni thinks he'll stay at home.**

The subjunctive is used in the dependent clause that follows verbs expressing volition, desire, doubt, opinion, or emotion:

avere paura che...	to be afraid that...
credere che...	to believe that...
desiderare che...	to want that...
dispiacere che...	to be sorry that...
dubitare che...	to doubt that...
non essere sicuro/certo che...	to be sure/certain that...
essere contento/felice che...	to be happy that...
pensare che...	to think that...
preferire che...	to prefer that...
sperare che...	to hope that...
volere che...	to want that...

The subjunctive is also used after the following impersonal expressions:

Bisogna che…	It is necessary that…
È necessario che…	It is necessary that…
È improbabile che…	It is improbable that…
È probabile che…	It is probable that…
È impossibile che…	It is impossible that…
È possibile che…	It is possible that…
È bene che…	It is good that…
È meglio che…	It is better that…
È importante che…	It is important that…
È ora che…	It is time that…
Pare che…	It seems that…
Sembra che…	It seems that…
Può darsi che…	It is possible that…
È un peccato che…	It is a shame that…
Si dice che…	Rumor has it/People say…

È meglio che tu parta. **It is better that you leave.**

Marco vuole che i suoi genitori vengano a cena. **Marco wants that his parents come to dinner.**

Below are the present subjunctive conjugations of regular *–are*, *–ere*, and *–ire* verbs.

parlare	ricevere	dormire	pulire
io parli	*riceva*	*dorma*	*pulisca*
tu parli	*riceva*	*dorma*	*pulisca*
lui/lei/Lei parli	*riceva*	*dorma*	*pulisca*
noi parliamo	*riceviamo*	*dormiamo*	*puliamo*
voi parliate	*riceviate*	*dormiate*	*puliate*
loro/Loro parlino	*ricevano*	*dormano*	*puliscano*

Below are the present subjunctive conjugations of some irregular verbs:

tenere	**rimanere**	**bere**
io tenga	rimanga	beva
tu tenga	rimanga	beva
lui/lei/Lei tenga	rimanga	beva
noi teniamo	rimaniamo	beviamo
voi teniate	rimaniate	beviate
loro/Loro tengano	rimangano	bevano

essere	**avere**
io sia	abbia
tu sia	abbia
lui/lei/Lei sia	abbia
noi siamo	abbiamo
voi siate	abbiate
loro/Loro siano	abbiano

dovere	**volere**	**potere**
io debba	voglia	possa
tu debba	voglia	possa
lui/lei/Lei debba	voglia	possa
noi dobbiamo	vogliamo	possiamo
voi dobbiate	vogliate	possiate
loro/Loro debbano	vogliano	possano

venire	**uscire**
io venga	esca
tu venga	esca
lui/lei/Lei venga	esca
noi veniamo	usciamo
voi veniate	usciate
loro/Loro vengano	escano

fare	**andare**
io faccia	vada
tu faccia	vada
lui/lei/Lei faccia	vada
noi facciamo	andiamo
voi facciate	andiate
loro/Loro facciano	vadano

stare	dire	dare
io stia	dica	dia
tu stia	dica	dia
lui/lei/Lei stia	dica	dia
noi stiamo	diciamo	diamo
voi stiate	diciate	diate
loro/Loro stiano	dicano	diano

conoscere	sapere
io conosca	sappia
tu conosca	sappia
lui/lei/Lei conosca	sappia
noi conosciamo	sappiamo
voi conosciate	sappiate
loro/Loro conoscano	sappiano

Exercise 12: What Do You Think?

Provide a logical ending to each statement.

1. *Io penso che la guerra…* ....

2. *I miei genitori vogliono che io…* ....

3. *Il mio miglior amico crede che io…* ....

4. *È necessario che mio fratello…* ....

5. *Ho paura che…* ....

6. *È importante che…* ....

7. *Può darsi che…* ....

8. *Il mio capo desidera che…* ....

9 *Noi siamo sicuri che…* ....

10. *Gli americani vogliono che…* ....

Exercise 13: Present Indicative or Present Subjunctive?

TRACK 59

Listen to Track 59 and repeat each sentence aloud. Then listen again, write down each sentence in the space provided, and indicate whether the sentence is in the present indicative or present subjunctive.

1. ....

....

2. ....

....

3. ....

....

4. ....

....

5. ....

....

6. ....

....

7. ....

....

8. ....

....

9. ....

....

10. ....

....

The Past Subjunctive

The past subjunctive is used when the action of the dependent clause happened in the past. It is a compound tense formed by pairing the present subjunctive of the verbs *avere* or *essere* with the past participle of the main verb. Let's review the present subjunctive of *avere* and *essere*:

essere	avere
io sia	*abbia*
tu sia	*abbia*
lui/lei/Lei sia	*abbia*
noi siamo	*abbiamo*
voi siate	*abbiate*
loro/Loro siano	*abbiano*

Penso che sia partito alle otto. ***I think he left at eight.***

È possibile che mio padre abbia sentito la notizia. ***It is possible that my father heard the news.***

Exercise 14: From Present to Past in the Subjunctive

TRACK 60

Listen to Track 60 and repeat each sentence. Then listen again and write down each sentence in the space provided. Finally, change the verb of the dependent clause from the present to the past subjunctive.

1. ....

....

2. ....

....

3. ....

....

4. ....

....

5. ....
   ....

6. ....
   ....

7. ....
   ....

8. ....
   ....

9. ....
   ....

10. ....
    ....

Let's Practice

Try to complete the following exercises without referring back in the text.

TRACK 61

Exercise 15: Recognizing Verb Tenses and Moods

Listen to each sentence in Track 61 and repeat. Then listen to the track again, write down each sentence, and identify the verb tense of the verb *dormire*.

1. ....
   ....

2. ....
   ....

3. ....
   ....

4. ....

....

5. ....

....

6. ....

....

7. ....

....

8. ....

....

9. ....

....

10. ....

....

Exercise 16: Recognizing Verb Tenses

Label the tense of each verb. Some of the tenses are from this part, others are from earlier sections.

1. *capivo* ....

2. *hanno chiamato* ....

3. *faceva* ....

4. *mangerebbero* ....

5. *erano andati* ....

6. *dica* ....

7. *darebbe* ....

8. *sarebbero andati* ....

9. *usciva* ....

10. *avranno mangiato* ....

Exercise 17: Practicing Verb Tenses

Conjugate the verbs in the subject and tense/mood requested.

1. *io, volere,* present conditional ....

2. *noi, dare,* present subjunctive ....

3. *voi, bere,* future ....

4. *Loro, chiedere,* past subjunctive ....

5. *tu, preferire,* future perfect ....

6. *lui, andare,* conditional perfect ....

7. *io, svegliarsi,* present conditional ....

8. *Lei, fare,* present subjunctive ....

9. *noi, stare,* future ....

10. *tu, avere,* conditional perfect ....

Exercise 18: More Tense and Mood Practice

Translate each of the following sentences. All of the tenses used are from this part.

1. *Vorrei un piatto di spaghetti al pomodoro.*

....

2. *Le mie sorelle saranno già partite.*

....

3. *Non credo che sia vero.*

....

4. *Mi sarebbe piaciuto vedere il film con voi.*

....

5. *Prenderemo la tua macchina stasera.*

....

6. *Vorremmo accompagnarti al supermercato.*

....

7. *Tutti i ragazzi andranno a Roma quest'estate.*

....

8. *È impossibile che Alberto non abbia capito.*

....

9. *Avresti voluto venire con noi.*

....

10. *Pioverà domani.*

....

Pronunciation Exercise: The Letters R and RR

The letter *r* (and the double *rr*) are perhaps the most difficult letters for non-native speakers of Italian to master. It is interesting to note that the English "r" is also very difficult for non-native speakers of English. Say aloud the following English words, focusing on the motions made by your mouth and tongue: "roar," "rice," "car," "hair," "roam," "right," "ring," "rack." You will have noticed that the English "r" is formed in the back of the mouth with the back of the tongue and that it is a soft, round sound. The Italian *r* is formed using the tip of the tongue on the upper palate behind the front teeth. For practice, try pronouncing the following English words, paying close attention to the placement of the tip of the tongue when pronouncing the letter "d," as in "dog," "dinner," "dart," and "duck."

Exercise 19: Pronunciation of the Letter R

Repeat each word.

raro	*ferie*	*forno*
Roma	*fortunato*	*ritornare*
caro	*morto*	*furbo*
foro	*recarsi*	*futuro*
povero	*reggere*	*rustico*

In Italian, the double *rr* is generally trilled. A trill is made by extending the tap that is made when pronouncing the single *r*.

Exercise 20: Pronunciation of the Letter RR

Repeat each word.

carro	*corretto*	*tradurre*
burro	*vorrei*	*correre*
sorriso	*berresti*	
birra	*porre*	

Exercise 21: Pronunciation of the Letters R and RR

Repeat each sentence.

1. *Per favore, vorrei una birra rossa.*

2. *Buon giorno, signor Verri. Vorrebbe del burro?*

3. *Riccardo corre perché ha parecchia fretta.*

4. *Vorrebbero partire.*

5. *Non riesco a tradurre la lettera di Roberto.*

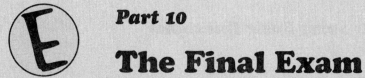

Part 10

The Final Exam

The final exam tests your cumulative knowledge. Many of the exercises integrate a number of different grammatical rules, so some of these exercises will be rather challenging. Try not to refer back to the explanations in the book unless absolutely necessary.

The Ultimate Test

Mastering these exercises is only the first step in developing your ability to read, write, speak, and understand Italian. Nothing is better, however, than getting firsthand experience by talking with native speakers of Italian, watching Italian movies, or reading Italian books, newspapers, and magazines.

TRACK 65

Exercise 1: Some Basic Questions

Answer the questions in complete sentences.

1. *Domanda:*

   ....

   Risposta:

   ....

2. *Domanda:*

   ....

   Risposta:

   ....

3. *Domanda:*

   ....

   Risposta:

   ....

4. *Domanda:*

   ....

   Risposta:

   ....

5. *Domanda:*

   ....

   Risposta:

   ....

6. *Domanda:*

   ....

Risposta:

....

7. *Domanda:*

....

Risposta:

....

8. *Domanda:*

....

Risposta:

....

9. *Domanda:*

....

Risposta:

....

10. *Domanda:*

....

Risposta:

....

11. *Domanda:*

....

Risposta:

....

Exercise 2: Avere and Essere

Complete the sentences with the correct form of *essere* or *avere*, according to the context.

1. *Lucia e io* .... *una bicicletta bianca.*

2. *Boston* .... *una bella città.*

3. *Maria e Giovanni* .... *studenti.*

4. *Tu e Davide* .... *di Roma.*

5. *Luciano e Luca* .... *una bella stanza.*

6. *Noi* .... *intelligenti.*

7. *Il bambino* .... *tre anni.*

8. *Tu* .... *un esame oggi?*

9. *Voi* .... *molti CD di Bob Dylan?*

10. *Lei, Signor Salvi,* .... *il libro d'italiano?*

Exercise 3: The Indefinite Article

Write the correct form of the indefinite article.

1. *Ecco* .... *piazza.*

2. *Ecco* .... *amico.*

3. *Ecco* .... *stadio.*

4. *Ecco* .... *stazione.*

5. *Ecco* .... *zaino.*

6. *Ecco* .... *amica.*

Exercise 4: The Definite Article

Write the definite article before the noun. Then write both article and noun in the plural.

1. .... *università* ....

2. .... *edificio* ....

3. .... *penna* ....

4. .... *libro* ....

5. .... *autobus* ....

6. .... *auto* ....

7. .... *classe* ....

8. .... *conversazione* ....

Exercise 5: Adjective Agreement

Complete with the correct form of the adjective in parentheses.

1. (grey) *L'automobile di papà è* ....

2. (English) *Marco ha due amici* ....

3. (old) *I cani di Antonio sono* ....

4. (green) *Gli occhi di Marcello sono* ....

5. (nice) *Mario è una persona* ....

6. (tall, blond) *Luisa e Marco sono* .... *e* ....

Exercise 6: Adjective Placement

Complete the sentences with the correct form of the adjective in parentheses. The adjective will come before or after the noun it modifies.

1. (yellow) *Marcello ha una* .... *Ford* ....

2. (Many) *Ci sono* .... *ristoranti* .... *in centro.*

3. (white) *Lei ha una* .... *casa* ....

4. (good) *Carlo e Marco sono* .... *amici* ....

5. (beautiful) *Lui è un* .... *ragazzo* ....

6. (long) *È un* .... *esame* ....

7. (same) *Io e Giovanna siamo nella* .... *classe* ....

8. (German) *Ho una* .... *macchina* ....

9. (old) *Giovanni è un* .... *amico* ....

10. (few) *Abbiamo* .... *amici* .... *in Florida.*

11. (good) *Marcello è un* .... *studente* ....

12. (Japanese) *Marco ha due* .... *amici* ....

13. (new) *Papà ha una* .... *automobile* ....

14. (nice) *Marcello ha degli* .... *amici* ....

Exercise 7: Article/Adjective/Noun Formation

Translate the article/adjective/noun into Italian, keeping in mind the placement of the adjective, either before or after the noun.

1. (a dear friend) *Carmela è* ....

2. (a red Ferrari) *Marcello ha* ....

3. (a young professor) *Lui è* ....

4. (Many Italian cities) .... *hanno delle belle piazze.*

5. (a new restaurant) *In Piazza dei Nobili c'è* ....

6. (an interesting book) *Lei ha* ....

7. (The same students) .... *sono in classe.*

8. (The other day) .... *ho visto un film con Roberto Benigni.*

9. (The White House) .... *è a Washington, DC.*

10. (a beautiful language) *L'italiano è* ....

11. (in the new restaurant downtown) *Papà mangia* ....

12. (many trees in the garden) *Ci sono* ....

Exercise 8: Bello

Replace the adjective *brutto* with *bello* in the following sentences.

1. *Che brutta cosa!* ....

2. *Che brutto giorno!* ....

3. *Che brutti occhi!* ....

4. *Che brutto libro!* ....

5. *Che brutto stadio!* ....

6. *Che brutti capelli!* ....

7. *Che brutto edificio!* ....

8. *Che brutti uffici!* ....

Exercise 9: Buono

Complete with the correct form of *buono*.

1. *Sono* .... *consigli.*

2. *È un* .... *caffè.*

3. *È una* .... *abitudine.*

4. *È un* .... *libro.*

5. *È un* .... *albergo.*

Exercise 10: Possessive Adjectives

Complete the sentences with the correct possessive adjective.

1. *Questa sera noi invitiamo* (your brothers) .... *alla festa.*

2. (Your books) .... *sono nella stanza* (of your brother) ....

3. *Linda e Mario parlano* (to their aunts) ....

4. (His brother) .... *è in Italia e* (his cousins) .... *sono in Francia.*

5. (My books) .... *sono* (on his table) ....

6. (Our car) .... *è dal meccanico.*

7. (Her daughters) .... *fanno un viaggio in Italia.*

8. (Your cousin) .... *non lavora il sabato e la domenica.*

9. *Sai che Marco non va alla festa con* (his girlfriend) ....

10. *Tu vedi* (his cars) ....

11. (Their grandfather) .... *vuole bene a* (his grandchildren) ....

12. *Penso di comprare dei fiori per* (my dear aunt) ....

13. (My exams) .... *sono difficili.*

14. *Gli studenti non fanno* (their homework) ....

15. (His sons) .... *sono intelligenti.*

16. (Their female friends) .... *non vengono con noi.*

Exercise 11: Verbs in the Present Tense

Complete the following sentences by providing the correct form of the appropriate verb in parentheses in the present tense.

1. (to look for) *Noi* .... *il numero di telefono del professore.*

2. (to be wrong) *Gli studenti* ....

3. (to be about to) *Loro* .... *finire l'esercizio.*

4. (to finish) *Maria* .... *il compito.*

5. (to live) *Questo semestre loro* .... *nel dormitorio.*

6. (to repeat) *Tu e Marco* .... *la spegazione.*

7. (to swim) *I bambini* .... *nella piscina.*

8. (to watch) *Tu e Maria* .... *la televisione.*

9. (to know) *Voi* .... *la fidanzata di Marcello.*

10. (to want) *Io* .... *andare al concerto di Bob Dylan.*

11. (to begin) *La lezione d'italiano* .... *alle 4.*

12. (to give back) *Tu* .... *il libro al professore.*

13. (to serve) *I camerieri* .... *il caffè ai clienti.*

14. (to work) *Voi* .... *in ufficio.*

15. (to close) *Noi* .... *la finestra.*

16. (to think about) *Tu* .... *tuo fratello?*

17. (to wait for) *Io* .... *il treno.*

18. (to play) *Noi* .... *tennis oggi.*

19. (to come) *Io* .... *alla festa domani sera.*

20. (to go out) *Loro* .... *spesso con le loro amiche.*

21. (to tell) *Tu* .... *sempre la verità?*

22. (to know) *Io non* .... *se Giovanni è uno studente.*

23. (to like) *Non mi* .... *gli spaghetti alla carbonara.*

24. (to succeed) *Marco non* .... *a capire la tua domanda.*

25. (to take a short trip) *Tu* .... *quest'estate?*

Exercise 12: Wanting

State three things you want to do but are unable to do because you have to do something else.

1. ....

2. ....

3. ....

Exercise 13: Andare, Fare, Stare, and Dare

Complete each sentence with the most appropriate verb: *andare, fare, stare,* or *dare.*

1. *Come* .... *tu oggi?*

2. *Quando* .... *una festa voi?*

3. *Noi* .... *in Italia ogni anno.*

4. *Che cosa* .... *tu sabato sera?*

5. *Io* .... *del tu ai miei amici.*

Exercise 14: Verb Conjugations

Conjugate the following verbs in the present tense.

	Restituire	Vedere	Dormire	Parlare
io				
tu				
lui/lei/Lei				
noi				
voi				
loro/Loro				

	Mangiare	Bere	Andare	Fare
io	....	....	....	....
tu	....	....	....	....
lui/lei/Lei	....	....	....	....
noi	....	....	....	....
voi	....	....	....	....
loro/Loro	....	....	....	....

Exercise 15: Translation

Translate into Italian.

1. Luca and Mario are learning to speak Italian.

   ....

2. I am from Providence. I think about my friends in Providence.

   ....

3. You are hot and the coffee is cold.

   ....

4. You and Maria feel like eating.

   ....

5. What kind of car do you have?

   ....

6. Which languages do you speak?

   ....

7. On Sundays Anna goes to church with Maria.

   ....

8. I am reading a book on Italian history.

   ....

9. After dinner, she takes a walk and then makes a phone call to Maria.

    ....

10. Sorry, but on Sunday I am going to the movies with Cristina.

    ....

11. Do you know John?

    ....

12. We go out with your son's friends.

    ....

13. You must be hungry. Do you want some pizza?

    ....

14. Do you know that my friend John is a student?

    ....

15. You can't watch TV now. You must study for your exam.

    ....

Exercise 16: Answering Questions

TRACK 81

Listen to each question, and then listen again and write down each question in the first blank provided. Answer the questions in complete sentences in Italian. Some questions will have more than one part to them.

1. *Domanda:*

    ....

    Risposta:

    ....

2. *Domanda:*

    ....

    Risposta:

    ....

3. *Domanda:*

   ....

   Risposta:

   ....

4. *Domanda:*

   ....

   Risposta:

   ....

5. *Domanda:*

   ....

   Risposta:

   ....

6. *Domanda:*

   ....

   Risposta:

   ....

7. *Domanda:*

   ....

   Risposta:

   ....

8. *Domanda:*

   ....

   Risposta:

   ....

9. *Domanda:*

   ....

   Risposta:

   ....

10. *Domanda:*

    ....

    Risposta:

    ....

Exercise 17: Direct Object Pronouns

TRACK 67

Listen to and repeat each sentence. Then listen again, writing each sentence. Finally, rewrite the sentences, changing the verb tense from present to past and substituting the direct object pronoun for the direct object.

1. ....
....

2. ....
....

3. ....
....

4. ....
....

5. ....
....

6. ....
....

7. ....
....

8. ....
....

Exercise 18: Direct and Indirect Object Pronouns

Rewrite the sentences substituting the direct object or indirect object pronoun for the direct object or indirect object.

1. *Ho parlato al mio professore stamattina.*

....

2. *Hai cercato il numero di telefono del professore.*

....

3. *Hanno dimenticato di telefonare a Stefano.*

....

4. *Non hai visto i tuoi amici.*

....

5. *Hai guardato la TV ieri sera.*

....

6. *Ha ordinato i ravioli.*

....

7. *Avete visto le vostre amiche sabato sera.*

....

8. *Abbiamo telefonato ai nostri nonni.*

....

9. *Ho incontrato Teresa al ristorante.*

....

Exercise 19: Double Object Pronouns

TRACK 68

Answer the questions in complete sentences in Italian, incorporating a double object pronoun in your answers.

1. *Domanda:*

....

Risposta:

....

2. *Domanda:*

....

Risposta:

....

3. *Domanda:*

....

Risposta:

....

4. *Domanda:*

....

Risposta:

....

5. *Domanda:*

....

Risposta:

....

6. *Domanda:*

....

Risposta:

....

7. *Domanda:*

....

Risposta:

....

8. *Domanda:*

....

Risposta:

....

9. *Domanda:*

....

Risposta:

....

10. *Domanda:*

....

Risposta:

....

Exercise 20: The Passato Prossimo

Fill in the blanks with the correct form of the *passato prossimo*.

1. *Venerdì scorso la mia famiglia* (to leave) .... *per New York in treno.*

2. *Mio padre e mia madre* (to travel) .... *in seconda classe.*

3. *Il mio amico* (to bring) .... *un po' di vino bianco.*

4. *Noi* (to drink) .... *il vino durante il viaggio.*

5. *Io* (to sleep) .... *durante il viaggio.*

6. *Quando il treno* (to arrive) .... *noi* (to climb off) .... *dal treno.*

7. *Io* (to want) .... *prendere un taxi.*

8. *I miei genitori* (to telephone) .... *al fratello di mio padre.*

9. *Maria e suo fratello* (to go out) .... *venerdì sera.*

10. *Mio zio* (to die) .... *l'anno scorso.*

11. *Le mie due sorelle* (to enter) .... *e hanno trovato una sorpresa.*

12. *Io* (to be born) .... *nel mese di ottobre.*

13. *Tu e Maria* (to go) .... *a sciare l'anno scorso.*

14. *Loro* (to work) .... *sabato scorso.*

15. *Maria e Elena non* (to be) .... *di Milano.*

Exercise 21: Now or Then?

Conjugate the verb in parentheses in the present or past tense, according to the time references indicated.

1. *Ieri mattina Marco* (to wake up) .... *alle 7 e* (to get up) .... *alle 7.30. Poi lui* (to prepare) .... *i bagagli per il viaggio ed* (to go) .... *all'aeroporto, dove* (to take) .... *il volo per Sardegna.*

2. *Stasera io* (to want) .... *andare al cinema con il mio amico. Il mio amico* (to be called) .... *Giovanni. Normalmente lui* (to get bored) .... *al cinema.*

Questa volta io e Giovanni (to have fun) .... *sicura-mente perché andiamo a vedere un film divertentissimo. Dopo il film (to stop)* .... *al bar a prendere un caffè.*

3. *Due giorni fa io (to work)* .... *fino a tardi e (to return)* .... *a casa alle undici. Io (to eat)* .... *velocemente, perché avevo molta fame. (to go)* .... *a letto alle undici e mezza e (to fall asleep)* .... *subito.*

Exercise 22: Answering Questions in the Passato Prossimo

TRACK 69

Listen to each question, then listen again, writing down each question in the first blank provided. Finally, answer the questions in complete sentences in Italian. Some questions will have more than one part to them.

1. *Domanda:*

   ....

   Risposta:

   ....

2. *Domanda:*

   ....

   Risposta:

   ....

3. *Domanda:*

   ....

   Risposta:

   ....

4. *Domanda:*

   ....

   Risposta:

   ....

5. *Domanda:*

   ....

Risposta:

....

6. *Domanda:*

....

Risposta:

....

7. *Domanda:*

....

Risposta:

....

8. *Domanda:*

....

Risposta:

....

9. *Domanda:*

....

Risposta:

....

Exercise 23: Conjugation Across the Tenses

Conjugate the verb *arrabbiarsi* in the requested tenses.

present	
io	....
tu	....
lui/lei/Lei	....
noi	....
voi	....
loro/Loro	....

imperfetto

io ....

tu ....

lui/lei/Lei ....

noi ....

voi ....

loro/Loro ....

passato prossimo

io ....

tu ....

lui/lei/Lei ....

noi ....

voi ....

loro/Loro ....

future

io ....

tu ....

lui/lei/Lei ....

noi ....

voi ....

loro/Loro ....

conditional

io ....

tu ....

lui/lei/Lei ....

noi ....

voi ....

loro/Loro ....

present subjunctive

io ....

tu ....

lui/lei/Lei ....

noi ....

voi ....

loro/Loro ....

Exercise 24: Translation Exercise

In the first space, translate the questions into Italian. In the second space, answer the questions in Italian. Then change the tense of your answer to the new tense listed.

1. Are you stopping at a newsstand before going to the office?

   Domanda: ....

   Risposta: ....

   Conditional: ....

2. Do you get angry when your friends don't call?

   Domanda: ....

   Risposta: ....

   Passato Prossimo: ....

3. Where do you like to eat?

   Domanda: ....

   Risposta: ....

   Imperfetto: ....

4. Did you enjoy yourself on Friday evening?

   Domanda: ....

   Risposta: ....

   Conditional Perfect: ....

5. How many times a week do you speak to your parents?

Domanda: ....

Risposta: ....

Future Perfect: ....

Exercise 25: Reciprocal Construction

Answer each question using the reciprocal construction, as in the example.

Marco ha visto i suoi cugini? Sì, Marco e i suoi cugini si sono visti.

1. *Marco ha parlato con il suo amico?*

    ....

2. *Elena ha visto suo cugino?*

    ....

3. *Hai scritto a tuo padre?*

    ....

4. *Giorgio ha telefonato al suo compagno?*

    ....

5. *Giuseppe ha chiamato i suoi amici?*

    ....

Exercise 26: Passato Prossimo or Imperfetto?

Complete the sentences using the *passato prossimo* or *imperfetto* of the verb in parentheses.

1. *Ieri pomeriggio tu e Maria* (to speak) .... *con i ragazzi che* (to play) .... *a calcio.*

2. *Quando mia moglie ed io* (to go out) .... *stamattina, il nostro gatto* (to sleep) .... *ancora.*

3. *Il mese scorso, tu e Lisa* (to go) .... *in Italia. Voi* (to enjoy oneself) .... *molto.*

4. *Quando loro* (to leave) .... (it was 8:30) ....

5. *Ieri a mezzogiorno Anna* (to stop) .... *al ristorante perché* (to be hungry) .... *e* (to be thirsty) ....

6. *Quando noi* (to arrive) .... *in biblioteca stamattina,* (to rain) ....

7. *Giovedì scorso io e Luciano* (to go) .... *in spiaggia, perché* (to be) .... *una bella giornata.*

Exercise 27: The Future Tense

Provide the future tense conjugation of the verb in parentheses.

1. (to pay attention) *Io non* .... *a quello che dice il professore.*

2. (to be able) *Marco non* .... *uscire, perché deve studiare.*

3. (to be thirsty) *Marcello, tu* ....

4. (to have to) *Voi* .... *fare attenzione in classe.*

5. (to address someone informally) *Io* .... *agli amici.*

6. (to drink) *Io non* .... *il caffè a colazione.*

7. (to be afraid) *Noi* ....

8. (to prepare) *Loro* .... *la colazione per i bambini.*

9. (to write) *Tu* .... *molte lettere agli amici?*

10. (to answer) *Io* .... *al telefono.*

11. (to leave) *Voi* .... *da casa.*

12. (to wake up) *I ragazzi* .... *molto presto.*

13. (to receive) *Tu e Maria* .... *molte email.*

14. (to offer) *Gianni* .... *un caffè al professore.*

15. (to believe) *Tu* .... *negli UFO?*

16. (to sleep) *Tutti gli studenti* .... *durante il viaggio.*

17. (to ask) *Che cosa* .... *tu?*

18. (to open) *La studentessa* .... *il libro a pagina dician-nove.*

19. (to follow) *I ragazzi* .... *il discorso.*

20. (to like) *Mi* .... *molto rivedere Parigi.*

Exercise 28: The Present Conditional

Provide the conditional tense conjugation of the verb in parentheses.

1. (to build) *Io e mia moglie* .... *una nuova casa se avessimo i soldi.*

2. (to ask a question) *Lo studente* .... *in classe ma è troppo timido.*

3. (to address someone formally) *Loro* .... *al professore.*

4. (to finish) *Loro* .... *le lasagne, ma non hanno più fame.*

5. (to understand) *I ragazzi non* .... *il discorso.*

6. (to clean) *Il mio amico* .... *più spesso se avesse il tempo.*

7. (to take a break) *Tu* .... *dopo la lezione.*

8. (to prefer) *Lui* .... *bere il caffè italiano.*

9. (to study) *Giovanni* .... *se avesse tempo.*

10. (to explain) *L'avvocato* .... *la legge al cliente.*

11. (to pay) *I miei amici* .... *il caffè.*

12. (to learn) *Noi* .... *l'italiano.*

13. (to return) *Tu* .... *in Italia l'anno prossimo.*

14. (to go) *Marco e Angela* .... *alla festa di Giovanni.*

15. (to get up) *Io* .... *molto tardi.*

Exercise 29: **Piacere**

Translate each sentence into Italian using the verb *piacere* in each sentence.

1. They liked us a lot.

   ....

2. We don't like foreign movies because we don't like to read subtitles.

   ....

3. They went out last night. He did not like her but she liked him.

   ....

4. She doesn't like his friends because they drink too much grappa.

   ....

5. I like to wash my car on Saturdays. I used to work on Sundays.

   ....

6. Marco and Lisa like to go out.

   ....

7. They don't like us because they don't know us.

   ....

8. I would like to eat in that restaurant.

....

9. I would be able to go to the party but I don't like parties.

....

10. I would have liked the professor but he didn't give me a good grade.

....

Exercise 30: Corretto o Incorretto?

Rewrite the following sentences so that they are grammatically correct.

1. *Io abiti in Roma.*

....

2. *Noi siamo mangiato nell nuova ristorante.*

....

3. *Ho prenduto un caffè al bar.*

....

4. *Pierino studava l'italiano.*

....

5. *Marcello e Maria avevono letto il libro.*

....

6. *Quella signora avranno sessant'anni.*

....

7. *Io e la mia moglie adreste in Italia.*

....

8. *Penso che lui è un'amico de Claudio.*

....

9. *Il mio fratello non crede che io sono andati alla festa.*

....

10. *È importante che tu vai stasera.*

....

Exercise 31: Listening and Translating

TRACK 70

Listen to each sentence. Then listen again and write each sentence as you hear it. Finally, go back and translate each sentence into English.

1. ....

....

2. ....

....

3. ....

....

4. ....

....

5. ....

....

6. ....

....

7. ....

....

8. ....

....

9. ....

....

10. ....

....

11. ....

....

12. ....

....

13. ....

....

14. ....

....

Exercise 32: From Indicative to Subjunctive

Change the following sentences from the indicative to the subjunctive by adding the subjunctive indicator in parentheses, as in the example.

Marco è intelligente. (Io credo che…)> Io credo che Marco sia intelligente.

1. *Mario e Silvia si sono sposati l'anno scorso. (Noi pensiamo che…)*

....

2. *Gianni si è arrabbiato. (È possibile che…)*

....

3. *Non hanno ancora fatto colazione. (Sembra che…)*

....

4. *I miei amici ed io non ci vediamo mai. (Peccato che…)*

....

5. *Tino ha mangiato la torta. (Pare che…)*

....

Verb Tables

essere

avere

parlare—regular –are verb

ricevere—regular –ere verb

dormire—regular –ire verb

andare	finire	piacere
bere	fare	stare
cercare	mangiare	potere
dare	mettere	uscire
dire	morire	venire
dovere	pagare	volere

essere (to be)

auxiliary verb

present indicative	**present subjunctive**
io sono	sia
tu sei	sia
lui, lei, Lei è	sia
noi siamo	siamo
voi siete	siate
loro, Loro sono	siano

passato prossimo (present perfect) indicative	**imperfect indicative**
io sono stato	ero
tu sei stato	eri
lui, lei, Lei è stato	era
noi siamo stati	eravamo
voi siete stati	eravate
loro, Loro sono stati	erano

future indicative	**present conditional**
io sarò	sarei
tu sarai	saresti
lui, lei, Lei sarà	sarebbe
noi saremo	saremmo
voi sarete	sareste
loro, Loro saranno	sarebbero

imperative	**imperfect subjunctive**
io —	fossi
tu sii	fossi
lui, lei, Lei sia	fosse
noi siamo	fossimo
voi siate	foste
loro, Loro siano	fossero

gerund	**past participle**
essendo	stato

avere (to have)

auxiliary verb

present indicative	**present subjunctive**
io ho	abbia
tu hai	abbia
lui, lei, Lei ha	abbia
noi abbiamo	abbiamo
voi avete	abbiate
loro, Loro hanno	abbiano

passato prossimo (present perfect) indicative	**imperfect indicative**
io ho avuto	avevo
tu hai avuto	avevi
lui, lei, Lei ha avuto	aveva
noi abbiamo avuto	avevamo
voi avete avuto	avevate
loro, Loro hanno avuto	avevano

future indicative	**present conditional**
io avrò	avrei
tu avrai	avresti
lui, lei, Lei avrà	avrebbe
noi avremo	avremmo
voi avrete	avreste
loro, Loro avranno	avrebbero

imperative	**imperfect subjunctive**
io —	avessi
tu abbi	avessi
lui, lei, Lei abbia	avesse
noi abbiamo	avessimo
voi abbiate	aveste
loro, Loro abbiano	avessero

gerund
avendo

past participle
avuto

parlare (to speak)

regular –are verb

present indicative	**present subjunctive**
io parlo	parli
tu parli	parli
lui, lei, Lei parla	parli
noi parliamo	parliamo
voi parlate	parliate
loro, Loro parlano	parlino

**passato prossimo
(present perfect)
indicative**

imperfect indicative

io ho parlato	parlavo
tu hai parlato	parlavi
lui, lei, Lei ha parlato	parlava
noi abbiamo parlato	parlavamo
voi avete parlato	parlavate
loro, Loro hanno parlato	parlavano

future indicative	**present conditional**
io parlerò	parlerei
tu parlerai	parleresti
lui, lei, Lei parlerà	parlerebbe
noi parleremo	parleremmo
voi parlerete	parlereste
loro, Loro parleranno	parlerebbero

imperative	**imperfect subjunctive**
io —	parlassi
tu parla	parlassi
lui, lei, Lei parli	parlasse
noi parliamo	parlassimo
voi parlate	parlaste
loro, Loro parlino	parlassero

gerund
parlando

past participle
parlato

ricevere (to receive)

regular –ere verb

present indicative	**present subjunctive**
io ricevo	riceva
tu ricevi	riceva
lui, lei, Lei riceve	riceva
noi riceviamo	riceviamo
voi ricevete	riceviate
loro, Loro ricevono	ricevano

**passato prossimo
(present perfect)
indicative**

imperfect indicative

io ho ricevuto	ricevevo
tu hai ricevuto	ricevevi
lui, lei, Lei ha ricevuto	riceveva
noi abbiamo ricevuto	ricevevamo
voi avete ricevuto	ricevevate
loro, Loro hanno ricevuto	ricevevano

future indicative	**present conditional**
io riceverò	riceverei
tu riceverai	riceveresti
lui, lei, Lei riceverà	riceverebbe
noi riceveremo	riceveremmo
voi riceverete	ricevereste
loro, Loro riceveranno	riceverebbero

imperative	**imperfect subjunctive**
io —	ricevessi
tu ricevi	ricevessi
lui, lei, Lei riceva	ricevesse
noi riceviamo	ricevessimo
voi ricevete	riceveste
loro, Loro ricevano	ricevessero

gerund
ricevendo

past participle
ricevuto

dormire (to sleep)

regular –ire verb

present indicative	**present subjunctive**
io dormo	dorma
tu dormi	dorma
lui, lei, Lei dorme	dorma
noi dormiamo	dormiamo
voi dormite	dormiate
loro, Loro dormono	dormano

**passato prossimo
(present perfect)
indicative**

imperfect indicative

io ho dormito	dormivo
tu hai dormito	dormivi

lui, lei, Lei ha dormito

noi abbiamo dormito

voi avete dormito

loro, Loro hanno dormito

dormiva

dormivamo

dormivate

dormivano

future indicative

io dormirò

tu dormirai

lui, lei, Lei dormirà

noi dormiremo

voi dormirete .

loro, Loro dormiranno

present conditional

dormirei

dormiresti

dormirebbe

dormiremmo

dormireste

dormirebbero

imperative

io —

tu dormi

lui, lei, Lei dorma

noi dormiamo

voi dormite

loro, Loro dormano

imperfect subjunctive

dormissi

dormissi

dormisse

dormissimo

dormiste

dormissero

gerund

dormendo

past participle

dormito

andare (to go)

irregular –are verb

present indicative

io vado

tu vai

lui, lei, Lei va

noi andiamo

voi andate

loro, Loro vanno

present subjunctive

vada

vada

vada

andiamo

andiate

vadano

**passato prossimo
(present perfect)
indicative**

io sono andato

tu sei andato

lui, lei, Lei è andato

noi siamo andati

voi siete andati

loro, Loro sono andati

imperfect indicative

andavo

andavi

andava

andavamo

andavate

andavano

future indicative

io andrò

tu andrai

lui, lei, Lei andrà

present conditional

andrei

andresti

andrebbe

noi andremo

voi andrete

loro, Loro andranno

andremmo

andreste

andrebbero

imperative

io —

tu va, vai, va'

lui, lei, Lei vada

noi andiamo

voi andate

loro, Loro vadano

imperfect subjunctive

andassi

andassi

andasse

andassimo

andaste

andassero

gerund

andando

past participle

andato

bere (to drink)

irregular –ere verb

present indicative

io bevo

tu bevi

lui, lei, Lei beve

noi beviamo

voi bevete

loro, Loro bevono

present subjunctive

beva

beva

beva

beviamo

beviate

bevano

**passato prossimo
(present perfect)
indicative**

io ho bevuto

tu hai bevuto

lui, lei, Lei ha bevuto

noi abbiamo bevuto

voi avete bevuto

loro, Loro hanno bevuto

imperfect indicative

bevevo

bevevi

beveva

bevevamo

bevevate

bevevano

future indicative

io berrò, beverò

tu berrai, beverai

lui, lei, Lei berrà, beverà

noi berremo, beveremo

voi berrete, beverete

loro, Loro berranno,
beveranno

present conditional

berrei, beverei

berresti, beveresti

berrebbe, beverebbe

berremmo, beveremmo

berreste, bevereste

berrebbero,
beverebbero

imperative

io —

tu bevi

lui, lei, Lei beva

imperfect subjunctive

bevessi

bevessi

bevesse

noi beviamo — bevessimo
voi bevete — beveste
loro, Loro bevano — bevessero

gerund — **past participle**
bevendo — bevuto

cercare (to look for)

spelling change –are verb (c>ch)

present indicative	**present subjunctive**
io cerco	cerchi
tu cerchi	cerchi
lui, lei, Lei cerca	cerchi
noi cerchiamo	cerchiamo
voi cercate	cerchiate
loro, Loro cercano	cerchino

**passato prossimo
(present perfect)**

indicative	**imperfect indicative**
io ho cercato	cercavo
tu hai cercato	cercavi
lui, lei, Lei ha cercato	cercava
noi abbiamo cercato	cercavamo
voi avete cercato	cercavate
loro, Loro hanno cercato	cercavano

future indicative	**present conditional**
io cercherò	cercherei
tu cercherai	cercheresti
lui, lei, Lei cercherà	cercherebbe
noi cercheremo	cercheremmo
voi cercherete	cerchereste
loro, Loro cercheranno	cercherebbero

imperative	**imperfect subjunctive**
io —	cercassi
tu cerca	cercassi
lui, lei, Lei cerchi	cercasse
noi cerchiamo	cercassimo
voi cercate	cercaste
loro, Loro cerchino	cercassero

gerund — **past participle**
cercando — cercato

dare (to give)

irregular –are verb

present indicative	**present subjunctive**
io do	dia
tu dai	dia
lui, lei, Lei dà	dia
noi diamo	diamo
voi date	diate
loro, Loro danno	diano

**passato prossimo
(present perfect)**

indicative	**imperfect indicative**
io avevo dato	davo
tu avevi dato	davi
lui, lei, Lei aveva dato	dava
noi avevamo dato	davamo
voi avevate dato	davate
loro, Loro avevano dato	davano

future indicative	**present conditional**
io darò	darei
tu darai	daresti
lui, lei, Lei darà	darebbe
noi daremo	daremmo
voi darete	dareste
loro, Loro daranno	darebbero

imperative	**imperfect subjunctive**
io —	dessi
tu dà, dai, da'	dessi
lui, lei, Lei dia	desse
noi diamo	dessimo
voi date	deste
loro, Loro diano	dessero

gerund — **past participle**
dando — dato

dire (to say, to tell)

irregular –ire verb

present indicative	**present subjunctive**
io dico	dica
tu dici	dica
lui, lei, Lei dice	dica
noi diciamo	diciamo
voi dite	diciate
loro, Loro dicono	dicano

**passato prossimo
(present perfect)
indicative**

io ho detto	**imperfect indicative**
tu hai detto	dicevo
lui, lei, Lei ha detto	dicevi
noi abbiamo detto	diceva
voi avete detto	dicevamo
loro, Loro hanno detto	dicevate
	dicevano

future indicative

	present conditional
io dirò	direi
tu dirai	diresti
lui, lei, Lei dirà	direbbe
noi diremo	diremmo
voi direte	direste
loro, Loro diranno	direbbero

imperative

	imperfect subjunctive
io —	dicessi
tu dì, di'	dicessi
lui, lei, Lei dica	dicesse
noi diciamo	dicessimo
voi dite	diceste
loro, Loro dicano	dicessero

gerund

	past participle
dicendo	detto

dovere (to have to, must)

irregular –ere verb

present indicative

	present subjunctive
io devo	debba
tu devi	debba
lui, lei, Lei deve	debba
noi dobbiamo	dobbiamo
voi dovete	dobbiate
loro, Loro devono, debbono	debbano

**passato prossimo
(present perfect)
indicative**

	imperfect indicative
io ho dovuto	dovevo
tu hai dovuto	dovevi
lui, lei, Lei ha dovuto	doveva
noi abbiamo dovuto	dovevamo
voi avete dovuto	dovevate
loro, Loro hanno dovuto	dovevano

future indicative

	present conditional
io dovrò	dovrei
tu dovrai	dovresti
lui, lei, Lei dovrà	dovrebbe
noi dovremo	dovremmo
voi dovrete	dovreste
loro, Loro dovranno	dovrebbero

imperative

	imperfect subjunctive
io —	dovessi
tu —	dovessi
lui, lei, Lei —	dovesse
noi —	dovessimo
voi —	doveste
loro, Loro —	dovessero

gerund

	past participle
dovendo	dovuto

finire (to finish)

irregular –ire verb (–ire>–isc–)

present indicative

	present subjunctive
io finisco	finisca
tu finisci	finisca
lui, lei, Lei finisce	finisca
noi finiamo	finiamo
voi finite	finiate
loro, Loro finiscono	finiscano

**passato prossimo
(present perfect)
indicative**

	imperfect indicative
io ho finito	finivo
tu hai finito	finivi
lui, lei, Lei ha finito	finiva
noi abbiamo finito	finivamo
voi avete finito	finivate
loro, Loro hanno finito	finivano

future indicative

	present conditional
io finirò	finirei
tu finirai	finiresti
lui, lei, Lei finirà	finirebbe
noi finiremo	finiremmo
voi finirete	finireste
loro, Loro finiranno	finirebbero

imperative	imperfect subjunctive
io —	finissi
tu finisci	finissi
lui, lei, Lei finisca	finisse
noi finiamo	finissimo
voi finite	finiste
loro, Loro finiscano	finissero

gerund	past participle
finendo	finito

fare (to do, to make)

irregular –are verb

present indicative	present subjunctive
io faccio	faccia
tu fai	faccia
lui, lei, Lei fa	faccia
noi facciamo	facciamo
voi fate	facciate
loro, Loro fanno	facciano

passato prossimo (present perfect) indicative	imperfect indicative
io ho fatto	facevo
tu hai fatto	facevi
lui, lei, Lei ha fatto	faceva
noi abbiamo fatto	facevamo
voi avete fatto	facevate
loro, Loro hanno fatto	facevano

future indicative	present conditional
io farò	farei
tu farai	faresti
lui, lei, Lei farà	farebbe
noi faremo	faremmo
voi farete	fareste
loro, Loro faranno	farebbero

imperative	imperfect subjunctive
io —	facessi
tu fa, fai, fa'	facessi
lui, lei, Lei faccia	facesse
noi facciamo	facessimo
voi fate	faceste
loro, Loro facciano	facessero

gerund	past participle
facendo	fatto

mangiare (to eat)

irregular –are verb (–ia– >–e–)

present indicative	present subjunctive
io mangio	mangi
tu mangi	mangi
lui, lei, Lei mangia	mangi
noi mangiamo	mangiamo
voi mangiate	mangiate
loro, Loro mangiano	mangino

passato prossimo (present perfect) indicative	imperfect indicative
io ho mangiato	mangiavo
tu hai mangiato	mangiavi
lui, lei, Lei ha mangiato	mangiava
noi abbiamo mangiato	mangiavamo
voi avete mangiato	mangiavate
loro, Loro hanno mangiato	mangiavano

future indicative	present conditional
io mangerò	mangerei
tu mangerai	mangeresti
lui, lei, Lei mangerà	mangerebbe
noi mangeremo	mangeremmo
voi mangerete	mangereste
loro, Loro mangeranno	mangerebbero

imperative	imperfect subjunctive
io —	mangiassi
tu mangia	mangiassi
lui, lei, Lei mangi	mangiasse
noi mangiamo	mangiassimo
voi mangiate	mangiaste
loro, Loro mangino	mangiassero

gerund	past participle
mangiando	mangiato

morire (to die)

irregular –ire verb (–o– >–uo–)

present indicative	present subjunctive
io muoio	muoia
tu muori	muoia

lui, lei, Lei muore	muoia
noi moriamo	moriamo
voi morite	moriate
loro, Loro muoiono	muoiano

passato prossimo (present perfect) indicative — **imperfect indicative**

io sono morto	morivo
tu sei morto	morivi
lui, lei, Lei è morto	moriva
noi siamo morti	morivamo
voi siete morti	morivate
loro, Loro sono morti	morivano

future indicative — **present conditional**

io morirò, morrò	morirei, morrei
tu morirai, morrai	moriresti, morresti
lui, lei, Lei morirà, morrà	morirebbe, morrebbe
noi moriremo, morremo	moriremmo, morremmo
voi morirete, morrete	morireste, morreste
loro, Loro moriranno, morranno	morirebbero, morrebbero

imperative — **imperfect subjunctive**

io —	morissi
tu muori	morissi
lui, lei, Lei muoia	morisse
noi moriamo	morissimo
voi morite	moriste
loro, Loro muoiano	morissero

gerund — **past participle**

morendo	morto

pagare (to pay)

irregular –are verb (–g– >–gh–)

present indicative — **present subjunctive**

io pago	paghi
tu paghi	paghi
lui, lei, Lei paga	paghi
noi paghiamo	paghiamo
voi pagate	paghiate
loro, Loro pagano	paghino

passato prossimo (present perfect) indicative — **imperfect indicative**

io ho pagato	pagavo
tu hai pagato	pagavi
lui, lei, Lei ha pagato	pagava
noi abbiamo pagato	pagavamo
voi avete pagato	pagavate
loro, Loro hanno pagato	pagavano

future indicative — **present conditional**

io pagherò	pagherei
tu pagherai	pagheresti
lui, lei, Lei pagherà	pagherebbe
noi pagheremo	pagherebbero
voi pagherete	paghereste
loro, Loro pagheranno	pagherebbero

imperative — **imperfect subjunctive**

io —	pagassi
tu paga	pagassi
lui, lei, Lei paghi	pagasse
noi paghiamo	pagassimo
voi pagate	pagaste
loro, Loro paghino	pagassero

gerund — **past participle**

pagando	pagato

piacere (to please)

irregular –ere verb

present indicative — **present subjunctive**

io piaccio	piaccia
tu piaci	piaccia
lui, lei, Lei piace	piaccia
noi piacciamo	piacciamo
voi piacete	piacciate
loro, Loro piacciono	piacciano

passato prossimo (present perfect) indicative — **imperfect indicative**

io sono piaciuto	piacevo
tu sei piaciuto	piacevi
lui, lei, Lei è piaciuto	piaceva
noi siamo piaciuti	piacevamo
voi siete piaciuti	piacevate
loro, Loro sono piaciuti	piacevano

future indicative — **present conditional**

io piacerò	piacerei
tu piacerai	piaceresti
lui, lei, Lei piacerà	piacerebbe

noi piaceremo

piaceremmo

voi piacerete

piacereste

loro, Loro piaceranno

piacerebbero

imperative

imperfect subjunctive

io —

piacessi

tu piaci

piacessi

lui, lei, Lei piaccia

piacesse

noi piacciamo

piacessimo

voi piacete

piaceste

loro, Loro piacciano

piacessero

gerund

past participle

piacendo

piaciuto

potere (to be able to, can)

irregular –ere verb

present indicative

present subjunctive

io posso

possa

tu puoi

possa

lui, lei, Lei può

possa

noi possiamo

possiamo

voi potete

possiate

loro, Loro possono

possano

**passato prossimo
(present perfect)
indicative**

imperfect indicative

io ho potuto

potevo

tu hai potuto

potevi

lui, lei, Lei ha potuto

poteva

noi abbiamo potuto

potevamo

voi avete potuto

potevate

loro, Loro hanno potuto

potevano

future indicative

present conditional

io potrò

potrei

tu potrai

potresti

lui, lei, Lei potrà

potrebbe

noi potremo

potremmo

voi potrete

potreste

loro, Loro potranno

potrebbero

imperative

imperfect subjunctive

io —

potessi

tu —

potessi

lui, lei, Lei —

potesse

noi —

potessimo

voi —

poteste

loro, Loro —

potessero

gerund

past participle

potendo

potuto

stare (to stay, to feel)

irregular –are verb

present indicative

present subjunctive

io sto

stia

tu stai

stia

lui, lei, Lei sta

stia

noi stiamo

stiamo

voi state

stiate

loro, Loro stanno

stiano

**passato prossimo
(present perfect)
indicative**

imperfect indicative

io sono stato

stavo

tu sei stato

stavi

lui, lei, Lei è stato

stava

noi siamo stati

stavamo

voi siete stati

stavate

loro, Loro sono stati

stavano

future indicative

present conditional

io starò

starei

tu starai

staresti

lui, lei, Lei starà

starebbe

noi staremo

staremmo

voi starete

stareste

loro, Loro staranno

starebbero

imperative

imperfect subjunctive

io —

stessi

tu sta, stai, sta'

stessi

lui, lei, Lei stia

stesse

noi stiamo

stessimo

voi state

steste

loro, Loro stiano

stessero

gerund

past participle

stando

stato

venire (to come)

irregular –ire verb

present indicative	**present subjunctive**
io vengo	venga
tu vieni	venga
lui, lei, Lei viene	venga
noi veniamo	veniamo
voi venite	veniate
loro, Loro vengono	vengano

passato prossimo (present perfect) indicative	**imperfect indicative**
io sono venuto	venivo
tu sei venuto	venivi
lui, lei, Lei è venuto	veniva
noi siamo venuti	venivamo
voi siete venuti	venivate
loro, Loro sono venuti	venivano

future indicative	**present conditional**
io verrò	verrei
tu verrai	verresti
lui, lei, Lei verrà	verrebbe
noi verremo	verremmo
voi verrete	verreste
loro, Loro verranno	verrebbero

imperative	**imperfect subjunctive**
io —	venissi
tu vieni	venissi
lui, lei, Lei venga	venisse
noi veniamo	venissimo
voi venite	veniste
loro, Loro vengano	venissero

gerund	**past participle**
venendo	venuto

volere (to want)

irregular –ere verb

present indicative	**present subjunctive**
io voglio	voglia
tu vuoi	voglia
lui, lei, Lei vuole	voglia
noi vogliamo	vogliamo
voi volete	vogliate
loro, Loro vogliono	vogliano

passato prossimo (present perfect) indicative	**imperfect indicative**
io ho voluto	volevo
tu hai voluto	volevi
lui, lei, Lei ha voluto	voleva
noi abbiamo voluto	volevamo
voi avete voluto	volevate
loro, Loro hanno voluto	volevano

future indicative	**present conditional**
io vorrò	vorrei
tu vorrai	vorresti
lui, lei, Lei vorrà	vorrebbe
noi vorremo	vorremmo
voi vorrete	vorreste
loro, Loro vorranno	vorrebbero

imperative	**imperfect subjunctive**
io —	volessi
tu —	volessi
lui, lei, Lei —	volesse
noi —	volessimo
voi —	voleste
loro, Loro —	volessero

gerund	**past participle**
volendo	voluto

Appendix B

Italian to English Glossary

A

Italian	English
a	at, in, to
a volte	sometimes
abbastanza	enough, rather
l'abitante	inhabitant
abitare	to live
l'abitudine	habit, practice
accendere	to light
l'acciuga	anchovy
accompagnare	to accompany
l'acqua	water
addormentarsi	to fall asleep
adesso	now
l'aeroplano	airplane
l'aeroporto	airport
affittare	to rent
l'agenzia	agency
l'agenzia di viaggi	travel agency
l'aggettivo	adjective
aggressivo	aggressive
l'aglio	garlic
agosto	August
aiutare	to help
l'aiuto	help
l'albergo	hotel
l'albero	tree
alto	tall
altro	other
alzarsi	to get up
l'amica	female friend
l'amico	male friend
l'amore	love
ancora	still, yet, again
andare	to go
l'anniversario	anniversary
l'anno	year
annoiarsi	to get bored
antipatico	unpleasant
appena	as soon as
l'appuntamento	appointment
aprile	April
aprire	to open
l'aranciata	orange soda
arrabbiarsi	to get angry
arrivare	to arrive
l'arrosto	roast
asciugare	to dry
l'asciugatrice	clothes dryer
ascoltare	to listen (to)
aspettare	to wait (for)
assistere	to attend
l'astrologia	astrology
l'atteggiamento	attitude
attentamente	attentively
attento	attentive
l'attenzione	attention
l'attore	actor
l'aula	classroom
l'autobus	bus
l'automobile	automobile, car
l'autore	author
l'autorità	authority
l'autostrada	highway
l'autunno	fall, autumn
avaro	stingy
avere	to have
avere bisogno (di)	to need, have need (of)
avere caldo	to be hot
avere fame	to be hungry
avere freddo	to be cold
avere fretta	to be in a hurry
avere paura (di)	to be afraid (of)
avere ragione	to be right, correct
avere sete	to be thirsty
avere sonno	to be tired, sleepy
avere torto	to be wrong, incorrect
avere voglia di	to feel like
l'avvocato	lawyer
azzurro	blue

B

Italian	English
il bagaglio	luggage
ballare	to dance
la bambina	female child
i bambini	children
il bambino	male child
il bar	bar
la base	base
basso	short
la bellezza	beauty
bello	beautiful
bene	well
bere	to drink
bianco	white
la biblioteca	library
la bicicletta	bicycle
il biglietto	ticket
biondo	blonde
la birra	beer
il biscotto	cookie
bisogna	it is necessary
blu	blue
la bottiglia	bottle
bravo	good, capable
brutto	ugly
la bugia	lie
la bugia di convenienza	white lie
il buio	dark
buono	good
il burro	butter

C

Italian	English
cadere	to fall
il caffè	coffee
il cagnetto	puppy
il calcio	soccer
caldo	warm
il calendario	calendar
cambiare	to change
la camera	room
la cameriera	waitress
il cameriere	waiter
camminare	to walk
la campagna	country, countryside
canadese	Canadian
il cane	dog
il cantante	singer
cantare	to sing
la canzone	song
i capelli	hair
capire	to understand

il capo **boss**
il capoufficio **office manager**
la cappella **chapel**
il cappello **hat**
la carne **meat**
caro **dear, expensive**
il carro **cart**
la carta **paper**
la carta di credito **credit card**
la casa **house, home**
il casinò **casino**
la cassa **safe, case, check-out counter**
il cassiere **cashier**
castano **brown, brunette**
cattivo **bad**
il cavallo **horse**
il CD **compact disc**
celebrare **to celebrate**
celibe, scapolo **single man**
la cena **dinner**
cenare **to have dinner**
cento **one hundred**
cercare **to look for, search**
Che (cosa)? **What?**
Chi? **Who? Whom?**
chiaccherare **to chat**
chiamare **to call**
chiamarsi **to call oneself, be called**
chiaro **clear**
il chiasso **noise, racket**
la chiave **key**
chiedere **to ask**
la chiesa **church**
la chitarra **guitar**
chiudere **to close**
ciao **hello**
il cinema **cinema, movie theater**
cinese **Chinese**
il cioccolato **chocolate**
la città **city**
la civiltà **civilization**
la classe **class**
classico **classic**
il cliente **customer**
il clima **climate**

la colazione **breakfast**
il, la collega **colleague**
il colore **color**
come **like, as**
Come? **How? What?**
cominciare **to begin**
la commedia **play**
la compagna **female friend, companion**
la compagna di stanza **female roommate**
la compagnia **company, companionship**
il compagno **male friend, companion**
il compagno di stanza **male roommate**
il compito (a casa) **homework**
il compleanno **birthday**
comprare **to buy**
il computer **computer**
con **with**
il concerto **concert**
il condominio **condominium**
la conferenza **conference, lecture**
conoscere **to know, meet**
consigliare **to advise**
il consiglio **advice**
contento **happy**
il conto **check, bill**
la conversazione **conversation**
correre **to run**
corretto **correct**
il corso **course**
così **as, so**
costare **to cost**
costruire **to build**
la cravatta **necktie**
la creazione **creation**
credere **to believe**
crudo **raw, uncooked**
cucinare **to cook**
la cugina **female cousin**
il cugino **male cousin**
cuocere **to cook**
la cura **cure**

D _____
Italian **English**

da **from**
dare **to give**
dare del Lei **to address someone formally**
dare del tu **to address someone informally**
la data **date**
davanti a **in front of, before**
decidere **to decide**
desiderare **to want**
di **about, of, from (origin)**
di solito **usually**
la diagnosi **diagnosis**
il diario **diary**
dicembre **December**
difficile **difficult**
difficilmente **hard, hardly, with difficulty**
diffondere **to spread**
diligente **diligent**
diligentemente **diligently**
dire **to say, tell**
il disco **record album**
il discorso **speech, address**
discutere **to discuss**
disperatamente **desperately**
disperato **desperate**
dispiacere **to displease**
distendere **to spread**
la ditta **company, firm**
diventare **to become**
divertente **fun, enjoyable, amusing**
divertirsi **to have fun, enjoy oneself**
il dizionario **dictionary**
dolce **sweet**
il dolce **dessert**
il dollaro **dollar**
dolorosamente **painfully**
doloroso **painful**
la domanda **question**
domandare **to ask a question**
domani **tomorrow**
domenica **Sunday**
la donna **woman**
dopo **after, later**
dormire **to sleep**

il dormitorio **dormitory**
il dottore **male or female doctor**
la dottoressa **female doctor**
Dove? **Where?**
dovere **to have to, must**
dubitare **to doubt**
durante **during**

E

Italian	**English**

eccellente **excellent**
Eccolo! Eccoli! **Here it is! Here they are!**
economicamente **economically**
economico **economic, economical**
l'edicola **newsstand**
l'edificio **building**
elegante **elegant**
elegantemente **elegantly**
elettronico **electronic**
l'elezione **election**
l'email **e-mail**
l'energia **energy**
l'eroe **hero**
l'esame **exam**
l'esercizio **exercise**
essere **to be**
essere al verde **to be broke**
essere in gioco **to be at stake**
essere nelle nuvole **to daydream**
l'estate **summer**
estendere **to extend**
europeo **European**

F

Italian	**English**

la fabbrica **factory**
la faccia **face**
facile **easy**
facilmente **easily**
falso **false**
la famiglia **family**
famoso **famous**
fare **to do, make**
fare attenzione **to pay attention**
fare caldo **to be hot (weather)**
fare colazione **to have breakfast**
fare freddo **to be cold (weather)**
fare il bagno **to take a bath**

fare la doccia **to take a shower**
fare la guerra **to wage war**
fare la spesa **to go food shopping**
fare le spese **to go shopping**
fare un errore **to make a mistake**
fare un giro **to go for a ride**
fare un regalo **to give a gift**
fare un viaggio **to take a trip**
fare una domanda **to ask a question**
fare una foto **to take a picture**
fare una gita **to take a short trip**
fare una passeggiata **to take a walk**
fare una pausa **to take a break**
fare una telefonata **to make a telephone call**
la farina **flour**
la farmacia **pharmacy**
farsi la barba **to shave**
la fata **fairy**
favolosamente **fabulously**
favoloso **fabulous**
il favore **favor**
febbraio **February**
felice **happy**
le ferie **holiday, vacation**
fermare **to stop**
fermarsi **to stop (oneself)**
la festa **party**
festeggiare **to celebrate**
la fetta **slice**
la fidanzata **fiancée**
il fidanzato **fiancé**
fidarsi **to trust**
la figlia **daughter**
il figlio **son**
la fila **row**
il film **movie, film**
la filosofia **philosophy**
finale **final**
la finestra **window**
finire **to finish**
fino a **until**
fino a quando **in so far as**
il fiore **flower**
la foglia **leaf**
il fondo **bottom**

il formaggio **cheese**
il forno **oven**
la fotografia **photograph**
fra/tra **between**
il francese **French**
il fratellino **little brother**
il fratello **brother**
freddo **cold**
frequentare **to attend**
fresco **cool**
la frutta **fruit**
fumare **to smoke**
il fungo **mushroom**
il fuoco **fire**
fuori **out, outside**
furbo **shrewd**
il futuro **future**

G

Italian	**English**

la galleria **gallery, tunnel**
il garage **garage**
il gatto **cat**
il gelato **ice cream**
generoso **generous**
il genio **genius**
i genitori **parents**
gennaio **January**
gettare **to throw, toss**
il ghetto **ghetto**
il ghiaccio **ice**
già **already**
la giacca **jacket**
giallo **yellow**
il giapponese **Japanese**
il giardino **garden**
giocare (a) **to play (a sport or game)**
il giocatolo **toy**
il gioco **game**
il giornale **newspaper**
la giornata **day**
il giorno **day**
giovane **young**
giovedì **Thursday**
la gioventù **youth, young people**
giugno **June**
gonfiare **to inflate**
il governatore **governor**

grande **big, large**
grasso **fat**
il greco **Greek**
grigio **grey**
grosso **big**
guadagnare **to earn**
guardare **to look at, watch**
la guerra **war**
la guida **guide**
guidare **to drive**
il guscio **shell**
H

Italian **English**
l'hotel **hotel**
I

Italian **English**
l'idea **idea**
ieri **yesterday**
imparare **to learn**
importante **important**
impossibile **impossible**
improbabile **improbable**
in **at, in, to**
in anticipo **early**
in centro **downtown**
in ritardo **late**
incominciare **to begin**
incontrare **to meet**
incoraggiare **to encourage**
incorretto **incorrect**
l'indipendenza **independence**
l'informazione **information**
l'inglese **English**
innamorarsi **to fall in love**
l'insalata **salad, lettuce**
insegnare **to teach**
intelligente **intelligent**
intelligentemente **intelligently**
interessante **interesting**
inventare **to invent**
l'inverno **winter**
invitare **to invite**
io **I**
l'irlandese **Irish**
l'isola **island**
L

Italian **English**
il lago **lake**

le lasagne **lasagna**
lasciare **to leave**
il latte **milk**
laurearsi **to graduate**
lavare **to wash**
lavarsi **to wash up**
lavorare **to work**
le scale **stairs**
legare **to tie, bind**
leggere **to read**
leggero **light**
lei **she**
Lei **you (singular, formal)**
lento **slow**
il leone **lion**
la lettera **letter**
il letto **bed**
la lezione **lesson**
lì, là **there**
liberamente **freely**
libero **free**
la libreria **bookstore**
il libro **book**
la lingua **tongue, language**
il locale **place**
loro **they**
Loro **you (plural, formal)**
luglio **July**
lui **he**
lunedì **Monday**
lungo **long**
il luogo **place**
lussuoso **luxurious**
M

Italian **English**
la macchina **car, machine**
la madre **mother**
il maestro **teacher**
la maga **witch, sorceress**
maggio **May**
la maglietta **T-shirt**
il maglione **sweater**
magnificamente **magnificently**
magnifico **magnificent**
magro **thin**
mai, non mai **ever, never**
male **badly**
mancare **to miss, lack**

la mancia **tip**
mandare **to send**
mangiare **to eat**
la mano **hand**
il mare **sea**
il marito **husband**
marrone **brown**
martedì **Tuesday**
marzo **March**
la mattina **morning**
il meccanico **mechanic**
il medico **doctor, physician**
medio **middle**
meglio **better**
la mela **apple**
mentre **while**
mercoledì **Wednesday**
il mese **month**
la messa **mass**
il messaggio **message**
mettere **to put, place**
mettersi **to put on (oneself), to wear**
mezzanotte **midnight**
mezzogiorno **noon**
migliore **better, best**
mille **one thousand**
la minestra **soup**
la moglie **wife**
molti **many, a lot of**
molto **much, very**
la montagna **mountain**
il monumento **monument**
morire **to die**
mostrare **to show**
la moto **motorcycle**
il museo **museum**
la musica **music**
N

Italian **English**
il napoletano **Neapolitan**
nascere **to be born**
la nascita **birth**
il naso **nose**
il Natale **Christmas**
la nebbia **fog**
necessario **necessary**
il negozio **store**

nero **black**
nessuno **no one**
la neve **snow**
nevicare **to snow**
niente **nothing**
il nipote **grandson, nephew**
la nipote **granddaughter, niece**
noi **we**
noioso **boring**
noleggiare **to rent (a car)**
il nome **name, noun**
la nonna **grandmother**
i nonni **grandparents**
il nonno **grandfather**
normale **normal, regular**
la nostalgia **nostalgia**
la notizia **news**
la notte **night**
notturno **nocturnal**
novembre **November**
nubile **single woman**
il numero **number**
il numero di telefono **telephone number**
nuotare **to swim**
nuovo **new**
nuvoloso **cloudy**

O

Italian	English

l'occhio **eye**
l'odore **odor**
offrire **to offer**
l'oggetto **object**
oggi **today**
ogni **each, every**
ogni volta **each time**
ognuno **everyone**
l'olio **oil**
onesto **honest**
l'ora **hour, time**
l'orologio **wristwatch**
ortodosso **orthodox**
l'ospedale **hospital**
l'osteria **tavern, public house**
ottobre **October**

P

Italian	English

il pacco **package, parcel**

il padre **father**
pagare **to pay**
la pagina **page**
il paio **pair**
il panino **sandwich**
la panna **cream**
il papa **pope**
il papà **dad, daddy**
la pappa **country soup, baby food**
parcheggiare **to park**
il parcheggio **parking lot, parking space**
il parco **the park**
parecchio **a lot**
parere **to seem**
parlare **to speak**
la parola **word**
partecipare a **to participate**
particolare **particular**
particolarmente **particularly**
partire **to leave**
la partita **game, match**
la patente di guida **driver's license**
la paura **fear**
la pazienza **patience**
il peccato **sin**
peggiore **worse, worst**
la pena **punishment**
la penna **pen**
pensare **to think**
pensare a **to think about (someone or something)**
pensare di **to think about (doing something)**
per **for**
percento **percent**
la percentuale **percentage**
perché **why, because**
perdere **to lose**
perdersi **to get lost**
la persona **person**
pesante **heavy**
pessimo **very bad, horrible**
il pesce fish
il peso **weight**
il pezzo **piece**

piacere **to be pleasing, please**
il piano **plan, project**
il piano (di un edificio) **floor, story**
piano **slowly, softly**
il piatto **plate, dish**
la piazza **plaza, central square**
piccante **spicy**
piccolo **small, short**
il piede **foot**
pigro **lazy**
la pioggia **rain**
piovere **to rain**
la piscina **swimming pool**
più **most**
la pizza **pizza**
il pizzaiolo **pizza maker**
un po', poco **very little, a little**
pochi **few**
il podestà **governor, chief magistrate**
poi **then**
la politica **politics**
il politico **politician**
la polizia **police**
il pomeriggio **afternoon**
il pomodoro **tomato**
porre **to put**
la porta **door**
portare **to carry, bring, wear**
possibile **possible**
il posto **place**
potere **to be able to, can**
povero **poor**
pranzare **to have lunch**
il pranzo **lunch**
preferire **to prefer**
prendere **to take**
preoccuparsi **to worry**
la preoccupazione **worry, concern**
preparare **to prepare**
prepararsi **to prepare oneself**
il presidente **president**
prestare **to lend**
presto **soon, early**
prevedere **to foresee**
prima **before**
la primavera **spring(time)**

il primo **first**
probabile **probable**
probabilmente **probably**
il professore **professor (male)**
la professoressa **professor (female)**
il pronome **pronoun**
il prosciutto **prosciutto**
prossimo **next**
provare **to try**
la psicologia **psychology**
pubblico **public**
pulire **to clean**
il punto **point, period**
puntuale **punctual**

Q

Italian	English
il quaderno	**notebook**
qualcosa	**something**
Quale?	**Which?**
Quando?	**When?**
Quanto? Quanti?	**How much? How many?**
quello	**that**
questo	**this**
qui, qua	**here**

R

Italian	English
raccontare	**to tell, recount**
il racconto	**short story**
la ragazza	**girl, girlfriend**
il ragazzo	**boy, boyfriend**
ragionare	**to reason**
la ragione	**reason**
ragionevole	**reasonable**
rapidamente	**quickly**
rapido	**fast**
il rappresentante	**representative**
raramente	**rarely**
raro	**rare**
recarsi	**to go**
recente	**recent**
recentemente	**recently**
regalare	**to give a gift**
il regalo	**gift, present**
la regola	**rule**
rendere	**to give back, restore**
restare	**to stay, remain**

restituire **to give back**
ricco **rich**
ricevere **to receive**
riferire **to report, relate**
rimanere **to stay, remain**
ripetere **to repeat**
riposarsi **to rest**
rispettare **to respect**
rispondere **to respond, answer**
la risposta **answer**
il ristorante **restaurant**
ritornare **to return**
la riunione **meeting**
riuscire **to succeed**
la rivista **magazine**
il romanzo **novel**
rosso **red**
il rumore **noise**
il russo **Russian**

S

Italian	English
sabato	**Saturday**
il salame	**salami**
salire	**to climb, to walk upstairs**
il salotto	**living room**
salutarsi	**to greet (one another)**
la salute	**health**
salve	**hello**
salvo	**safe, unharmed**
sano	**healthy**
sapere	**to know a fact, know how do something**
il sassofono	**saxophone**
sbadigliare	**to yawn**
sbagliarsi	**to be wrong, to make a mistake**
sbagliato	**wrong, incorrect**
lo scaffale	**shelf**
la scarpa	**shoe**
scegliere	**to choose**
la scelta	**choice**
la scena	**scene**
scendere	**to descend, climb off, to walk downstairs**
la scheda	**card, file**
lo schema	**scheme, pattern**
lo scherzo	**joke**

schiacciare **to crush, squish**
lo schiavo **slave**
schiuma **foam, froth**
lo scialle **shawl**
sciare **to ski**
la sciarpa **scarf**
scientifico **scientific**
la scienza **science**
lo scienziato **scientist**
la scimmia **monkey**
scintillare **to shine, sparkle**
sciocco **foolish**
sciogliersi **to loosen, melt**
lo sciopero **strike**
sciupare **to spoil**
sconsigliare **to dissuade**
scoprire **to discover**
scorso **last, past**
la scrivania **desk**
scrivere **to write**
lo scultore **sculptor**
la scuola **school**
la scusa **excuse**
scusarsi **to apologize**
lo sdegno **disdain**
sdraiato **stretched out, lying down**
il secolo **century**
secondo **second**
sedersi **to sit**
seguente **following**
seguire **to follow**
sembrare **to seem**
il semestre **semester**
sempre **always**
sensato **sensible**
sensibile **sensitive**
sentire **to hear, to feel**
sentirsi **to feel**
senza **without**
il senzatetto **homeless person**
la sera **evening**
sereno **serene, nice, clear**
servire **to serve**
settembre **September**
la settimana **week**
sfidare **to challenge**
la sfilata **parade, show**

la sfortuna **misfortune**
sgarbato **rude**
sgretolarsi **to crumble to pieces**
sicuramente **certainly**
sicuro **certain, safe**
la sigaretta **cigarette**
il sigaro **cigar**
la signora **madam, lady, Ms., Mrs.**
il signore **gentleman, Mr.**
la signorina **young lady, miss, Ms.**
simpatico **nice, agreeable**
la sinagoga **synagogue**
sincero **sincere**
il sindaco **mayor**
la situazione **situation**
slegare **to untie**
slogarsi **to dislocate**
lo smalto **fingernail polish**
smettere **to quit**
snello **thin**
snodare **to untie**
sognare **to dream**
il sogno **dream**
i soldi **money**
il sole **sun**
sopra **on, over, above**
la sorella **sister**
la sorellina **little sister**
sorridere **to smile**
il sorriso **smile**
sotto **under, beneath, below**
i sottotitoli **subtitles**
lo spagnolo **Spanish**
lo spago **string**
lo spazio **space**
lo specchio **mirror**
spedire **to send**
spendere **to spend**
sperare **to hope**
spesso **often**
la spiaggia **beach**
spiegare **to explain**
la spiegazione **explanation**
gli spinaci **spinach**
sporco **dirty**

lo sport **sport**
sposarsi **to get married**
la squadra **team**
lo squarcio **gash**
squillare **to ring**
sregolato **disorderly**
lo stadio **stadium**
stamattina **this morning**
stampare **to print**
stanco **tired**
stanotte **tonight**
la stanza **room**
stare **to be, stay**
stare per **to be about to**
stare zitto **to be quiet**
stasera **this evening, tonight**
lo stato **condition, state**
la statua **statue**
la stazione **station**
stendere **to extend, spread**
lo stesso **same**
la storia **history**
la strada **street, road**
straordinario **extraordinary**
la strega **witch**
stretto **tight**
lo strumento musicale **musical instrument**
lo studente **male student**
la studentessa **female student**
studiare **to study**
lo studio **study, studio**
studioso **studious, diligent**
stupido **stupid**
su **on**
subito **right away**
sufficiente **sufficient**
suggerire **to suggest**
la suocera **mother-in-law**
il suocero **father-in-law**
suonare **to play (an instrument), to ring (a bell)**
il supermercato **supermarket**
svegliare **to waken**
svegliarsi **to wake up**
sviluppare **to develop**
la Svizzera **Switzerland**
svizzero **Swiss**

T

Italian	English
il tabaccaio	**tobacconist**
tanto, tanti	**so much, so many**
tardi	**late**
il tassì	**taxi**
il tavolo	**table**
il teatro	**theater**
il tedesco	**German**
telefonare	**to call**
la telefonata	**telephone call**
il telefono	**telephone**
il telegiornale	**television news**
la televisione	**television**
il tempo	**weather, time**
tenere	**to keep**
il tennis	**tennis**
tirare	**to pull**
tornare	**to return**
la torta	**cake**
tra/fra	**between, among**
tradurre	**to translate**
tranquillamente	**peacefully**
tranquillo	**peaceful**
il treno	**train**
la tribù	**tribe**
triste	**sad**
tristemente	**sadly**
troppo, troppi	**too much, too many**
trovare	**to find**
tu	**you (singular, informal)**
il, la turista	**tourist**

U

Italian	English
ubbidire	**to obey**
l'ufficio	**office**
l'ufficio postale	**post office**
ultimo	**last, latest**
l'università	**university**
l'uomo	**man, humankind**
usato	**used**
uscire	**to go out**

V

Italian	English
la vacanza	**vacation**
il vapore	**steam, vapor**

vario **various**

il vaso **vase**

vecchio **old**

vedere **to see**

veloce **quick, fast**

velocemente **rapidly**

vendere **to sell**

venerdì **Friday**

venire **to come**

il vento **wind**

il verbo **verb**

verde **green**

la verità **truth**

vero **true**

vestire **to dress**

vestirsi **to get dressed**

i vestiti **clothes**

la via **street**

viaggiare **to travel**

il viaggio **trip, journey**

vicino **close**

il vicino di casa **neighbor**

il vigliacco **coward**

vincere **to win**

il vino **wine**

la virgola **comma**

visitare **to visit**

il vitello **veal**

vivere **to live**

il vocabolario **vocabulary, dictionary**

la voce **voice**

voi **you (plural, informal)**

volere **to want, owe**

il volo **flight**

la volta **time, turn**

il voto **grade**

il vulcano **volcano**

vuoto **empty**

Z

Italian **English**

lo zaino **backpack**

la zebra **zebra**

lo zero **zero**

la zia **aunt**

lo zio **uncle**

lo zoo **zoo**

lo zucchero **sugar**

lo zucchino **zucchini**

la zuppa **soup**

Appendix C

English to Italian Glossary

A

English   Italian

a lot   **parecchio**

about, of   **di**

to accompany   **accompagnare**

actor   **l'attore**

address someone formally   **dare del Lei**

address someone informally   **dare del tu**

adjective   **l'aggettivo**

advice   **il consiglio**

to advise   **consigliare**

after, later   **dopo**

afternoon   **il pomeriggio**

again   **di nuovo ancora**

agency   **l'agenzia**

aggressive   **aggressivo**

airplane   **l'aereoplano**

airport   **l'aeroporto**

already   **già**

always   **sempre**

anchovy   **l'acciuga**

anniversary   **l'anniversario**

answer   **la risposta**

to apologize   **scusarsi**

apple   **la mela**

appointment   **l'appuntamento**

April   **aprile**

aranciata, orange soda   **l'aranciata**

to arrive   **arrivare**

as soon as   **appena**

to ask   **chiedere**

to ask a question   **domandare, fare una domanda**

astrology   **l'astrologia**

at, in, to   **a, in**

to attend   **assistere, frequentare**

attention   **l'attenzione**

attentive   **attento**

attentively   **attentamente**

attitude   **l'atteggiamento**

August   **agosto**

aunt   **la zia**

author   **l'autore**

authority   **l'autorità**

B

English   Italian

backpack   **lo zaino**

bad   **cattivo**

bad, badly   **male**

bar   **il bar**

base   **la base**

to be, stay   **stare**

to be   **essere**

to be able to, can   **potere, riuscire (a)**

to be about to   **stare per**

to be afraid (of)   **avere paura (di)**

to be at stake   **essere in gioco**

to be born   **nascere**

to be broke   **essere al verde**

to be cold   **avere freddo**

to be cold (weather)   **fare freddo**

to be hot   **avere caldo**

to be hot (weather)   **fare caldo**

to be hungry   **avere fame**

to be in a hurry   **avere fretta**

to be pleasing, please   **piacere**

to be quiet   **stare zitto**

to be right, correct   **avere ragione**

to be thirsty   **avere sete**

to be tired, sleepy   **avere sonno**

to be wrong   **sbagliarsi**

to be wrong, incorrect   **avere torto**

beach   **la spiaggia**

beautiful   **bello**

beauty   **la bellezza**

because   **perché**

to become   **diventare**

bed   **il letto**

beer   **la birra**

before   **prima**

to begin   **cominciare, incominciare**

to believe   **credere**

best   **migliore**

better   **meglio**

between   **fra, tra**

bicycle   **la bicicletta**

big, large   **grande, grosso**

birth   **la nascita**

birthday   **il compleanno**

black   **nero**

blonde   **biondo**

blue   **azzurro, blu**

book   **il libro**

bookstore   **la libreria**

boring   **noioso**

boss   **il capo**

bottle   **la bottiglia**

bottom   **il fondo**

boy, boyfriend   **il ragazzo**

breakfast   **la colazione**

brother   **il fratello**

brown   **marrone, castano**

to build   **costruire**

building   **l'edificio**

bus   **l'autobus**

butter   **il burro**

to buy   **comprare**

by   **da**

C

English   Italian

cake   **la torta**

calendar   **il calendario**

to call   **chiamare, telefonare**

to call oneself, be called   **chiamarsi**

Canadian   **canadese**

car   **l'automobile, la macchina**

card, file   **la scheda, il file**

to carry, bring, wear   **portare**

cart   **il carro**

cashier   **il cassiere**

casino   **il casinò**

cat   **il gatto**

to celebrate   **celebrare, festeggiare**

century   **il secolo**

certain, safe   **sicuro, certo**

certainly   **sicuramente, certamente**

to challenge   **sfidare**

to change **cambiare**

chapel **la cappella**

to chatter **chiacchierare**

check, bill **il conto**

cheese **il formaggio**

chestnut **castagna**

child (female) **la bambina**

child (male) **il bambino**

children **i bambini**

Chinese **cinese**

chocolate **il cioccolato**

choice **la scelta**

to choose **scegliere**

Christmas **il Natale**

church **la chiesa**

cigar **il sigaro**

cigarette **la sigaretta**

cinema, movie theater
il cinema

city **la città**

civilization **la civiltà**

class **la classe**

classic **classico**

classroom **l'aula**

to clean **pulire**

clear **chiaro**

climate **il clima**

to climb **salire**

close **vicino**

to close **chiudere**

clothes **i vestiti**

clothes dryer **l'asciugatrice**

cloudy **nuvoloso**

coffee **il caffè**

cold **freddo**

colleague **il, la collega**

color **il colore**

to come **venire**

comma **la virgola**

compact disc **il CD**

company, companionship **la
compagnia**

company, firm **la ditta**

computer **il computer**

concert **il concerto**

condition **la condizione**

condominium **il condominio**

conference, lecture **la conferenza**

conference **il congresso, il
convegno**

conversation **la conversazione**

to cook **cucinare, cuocere**

cookie **il biscotto**

cool **fresco**

correct **corretto, giusto**

to cost **costare**

country, countryside **la campagna**

country soup, baby food **la pappa**

course **il corso**

coward **il vigliacco**

cream **la panna**

creation **la creazione**

credit card **la carta di credito**

to crumble to pieces **sgretolarsi**

to crush, squish **schiacciare**

cure **la cura**

customer **il cliente**

D

English **Italian**

dad, daddy **il papà**

to dance **ballare**

dark **buio, il buio**

date **la data**

daughter **la figlia**

day **la giornata, il giorno**

to daydream **essere nelle nuvole**

dear, expensive **caro**

December **dicembre**

to decide **decidere**

to descend, climb off **scendere**

desk **la scrivania**

desperate **disperato**

desperately **disperatamente**

dessert **il dolce**

to develop **sviluppare**

diagnosis **la diagnosi**

diary **il diario**

dictionary **il dizionario**

to die **morire**

difficult **difficile**

difficultly **difficilmente**

diligent **diligente, studioso**

diligently **diligentemente**

dinner **la cena**

dirty **sporco**

to discover **scoprire**

to discuss **discutere**

disdain **lo sdegno**

to dislocate **slogarsi**

disorderly **sregolato**

to displease **dispiacere (a)**

to dissuade **sconsigliare,
dissuadere**

to do, make **fare**

doctor **il dottore**

doctor, physician **il medico**

dog **il cane**

dollar **il dollaro**

door **la porta**

dormitory **il dormitorio**

to doubt **dubitare**

downtown **in centro**

dream **il sogno**

to dream **sognare**

to dress **vestire**

to drink **bere**

to drive **guidare**

driver's license **la patente di
guida**

to dry **asciugare**

during **durante**

E

English **Italian**

each, every **ogni**

each time **ogni volta**

early **in anticipo, presto**

to earn **guadagnare**

easily **facilmente**

easy **facile**

to eat **mangiare**

economic, economical **economico**

economically **economicamente**

election **l'elezione**

electronic **elettronico**

elegant **elegante**

elegantly **elegantemente**

e-mail **l'email**

empty **vuoto**

to encourage **incoraggiare**

energy **l'energia**

English **inglese, l'inglese**

enough, rather **abbastanza**

European **europeo**

evening **la sera**

ever **mai**
everyone **ognuno**
exam **l'esame**
excellent **eccellente**
excuse **la scusa**
exercise **l'esercizio**
to explain **spiegare**
explanation **la spiegazione**
to extend, spread **estendere (un invito), prolungare, stendere**
extraordinary **straordinario**
eye **l'occhio**
F

English **Italian**
fabulous **favoloso**
fabulously **favolosamente**
face **la faccia**
factory **la fabbrica**
fairy **la fata**
fall, autumn **l'autunno**
to fall **cadere**
to fall asleep **addormentarsi**
to fall in love **innamorarsi**
false **falso**
family **la famiglia**
famous **famoso**
fast **rapido**
fat **grasso**
father **il padre**
father-in-law **il suocero**
favor **il favore**
fear **la paura**
February **febbraio**
to feel **sentirsi**
to feel like **avere voglia di**
few, a little, very little **pochi, poco, un po'**
a little, very little **poco, un po'**
fiancé **il fidanzato**
fiancée **la fidanzata**
final **finale**
to find **trovare**
fingernail polish **lo smalto (delle unghie)**
to finish **finire**
fire **il fuoco**
first **primo**
fish **il pesce**

flight **il volo**
floor **il piano, il pavimento**
flour **la farina**
flower **il fiore**
foam, froth **schiuma**
fog **la nebbia**
to follow **seguire**
following **seguente**
foolish **sciocco**
foot **il piede**
for **per**
to foresee **prevedere**
free **libero**
freely **liberamente**
French **il francese**
Friday **venerdì**
friend, companion (female) **la compagna, l'amica**
friend, companion (male) **il compagno, l'amico**
from (origin) **da/di**
fruit **la frutta**
fun, enjoyable **divertente**
future **il futuro**
G

English **Italian**
gallery **la galleria**
game **il gioco**
game, match **la partita**
garage **il garage**
garden **il giardino**
garlic **l'aglio**
gash **lo squarcio**
generous **generoso**
genius **il genio**
gentleman, mister **il signore**
German **tedesco, il tedesco**
to get angry **arrabbiarsi**
to get bored **annoiarsi**
to get dressed **vestirsi**
to get lost **perdersi**
to get married **sposarsi**
to get up **alzarsi**
ghetto **il ghetto**
gift, present **il regalo**
girl, girlfriend **la ragazza**
to give **dare**

to give a gift **fare un regalo (a), regalare (a)**
to give back **restituire (a), rendere (a)**
to go **andare, recarsi**
to go food shopping **fare la spesa**
to go for a ride **fare un giro**
to go out **uscire**
to go shopping **fare le spese**
good **buono**
good, capable **bravo**
governor **il governatore**
grade **il voto**
to graduate **laurearsi, diplomarsi**
granddaughter, niece **la nipote**
grandfather **il nonno**
grandmother **la nonna**
grandparents **i nonni**
grandson, nephew **il nipote**
Greek **greco, il greco**
green **verde**
to greet (one another) **salutarsi**
grey **grigio**
guide **la guida**
guitar **la chitarra**
H

English **Italian**
habit, practice **l'abitudine**
hair **i capelli**
hand **la mano**
happy **contento, felice**
hat **il cappello**
to have **avere**
to have breakfast **fare colazione**
to have dinner **cenare**
to have fun, enjoy oneself **divertirsi**
to have lunch **pranzare**
to have to, must **dovere**
he **lui**
health **la salute**
healthy **sano**
to hear **sentire**
heavy **pesante**
hello **ciao, salve**
help **l'aiuto**
to help **aiutare**
here **qui, qua**

Here it is! Here they are! **Ecco!**

hero **l'eroe**

highway **l'autostrada**

history **la storia**

holiday, vacation **le ferie**

homeless person **il senzatetto**

homework **il compito**

honest **onesto**

to hope **sperare**

horse **il cavallo**

hospital **l'ospedale**

hotel **l'albergo, l'hotel**

hour, time **l'ora**

house **la casa**

How? What? **Come?**

how, what, like **come**

how much, how many **quanto, quanti**

husband **il marito**

I	
English	**Italian**

I **io**

ice **il ghiaccio**

ice cream **il gelato**

idea **l'idea**

important **importante**

impossible **impossibile**

improbable **improbabile**

in front of **davanti a, di fronte a**

incorrect **incorretto, scorretto**

independence **l'indipendenza**

to inflate **gonfiare**

information **l'informazione**

inhabitant **l'abitante**

intelligent **intelligente**

intelligently **intelligentemente**

interesting **interessante**

to invent **inventare**

to invite **invitare**

Irish **irlandese, l'irlandese**

island **l'isola**

J	
English	**Italian**

jacket **la giacca**

January **gennaio**

Japanese **giapponese, il giapponese**

joke **lo scherzo**

July **luglio**

June **giugno**

K	
English	**Italian**

to keep **tenere**

key **la chiave**

to know a fact, know how to do something **sapere**

to know, meet **conoscere**

L	
English	**Italian**

lake **il lago**

lasagna **le lasagne**

last **ultimo**

last, latest, past **scorso**

late **in ritardo, tardi**

lawyer **l'avvocato**

lazy **pigro**

leaf **la foglia**

to learn **imparare**

to leave **lasciare, partire**

to lend **prestare**

lesson **la lezione**

letter **la lettera**

library **la biblioteca**

lie **la bugia**

light **leggero**

to light **accendere**

lion **il leone**

to listen (to) **ascoltare**

little brother **il fratellino**

little sister **la sorellina**

to live **abitare, vivere**

living room **il salotto, il soggiorno**

long **lungo**

to look at, watch **guardare**

to look for, search **cercare**

to loosen, melt **sciogliersi**

to lose **perdere**

love **l'amore**

luggage **il bagaglio**

lunch **il pranzo**

luxurious **lussuoso**

M	
English	**Italian**

madam, lady **la signora**

magazine **la rivista**

magnificent **magnifico**

magnificently **magnificamente**

to make a mistake **fare un errore**

to make a telephone call **fare una telefonata**

man **l'uomo**

many, much, a lot **molto, molti**

March **marzo**

mass **la messa**

May **maggio**

mayor **il sindaco**

meat **la carne**

mechanic **il meccanico**

to meet **incontrare**

meeting **la riunione**

message **il messaggio**

middle **medio**

midnight **la mezzanotte**

milk **il latte**

mirror **lo specchio**

misfortune **la sfortuna**

miss, Ms. **la signorina**

to miss, lack **mancare**

Monday **lunedì**

money **i soldi**

monkey **la scimmia**

month **il mese**

monument **il monumento**

morning **la mattina**

most **più, la maggior parte**

mother **la madre**

mother-in-law **la suocera**

motorcycle **la moto(cicletta)**

mountain **la montagna**

movie, film **il film**

Mrs., madam **la signora**

Ms., miss **la signorina**

museum **il museo**

mushroom **il fungo**

music **la musica**

musical instrument **lo strumento musicale**

N	
English	**Italian**

name, noun **il nome**

Neapolitan **napoletano, il napoletano**

necessary **necessario**

necktie **la cravatta**

to need, have need (of) **avere bisogno (di)**

neighbor **il vicino di casa**

never **non mai**

new **nuovo**

news **la notizia**

newspaper **il giornale**

newsstand **l'edicola**

next **prossimo**

nice, agreeable **simpatico**

night **la notte**

no longer **più, non più**

no one **nessuno**

nocturnal **notturno**

noise **chiasso, il rumore**

noon **mezzogiorno**

normal **normale**

nose **il naso**

nostalgia **la nostalgia**

notebook **il quaderno**

nothing **niente**

novel **il romanzo**

November **novembre**

now **adesso, ora**

number **il numero**

O

English	Italian

to obey **ubbidire**

object **l'oggetto**

ocean **il mare**

October **ottobre**

odor **l'odore**

to offer **offrire**

office **l'ufficio**

office manager **il capoufficio**

often **spesso**

oil **l'olio**

old **vecchio**

on **su, sopra**

one hundred **cento**

one thousand **mille**

to open **aprire**

orthodox **ortodosso**

other **altro**

out, outside **fuori**

oven **il forno**

to owe **dovere (a qualcuno)**

P

English	Italian

package, parcel **il pacco**

page **la pagina**

painful **doloroso**

painfully **dolorosamente**

pair **il paio**

paper **la carta**

parade, show **la sfilata**

parents **i genitori**

park **il parco**

to park **parcheggiare**

parking lot, space **il parcheggio**

to participate **partecipare**

particular **particolare**

particularly **particolarmente**

party **la festa**

patience **la pazienza**

to pay **pagare**

to pay attention **fare attenzione**

peaceful **tranquillo**

peacefully **tranquillamente**

pen **la penna**

percent **percento**

percentage **la percentuale**

person **la persona**

pharmacy **la farmacia**

philosophy **la filosofia**

photograph **la fotografia**

piece **il pezzo**

pizza **la pizza**

pizza maker **il pizzaiolo**

place **il locale, il luogo, il posto**

plan **il progetto, il piano**

plate, dish **il piatto**

play **la commedia**

to play (a sport or game) **giocare a**

to play (an instrument) **suonare**

plaza, central square **la piazza**

point, period **il punto**

police **la polizia**

politician **il politico**

politics **la politica**

pool **la piscina**

poor **povero**

pope **il papa**

possible **possibile**

post office **l'ufficio postale**

to prefer **preferire**

to prepare **preparare**

to prepare oneself **prepararsi**

president **il presidente**

to print **stampare**

probable **probabile**

probably **probabilmente**

professor (male) **il professore**

professor (female) **la professoressa**

pronoun **il pronome**

prosciutto **il prosciutto**

psychology **la psicologia**

public **pubblico**

to pull **tirare**

punctual **puntuale**

punishment **la pena**

puppy **il cagnetto**

to put **porre**

to put, place **mettere**

to put on (oneself) **mettersi**

Q

English	Italian

question **la domanda**

quick, fast **veloce**

quickly **rapidamente**

to quit **smettere, licenziarsi**

R

English	Italian

rain **la pioggia**

to rain **piovere**

rapidly **velocemente**

rare **raro**

rarely **raramente**

raw, uncooked **crudo**

to read **leggere**

reason **la ragione**

to reason **ragionare**

reasonable **ragionevole**

to receive **ricevere**

recent **recente**

recently **recentemente, di recente**

record album **il disco**

red **rosso**

to remain **rimanere**

to rent **affittare**

to rent (a car) **noleggiare**

to repeat **ripetere**
to report, relate **riferire**
representative **il rappresentante**
to respect **rispettare**
to respond, answer **rispondere**
to rest **riposarsi**
restaurant **il ristorante**
to return **ritornare, tornare**
rich **ricco**
right away **subito**
to ring **squillare**
road **la strada**
roast **l'arrosto**
room **la camera, la stanza**
roommate **il/la compagno/
  a di stanza**
row **la fila**
rude **sgarbato**
rule **la regola**
to run **correre**
Russian **russo, il russo**

S

English Italian
sad **triste**
sadly **tristemente**
safe, case, check-out counter **la
  cassa**
safe, unharmed **salvo**
salad **l'insalata**
salami **il salame**
same **stesso, lo stesso**
sandwich **il panino**
Saturday **sabato**
saxophone **il sassofono**
to say, tell **dire**
scarf **la sciarpa**
scene **la scena**
scheme, pattern **lo schema, il
  modello**
school **la scuola**
science **la scienza**
scientific **scientifico**
scientist **lo scienziato**
sculptor **lo scultore**
second **secondo**
to see **vedere**
to seem **parere, sembrare**
to sell **vendere**

semester **il semestre**
to send **mandare, spedire**
sensible **sensato**
sensitive **sensibile**
September **settembre**
serene, nice **sereno**
to serve **servire**
to shave **fare/farsi la barba**
shawl **lo scialle**
she **lei**
shelf **lo scaffale**
shell **il guscio**
to shine, sparkle **scintillare,
  brillare**
shoe **la scarpa**
short **basso, piccolo**
short story **il racconto**
to show **mostrare**
shrewd **furbo**
sin **il peccato**
sincere **sincero**
to sing **cantare**
singer **il cantante**
single (man) **celibe, scapolo**
single (woman) **nubile**
sister **la sorella**
to sit **sedersi**
situation **la situazione**
to ski **sciare**
slave **lo schiavo**
to sleep **dormire**
slice **la fetta**
slow **lento**
slowly, softly **piano**
small **piccolo**
smile **il sorriso**
to smile **sorridere**
to smoke **fumare**
snow **la neve**
to snow **nevicare**
so **così**
so much, so many **tanto, tanti**
soccer **il calcio**
something **qualcosa**
sometimes **a volte**
son **il figlio**
song **la canzone**
soon, early **presto**

soup **la minestra, la zuppa**
space **lo spazio**
Spanish **spagnolo, lo spagnolo**
to speak **parlare**
speech, address **il discorso**
to spend **spendere**
spicy **piccante**
spinach **gli spinaci**
to spoil **sciupare, viziare**
sport **lo sport**
spread **diffondere, distendere**
spring(time) **la primavera**
stadium **lo stadio**
stairs **le scale**
state **lo stato, la condizione**
station **la stazione**
statue **la statua**
to stay, remain **restare, rimanere**
steam, vapor **il vapore**
still, yet **ancora**
stingy **avaro**
to stop **fermare**
to stop (oneself) **fermarsi**
store **il negozio**
street **la strada, la via**
stretched out, lying down **sdraiato**
strike **lo sciopero**
string **lo spago**
studious **studioso**
study, studio **lo studio**
to study **studiare**
stupid **stupido**
subtitles **i sottotitoli**
to succeed **riuscire, avere
  successo**
sufficient **sufficiente**
sugar **lo zucchero**
to suggest **suggerire**
summer **l'estate**
sun **il sole**
Sunday **domenica**
supermarket **il supermercato**
sweater **il maglione**
to swim **nuotare**
swimming pool **la piscina**
Swiss **svizzero**
Switzerland **la Svizzera**
synagogue **la sinagoga**

T

English	Italian
table	**il tavolo**
to take	**prendere**
to take a bath	**fare il bagno**
to take a break	**fare una pausa**
to take a picture	**fare una foto**
to take a short trip	**fare una gita**
to take a shower	**fare la doccia**
to take a trip	**fare un viaggio**
to take a walk	**fare una passeggiata**
tall	**alto**
tavern, public house	**l'osteria, la trattoria**
taxi	**il tassì**
to teach	**insegnare**
teacher	**il maestro**
team	**la squadra**
telephone	**il telefono**
telephone call	**la telefonata**
telephone number	**il numero di telefono**
television	**la televisione**
television news	**il telegiornale**
to tell, recount	**raccontare**
tennis	**il tennis**
that	**quello, il quale, la quale, che**
theater	**il teatro**
then	**poi**
there	**lì, là**
they	**loro**
thin	**magro, snello**
to think	**pensare**
to think about (doing something)	**pensare di**
to think about (someone or something)	**pensare a**
this	**questo**
this evening, tonight	**stasera**
this morning	**stamattina**
to throw, toss	**gettare**
Thursday	**giovedì**
ticket	**il biglietto**
to tie, bind	**legare**
tight	**stretto**
time	**il tempo**
tip	**la mancia**
tired	**stanco**
tobacconist	**il tabaccaio**
today	**oggi**
tomato	**il pomodoro**
tomorrow	**domani**
tongue, language	**la lingua**
tonight	**stanotte**
too much, too many	**troppo, troppi**
tourist	**il, la turista**
toy	**il giocatolo**
train	**il treno**
to translate	**tradurre**
to travel	**viaggiare**
travel agency	**l'agenzia di viaggi**
tree	**l'albero**
tribe	**la tribù**
trip	**il viaggio**
true	**vero**
to trust	**fidarsi**
truth	**la verità**
to try	**provare a, cercare di**
T-shirt	**la maglietta**
Tuesday	**martedì**

U

English	Italian
ugly	**brutto**
uncle	**lo zio**
under, below, beneath	**sotto**
to understand	**capire**
university	**l'università**
unpleasant	**antipatico, spiacevole**
to untie	**slegare, snodare**
until	**fino a**
used	**usato**
usually	**di solito**

V

English	Italian
vacation	**la vacanza**
various	**vario**
vase	**il vaso**
veal	**il vitello**
verb	**il verbo**
to visit	**visitare**
vocabulary	**il vocabolario, il dizionario**
voice	**la voce**
volcano	**il vulcano**

W

English	Italian
to wage war	**fare la guerra**
to wait (for)	**aspettare**
waiter	**il cameriere**
waitress	**la cameriera**
to wake up	**svegliarsi**
to waken	**svegliare**
to walk	**camminare**
to want	**desiderare, volere**
war	**la guerra**
warm	**caldo**
to wash	**lavare**
to wash up	**lavarsi**
water	**l'acqua**
we	**noi**
weather	**il tempo, il clima**
Wednesday	**mercoledì**
week	**la settimana**
weight	**il peso**
well	**bene**
What?	**Che (cosa)?**
When?	**Quando?**
Where?	**Dove?**
Which?	**Quale? Che?**
while	**mentre**
white	**bianco**
white lie	**la bugia di convenienza**
Who? Whom?	**Chi?**
Why?	**Perché?**
wife	**la moglie**
to win	**vincere**
wind	**il vento**
window	**la finestra**
wine	**il vino**
winter	**l'inverno**
witch	**la strega, la maga**
with	**con**
without	**senza**
word	**la parola**
to work	**lavorare**
worry, concern	**la preoccupazione**
to worry	**preoccuparsi**
worst	**pessimo**
wristwatch	**l'orologio**

to write   *scrivere*
wrong, incorrect   *sbagliato*

Y
_____

English   *Italian*
to yawn   *sbadigliare*
year   *l'anno*
yellow   *giallo*
yesterday   *ieri*
you (plural, formal)   *Loro*
you (plural, informal   *voi*
   and formal)
you (singular, formal)   *Lei*
you (singular, informal)   *tu*
young   *giovane*
youth   *la gioventù*

Z
_____

English   *Italian*
zebra   *la zebra*
zero   *lo zero*
zoo   *lo zoo*
zucchini   *lo zucchino*

Appendix D

Answer Key

Part 1: Nouns, Articles, and Adjectives

Exercise 1: Translation

1. doctor
2. energy
3. station
4. philosophy
5. automobile
6. University of Perugia
7. prosciutto from Parma
8. post office
9. train
10. bicycle

Exercise 2: Listening Comprehension

Noun	Gender
1. *libro*	masculine
2. *studentessa*	feminine
3. *anniversario*	masculine
4. *ufficio*	masculine
5. *strada*	feminine
6. *bicicletta*	feminine
7. *chiesa*	feminine
8. *fratello*	masculine
9. *sorella*	feminine
10. *casa*	feminine
11. *cugino*	masculine
12. *amico*	masculine
13. *cugina*	feminine
14. *ragazza*	feminine
15. *bambino*	masculine

Exercise 3: Making Nouns Plural

1. *calendario*	*calendari*
2. *stazione*	*stazioni*
3. *dottore*	*dottori*
4. *giorno*	*giorni*
5. *ragione*	*ragioni*
6. *tedesco*	*tedeschi*
7. *albergo*	*alberghi*
8. *auto(mobile)*	*auto (mobili)*
9. *amico*	*amici*
10. *studente*	*studenti*
11. *bar*	*bar*
12. *caffè*	*caffè*
13. *stadio*	*stadi*
14. *attore*	*attori*
15. *libro*	*libri*

Exercise 4: Listening Comprehension

Noun	Plural
1. *libro*	*libri*
2. *aeroporto*	*aeroporti*
3. *fratello*	*fratelli*
4. *sorella*	*sorelle*
5. *pizza*	*pizze*
6. *dottore*	*dottori*
7. *diario*	*diari*
8. *figlio*	*figli*
9. *amica*	*amiche*
10. *politico*	*politici*
11. *città*	*città*
12. *sport*	*sport*
13. *cinema (tografo)*	*cinema (tografi)*
14. *ragazza*	*ragazze*
15. *ragazzo*	*ragazzi*

Exercise 5: Singular to Plural and Plural to Singular

1. *calendari*	*calendario*
2. *televisione*	*televisioni*
3. *pizze*	*pizza*
4. *amiche*	*amica*
5. *amico*	*amici*
6. *caffè*	*caffè*
7. *autori*	*autore*
8. *albergo*	*alberghi*
9. *negozio*	*negozi*
10. *casa*	*case*

Exercise 6: Articles and Nouns

1. *un amico*
2. *un'amica*
3. *un tassì*
4. *una mela*
5. *uno studente*
6. *una studentessa*
7. *uno zoo*
8. *un'università*
9. *un attore*
10. *una conversazione*

Exercise 7: Articles and Nouns

Noun	Plural
1. *il libro*	*i libri*
2. *lo studente*	*gli studenti*
3. *la ragazza*	*le ragazze*
4. *l'amico*	*gli amici*
5. *lo zucchero*	*gli zuccheri*
6. *la casa*	*le case*
7. *la mela*	*le mele*
8. *l'università*	*le università*
9. *l'attore*	*gli attori*
10. *lo sport*	*gli sport*

Exercise 8: Adjectives

1. *Stefano è alto. Suo fratello Gianni è* basso.
2. *Marina è intelligente. La sua amica Grazia è* stupida.
3. *Zio Alberto e zia Barbara sono generosi. I miei cugini sono* avari.
4. *Il capo di Monica è simpatico. Il capo di Massimo è* antipatico.
5. *Le sorelle di Giovanni non sono vecchie. Sono* giovani.
6. *La casa non è piccola. È* grande.
7. *I film non sono interessanti. Sono* noiosi.
8. *Il cane di Stefano non è grasso. È* magro.
9. *Le macchine non sono belle. Sono* brutte.
10. *Bill Gates è ricco. Tu sei* povero.

Exercise 9: Adjective Placement

1. *Mio zio ha due <u>vecchie</u> case in campagna.*
2. *Abita vicino a un <u>piccolo</u> lago.*
3. *L'italiano non è una lingua <u>difficile</u>.*
4. *Parlo di un <u>altro</u> libro.*
5. *Ogni giorno vedo gli <u>stessi</u> studenti.*
6. *Ieri ho visto un film <u>stupido</u>.*
7. *Elena è una <u>bella</u> ragazza.*
8. *Tre <u>ricchi</u> signori mangiano al ristorante.*
9. *Noi abbiamo due <u>simpatiche</u> amiche.*
10. *È una <u>nuova</u> idea.*

Exercise 10: *Molto, tanto, troppo, poco*

1. *Noi abbiamo <u>molti</u> amici.*
2. *Mio padre ha <u>poca</u> pazienza.*
3. *Il mio capoufficio ha <u>poche</u> idee buone.*
4. *Non voglio mangiare <u>troppi</u> grassi.*
5. *Lui ha <u>tanti</u> cugini in Italia.*

Exercise 11: Adverbs

1. *Mio fratello è un uomo <u>molto</u> simpatico.*
2. *Maria è una persona <u>abbastanza</u> sincera.*
3. *Tu e Antonio siete ragazzi <u>poco</u> intelligenti.*
4. *Lui ha dei cugini <u>troppo</u> curiosi.*
5. *Lui abita in una casa <u>tanto</u> bella.*

Exercise 12: *Tutto*

1. *Io studio <u>tutta la</u> sera.*
2. *<u>Tutti i</u> vini italiani sono buoni.*
3. *Ho letto <u>tutti i</u> racconti di Alberto Moravia.*
4. *Mio fratello ha pulito <u>tutta la</u> casa.*
5. *<u>Tutte le</u> ragazze sono simpatiche.*

Exercise 13: Each and Every

1. *ogni ragazzo*
2. *ogni casa*
3. *ogni bottiglia*
4. *ogni giorno*
5. *ogni studente*

Exercise 14: Indefinite Articles

1. *un libro*
2. *un amico*
3. *uno zoo*
4. *uno studente*
5. *una casa*
6. *un'amica*
7. *una zebra*
8. *una studentessa*

Exercise 15: Definite Articles

1. *il giardino*		*i giardini*
2. *l'albero*		*gli alberi*
3. *lo zero*		*gli zeri*
4. *lo studio*		*gli studi*
5. *la casa*		*le case*
6. *l'autostrada*		*le autostrade*

Exercise 16: Correct or Incorrect?

1. *<u>la</u> stessa ragazza*
2. *<u>una</u> città europea*
3. *<u>l'altro</u> giorno*
4. *due <u>fiori gialli</u>*
5. *tre <u>giovani</u> fratelli*
6. *<u>una bella</u> città*
7. *i nuovi <u>calendari</u>*
8. *<u>un</u> dottore <u>intelligente</u>*
9. *<u>i</u> ragazzi <u>simpatici</u>*
10. *un libro interessante*

Exercise 17: Il Signor Gori

1. *Il signor Gori abita a Pistoia.*
2. *La casa del signor Gori è gialla.*
3. *La casa ha due piani.*
4. *I suoi vicini di casa sono abbastanza simpatici.*
5. *È rossa.*
6. *Ha due figli.*
7. *Sono giovani e studiosi.*

Exercise 18: Opposites

1. *I film di Robin Williams sono interessanti.*
2. *L'italiano è una lingua facile.*
3. *Gli edifici di Manhattan sono alti.*
4. *I giovani di oggi sono attivi.*
5. *I suoceri di Massimo sono simpatici.*
6. *Lassie è un cane intelligente.*
7. *Bob Dylan è vecchio.*

Exercise 19: From Italian to English

1. Stephen King is a very famous author.
2. The *Divine Comedy* is long and interesting.
3. Bill Gates is a generous man.
4. Doctor Rossi is very nice and has many friends.
5. All of the universities in Italy are old.

Part 2: Subject Pronouns, Avere *and* Essere

Exercise 1: The Correct Subject Pronouns

1. *voi*
2. *Lei*
3. *Voi or Loro*
4. *tu*

Exercise 2: *Massimo è di Quarrata*

1. *(Tu e Adriano) Tu e Adriano siete di Quarrata.*
2. *(Silverio e lo zio Marco) Silverio e lo zio Marco sono di Quarrata.*
3. *(Monica) Monica è di Quarrata.*
4. *(Alessio ed io) Alessio ed io siamo di Quarrata.*
5. *(Bruno) Bruno è di Quarrata.*

Exercise 3: *D'accordo!* (Agreed!)

1. *Tom Cruise è un attore americano.*
2. *Roma è una città in Italia.*
3. *D'accordo.*
4. *Leonardo è di Vinci.*
5. *D'accordo.*

Exercise 4: Singular to Plural and Plural to Singular

1. *Tu sei intelligente.*
2. *La ragazza italiana è molto simpatica.*
3. *Noi siamo molto sinceri.*
4. *La chiesa italiana è vecchia e bella.*
5. *L'amico di Stefano è alto e biondo.*

Exercise 5: *Avere*

1. *Lei, signor Buonanno, ha una casa al mare?*
2. *Tu e Marcello avete dei colleghi simpatici.*
3. *Homer Simpson ha tre figli.*
4. *Io ho un fratello.*
5. *Marco ed io abbiamo amici in California.*

Exercise 6: More with *Avere*

1. *Sì, ho una macchina tedesca.*
   No, non ho una macchina tedesca.
2. *Sì, ho un cane (un gatto). Si chiama* (name).
   No, non ho un cane (un gatto).
3. *Ho i capelli castani (biondi).*
4. *Ho* (number) *cugini.*
5. *Sì, ho un condominio in Florida.*
   Non, non ho un condominio in Florida.

Exercise 7: Informal Idiomatic Expressions with *Avere*

1. *Hai sete?*
2. *Hai caldo?*
3. *Hai paura?*
4. *Hai bisogno di una nuova macchina?*
5. *Hai voglia di parlare?*

Exercise 8: Formal Idiomatic Expressions with *Avere*

1. *Ha sete?*
2. *Ha caldo?*
3. *Ha paura?*
4. *Ha bisogno di una nuova macchina?*
5. *Ha voglia di parlare?*

Exercise 9: *La mia città*

1. *C'è un ristorante cinese a* (my city).
2. *Ci sono* (number) *abitanti a* (my city).
3. *C'è un'università a* (my city).
4. *Ci sono ristoranti italiani a* (my city).
5. *C'è una biblioteca pubblica a* (my city).

Exercise 10: On Tour

1. *Ecco la chiesa!*
2. *Ecco la sinagoga!*
3. *Ecco il parco!*
4. *Ecco il ristorante italiano!*
5. *Ecco la casa del sindaco!*

Exercise 11: *Buono*

1. *Maria e Enza sono due **buone** ragazze.*
2. *Sono **buone** amiche.*
3. *È un **buon** caffè.*
4. *È una **buon'amica**.*
5. *È un **buon** libro.*
6. *È un **buon** albergo.*

Exercise 12: *Bello*

1. Che **bella** cosa!
2. Che **bel** giorno!
3. Che **begli** occhi!
4. Che **bel** libro!
5. Che **bella** storia!
6. Che **bei** capelli!
7. Che **bell'edificio**!
8. Che **begli** uffici!

Exercise 13: Numbers

Number		Spelling
1.	17	*diciassette*
2.	2	*due*
3.	11	*undici*
4.	8	*otto*
5.	19	*diciannove*
6.	23	*ventitrè*
7.	38	*trentotto*
8.	100	*cento*
9.	40	*quaranta*
10.	1,000	*mille*

Exercise 14: Answering Questions

1. *Ho (number) anni.*
2. *Ho molti amici.*
3. *Ho due macchine.*
4. *Ho (number) fratelli (sorelle).*
5. *Ci sono (number) musei a New York.*
6. *Ho molta pazienza.* or *Ho poca pazienza.*
7. *Un caffè a Starbucks costa (dollar amount).*

Exercise 15: Habitual Actions

1. habitual
2. habitual
3. once
4. once
5. habitual

Exercise 16: Asking and Answering Questions

1. *Domanda: Hai un marito (una moglie)?*
   Do you have a husband (wife)?
   Risposta: Sì, ho un marito (una moglie).
   No, non ho un marito (una moglie).
2. *D: Come si chiama?* What's his/her name?
   R: Si chiama (name).
3. *D: Com'è?* What is he/she like?
   R: Answers vary.
4. *D: Ha gli occhi azzurri?* Does he/she have blue eyes?
   R: Ha gli occhi azzurri. Or *Non ha gli occhi azzurri.*
5. *D: Tu hai una macchina?* Do you have a car?
   R: Sì, ho una macchina. Or *Non ho una macchina.*
6. *D: Com'è la macchina?* What's your car like?
   R: Answers vary.
7. *D: Di dove sei?* Where are you from?
   R: Sono di (name of your city).
8. *D: Hai molti amici?* Do you have many friends?
   R: Sì, ho molti amici.
9. *D: Ci sono molti ristoranti italiani nella tua città?*
   Are there many Italian restaurants in your city?
   R: Sì, ci sono (Non ci sono) molti ris-
   toranti italiani nella mia città.
10. *D: C'è un aeroporto nella tua città?* Is
    there an airport in your city?
    R: Sì, c'è un aeroporto (non c'è un aero-
    porto) nella mia città.
11. *D: C'è un parco nella tua città?* Is there a park in your city?
    R: Sì, c'è un parco (non c'è un parco) nella mia città.
12. *D: Hai un cane o un gatto?* Do you have a dog or a cat?
    R: Sì, ho un cane (un gatto). or
    Non ho un cane (un gatto).
13. *D: Come si chiama?* What is its name?
    R: Si chiama (name).
14. *D: Quanti anni ha?* How old is it?
    R: Ha (number) anni.
15. *D: È intelligente?* Is it an intelligent dog/cat?
    R: Sì, è intelligente. or *Non è intelligente.*
16. *D: Hai molti libri?* Do you have many books?
    R: Sì, ho molti libri. or *Non ho molti libri.*
17. *D: Quanti libri hai?* How many books do you have?
    R: Ho (number) libri.

Part 3: First Conjugation Verbs, Prepositions, and Telling Time

Exercise 1: Conjugating–*Are* Verbs

1. *Io guardo la televisione.*
2. *Noi guardiamo…*
3. *Voi guardate…*
4. *Tu guardi…*
5. *Pietro ed io guardiamo…*
6. *Tutti i miei cugini guardano…*

1. *Noi parliamo italiano e inglese.*
2. *Mio padre parla…*
3. *Tu e Elena parlate…*
4. *Loro parlano…*
5. *Ogni studente parla…*
6. *I figli del signor Gianni parlano…*

1. *Tutti gli studenti lavorano il venerdì?*
2. *Loro lavorano…*
3. *Mio fratello ed io lavoriamo…*

4. *Gli avvocati lavorano…*
5. *Gianni lavora…*
6. *Marcello ed il suo amico lavorano…*

1. *Voi non aspettate il treno.*
2. *Marco e Angela non aspettano…*
3. *Tu e Marco non aspettate…*
4. *Loro non aspettano…*
5. *I miei amici ed io non aspettiamo…*
6. *Tutte le ragazze non aspettano…*

Exercise 2: Translation Exercise Using –*Are* Verbs

1. *Io imparo a parlare italiano.*
2. *Loro incominciano a lavorare venerdì.*
3. *Noi pensiamo di mangiare nel nuovo ristorante.*
4. *I ragazzi desiderano spiegare la situazione.*
5. *Il professore parla con uno studente.*
6. *John abita a Boston. Pensa di lavorare a San Diego.*
7. *Tu giochi a tennis? Desideri giocare a tennis con Marco?*
8. *Lui ha paura degli altri bambini.*
9. *Noi abbiamo voglia di mangiare la pizza.*
10. *Tu e John non avete bisogno del computer oggi.*

Exercise 3: Listening Comprehension with –*Are* Verbs

1. *abitare*	to live
2. *ascoltare*	to listen/to listen to
3. *arrivare*	to arrive
4. *aspettare*	to wait/to wait for
5. *cantare*	to sing
6. *comprare*	to buy
7. *desiderare*	to want/to wish/to desire
8. *domandare*	to ask a question
9. *frequentare*	to attend
10. *giocare (a)*	to play (a sport or game)
11. *guardare*	to look at/to watch
12. *imparare (a + infinitive)*	to learn (to do something)
13. *(in)cominciare (a + infinitive)*	to begin (to do something)
14. *insegnare (a + infinitive)*	to teach (to do something)
15. *lavorare*	to work
16. *mangiare*	to eat
17. *pagare*	to pay
18. *parlare (a)/(di)*	to speak (to/of)
19. *pensare (a)/(di)*	to think about someone or about doing something
20. *portare*	to wear or to carry
21. *spiegare*	to explain
22. *suonare*	to play (an instrument) or to ring
23. *trovare*	to find

Exercise 4: Correct or Incorrect?

1. *Noi pensiamo <u>di</u> mangiare in un ristorante.*
2. *Alfredo non ha molt<u>a</u> pazienza.*
3. correct
4. *Dove aspettate il treno?*
5. correct
6. *Penso a mio fratello. Lui è al verde.*
7. *Io lavor<u>o</u> il martedì.*
8. *Tu pag<u>hi</u> il conto?*
9. correct
10. *Hai voglia di stud<u>ia</u>re l'italiano?*

Exercise 5: *Andare, Fare, Dare,* and *Stare*

1. *Io <u>vado</u> a un concerto stasera.*
2. *Noi <u>facciamo</u> attenzione quando parla.*
3. *Tu e Mario <u>state</u> a casa oggi?*
4. *Che cosa desiderate <u>fare</u> stasera?*
5. *Chi <u>dà</u> il libro al professore?*
6. *Dove <u>andiamo</u> noi in vacanza?*
7. *Marcello, come <u>stai</u> tu?*
8. *Loro <u>danno</u> informazioni ai turisti.*
9. *Mia moglie ed io non desideriamo <u>fare</u> gli spaghetti.*
10. *Lei <u>fa</u> colazione alle 8 ogni mattina.*

Exercise 6: *Andare, Fare, Dare,* and *Stare*

1. *Come <u>stanno</u> Loro oggi?*
2. *Che cosa <u>fai</u> tu?*
3. *Io <u>vado</u> a mangiare al ristorante.*
4. *La madre <u>dà</u> dei soldi a suo figlio.*

Exercise 7: Idiomatic Expressions with *Fare*

1. *Io faccio attenzione quando lui parla.*
2. *Tu fai la doccia.*
3. *Lui fa colazione.*
4. *Noi non facciamo molte domande.*
5. *Tu e John fate una foto.*
6. *Loro fanno una gita.*
7. *Io faccio una passeggiata il lunedì.*
8. *Lui fa troppe domande.*
9. *Noi facciamo la spesa il sabato.*
10. *Fa freddo fuori!*

Exercise 8: Question Words

1. *<u>Come</u> stai?*
2. *<u>Dove</u> vai stasera?*
3. *<u>Quanti</u> libri desideri comprare?*
4. *<u>Perché</u> fai così?*
5. *<u>Quale</u> film desideri vedere questo fine settimana?*
6. *<u>Che cosa</u> pensi di fare per il compleanno di Cristina?*
7. *<u>Quanta</u> pazienza ha tuo padre?*
8. *<u>Quanto</u> costa una nuova BMW?*

9. _Quando_ fai un viaggio in Italia?
10. _Quali_ vini sono buoni?

Exercise 9: Prepositions

1. Marcello abita _a_ Roma.
2. Il fratello _di_ Massimo si chiama Adriano.
3. Gli studenti studiano _in_ biblioteca.
4. Telefono _a_ mia madre ogni domenica.
5. Non mi piace la pizza _con_ le acciughe.

Exercise 10: _Un Viaggio in Italia_

1. John va in Italia quest'estate.
2. John viaggia con sua moglie.
3. 'La creazione dell'uomo' è nella Cappella Sistina, a Roma.
4. 'La nascita di Venere' è nella Galleria degli Uffizi, a Firenze.
5. Vanno al lago di Como.

Exercise 11: Articulated Prepositions

1. del signor Romeo
2. in un edificio
3. in centro
4. del computer
5. a Denver
6. i libri di Franco
7. nelle chiese
8. in biblioteca
9. dall'altra ragazza
10. nelle aule
11. dell'elezione
12. tra due libri
13. con lo zucchero
14. in un nuovo ristorante
15. con un amico

Exercise 12: Translation

1. Io abito in una casa piccola.
2. Il professore spiega la lezione agli studenti.
3. La conferenza è in un albergo in centro.
4. Oggi John è a casa.
5. I libri di Francesco sono sul letto.
6. I giocatoli dei bambini sono nel salotto.
7. Di chi è questa penna?
8. È la penna dell'avvocato.
9. Ecco gli amici di John.
10. Il regalo è dall'amico di John.
11. Ci sono molti fiori sugli alberi.
12. Peter lavora in un ristorante in centro.
13. Il calendario è tra due libri sulla scrivania.
14. È un buon amico di Boston.

15. I bambini portano molti regali al maestro.
16. Loro lavorano negli Stati Uniti.
17. Loro arrivano con il treno da New York.
18. Il treno arriva alla stazione alle nove stasera.
19. Io ascolto la musica quando lavoro.
20. Compri molti vestiti nei nuovi negozi in via Newbury?

Exercise 13: Telling Time

1. Sono le cinque e diciassette.
2. Sono le tre e otto.
3. Sono le quattordici e ventiquattro.
4. Sono le otto e trenta.
5. Sono le dodici e quarantacinque.
6. Sono le diciotto e quarantaquattro.
7. È l'una e quindici.
8. È mezzanotte.
9. Sono le sei e nove.
10. È l'una e cinquantacinque.

Exercise 14: At What Time?

1. Sono le (time).
2. Mangio alle (time)
3. Vado a letto alle (time).
4. Vado al lavoro alle (time).
5. Sono a casa alle (time).

Exercise 15: Verb Conjugations

	Mangiare	_Pagare_	_Parlare_
io	mangio	pago	parlo
tu	mangi	paghi	parli
lui/lei	mangia	paga	parla
noi	mangiamo	paghiamo	parliamo
voi	mangiate	pagate	parlate
loro	mangiano	pagano	parlano

	Dare	_Fare_	_Andare_
io	do	faccio	vado
tu	dai	fai	vai
lui/lei	dà	fa	va
noi	diamo	facciamo	andiamo
voi	date	fate	andate
loro	danno	fanno	vanno

	Stare	_Incominciare_	_Giocare_
io	sto	incomincio	gioco
tu	stai	incominci	giochi
lui/lei	sta	incomincia	gioca
noi	stiamo	incominciamo	giochiamo
voi	state	incominciate	giocate
loro	stanno	incominciano	giocano

Exercise 16: Articulated Prepositions

	il	lo	l'	la	l'	i	gli	le
a	al	allo	all'	alla	all'	ai	agli	alle
da	dal	dallo	dall'	dalla	dall'	dai	dagli	dalle
di	del	dello	dell'	della	dell'	dei	degli	delle
in	nel	nello	nell'	nella	nell'	nei	negli	nelle
su	sul	sullo	sull'	sulla	sull'	sui	sugli	sulle

Exercise 17: Present Tense Verbs

1. aspettiamo
2. imparano
3. mangi
4. guardate
5. giochiamo
6. spieghiamo
7. penso agli (a+gli)
8. compra
9. studi
10. incomincia
11. ascoltiamo
12. frequentano
13. insegno
14. paghiamo
15. desiderano

Exercise 18: Answering Questions

1. *Quando sei al verde, a chi chiedi i soldi?*
   When you're broke, whom do you ask for money?
1. *Quando sono al verde, chiedo soldi a…* (Answers vary.)
2. *Quanti e quali sono i giorni della settimana?*
   How many, and what are the days of the week?
2. *Ci sono sette giorni in una settimana: lunedì, mart-edì, mercoledì, giovedì, venerdì, sabato e domenica.*
3. *Che cosa fai stasera quando finisci di fare gli esercizi d'italiano?*
   What are you going to do this evening when you finish the Italian exercises?
3. *Quando finisco gli esercizi, io…* (Answers vary.)
4. *Quanti cugini hai? Come si chiamano? Dove abitano?*
   How many cousins do you have? What are their names? Where do they live?
4. *Io ho (number) cugini. Si chiamano (names). Abitano a (city).*

Part 4: Second and Third Conjugation Verbs and Adverbs

Exercise 1: Conjugating –*Ere* Verbs

1. scriviamo
2. credete
3. prendo
4. vendere
5. perde
6. discutete
7. conosciamo
8. assistono
9. metto
10. chiude

Exercise 2: Reading Comprehension

Ogni mattina <u>prendo</u> un caffè al bar vicino a casa mia. Quando sono al bar <u>vedo</u> i miei vicini di casa; di solito noi <u>discutiamo</u> di politica, di musica, o delle notizie del giorno. Quando non partecipo alla conversazione, <u>leggo</u> il giornale. <u>Chiedo</u> il conto, pago, e vado in ufficio.

Exercise 3: Working with –*Ere* Verbs

1. prendiamo
2. riceve
3. rispondete
4. decidiamo
5. discutono
6. vendo
7. perde
8. chiedi
9. chiude
10. credono

Exercise 4: Answering Questions

1. *Fino a che ora dormi il sabato mattina?*
   Until what time do you sleep on Saturday mornings?
1. *Io dormo fino alle (time) il sabato mattina.*
2. *Quando ricevi un'email da un collega, rispondi subito?*
   When you receive an e-mail from a colleague, do you answer it right away?
2. *Quando ricevo un email, (non) rispondo subito.*
3. *A che ora esci dall'ufficio il venerdì pomeriggio?*
   At what time do you leave the office on Friday afternoons?
3. *Il venerdì pomeriggio io esco dall'ufficio alle (time).*
4. *Tu segui la politica? Discuti di politica con la tua famiglia?*
   Do you follow politics? Do you discuss politics with your family?
4. *Io (non) seguo la politica. Io (non) discuto di politica con la mia famiglia.*
5. *Tu ascolti la musica classica?*
   Do you listen to classical music?
5. *Io (non) ascolto la musica classica.*

Exercise 5: Change the Subject

1. *Marco sceglie un regalo per Martina.*
2. *Tutti i miei amici scelgono un regalo per Martina.*
3. *Tu e Marta scegliete un regalo per Martina.*
4. *Io scelgo un regalo per Martina.*

Exercise 6: Questions and Answers

1. *Io preferisco il ristorante italiano (il ristorante cinese).*
2. *Quando finisco di mangiare, (non) prendo un caffè.*
3. *(Non) capisco l'italiano.*
4. *Suggerisco (name of film).*
5. *Il venerdì pomeriggio finisco di lavorare alle (time).*

Exercise 7: Listening Comprehension

1. *Elena e Caterina non vengono alla festa perché escono con Mariella.*
2. *Tu e Mario non venite alla festa perché uscite con Mariella.*
3. *Io non vengo alla festa perché esco con Mariella.*
4. *Gli altri ragazzi e io non veniamo alla festa perché esce con Mariella.*
5. *Il signor Giovanni non viene alla festa perché esce con Mariella.*

Exercise 8: *Dovere, Potere,* and *Volere*

1. *Tu non puoi comprare una nuova Mercedes perché devi...*
2. *Davide e Maria non possono fare un viaggio in Inghilterra perché devono...*
3. *I miei amici non possono andare al cinema perché devono...*
4. *Lui non può ascoltare la musica perché deve...*
5. *Elena ed io non possiamo visitare Venezia perché dobbiamo...*

Exercise 9: *Conoscere*

io conosco	*noi conosciamo*
tu conosci	*voi conoscete*
lui conosce	*loro conoscono*
lei conosce	*Loro conoscono*
Lei conosce	

Exercise 10: *Sapere* or *Conoscere?*

1. *sa*
2. *conoscono*
3. *sapete*
4. *sappiamo*
5. *conoscere*
6. *sai*
7. *so, so*
8. *conosce*
9. *sanno*
10. *sapere*

Exercise 11: Time Expressions

1. *Gli aeroplani partono in ritardo dall'aeroporto di Boston.*
2. *Spesso mangio fuori in un ristorante con la mia famiglia.*
3. *Telefono a mia madre una volta alla settimana.*
4. *Leggo un libro di tanto in tanto.*
5. *Guardo la televisione tutte le sere.*
6. *Vado al cinema raramente.*
7. *Vado in vacanza in Europa ogni anno.*
8. *I politici dicono la verità ogni tanto.*
9. *Esco con i miei amici spesso.*
10. *Vado a teatro tutte le sere.*

Exercise 12: From Adjective to Adverb

1. *facilmente*
2. *raramente*
3. *disperatamente*
4. *recentemente*
5. *magnificamente*
6. *difficilmente*
7. *diligentemente*
8. *dolorosamente*
9. *tranquillamente*
10. *economicamente*

Exercise 13: More with Adverbs

1. *Andrea Boccelli è un buon cantante. Lui canta <u>bene</u>.*
2. *Sto attento quando lui parla. Io ascolto <u>attentamente</u>.*
3. *L'italiano per me è facile. Parlo italiano <u>facilmente</u>.*
4. *Il signor Ferragamo ha molti vestiti eleganti. Lui si veste <u>elegantemente</u>.*
5. *Giovanni è disperato perché non trova le chiavi della macchina. Cerca le chiavi <u>disperatamente</u>.*

Exercise 14: Conjugation

1. *Tu <u>scrivi</u> molte lettere agli amici?*
2. *Io <u>rispondo</u> al telefono in casa mia.*
3. *I camerieri <u>servono</u> il caffè ai clienti.*
4. *Voi <u>partite</u> da casa.*
5. *Noi chiudiamo la finestra.*
6. *Gli studenti <u>leggono</u> il libro d'italiano.*
7. *Tu e Maria <u>ricevete</u> molti messaggi elettronici.*
8. *Gianni <u>offre</u> un caffè al professore.*
9. *Tu <u>credi</u> negli UFO?*
10. *Tutti gli studenti <u>dormono</u> in biblioteca?*
11. *Che cosa <u>metti</u> tu nel caffè?*
12. *Tu e gli altri ragazzi <u>ripetete</u> la domanda.*
13. *La mia amica <u>apre</u> la finestra.*
14. *Gli studenti <u>spediscono</u> dei messaggi elettronici.*
15. *Noi <u>facciamo colazione</u> ogni mattina.*
16. *Gina e Lorenzo <u>fanno una foto</u> della statua.*
17. *Voi <u>restituite</u> il libro al professore.*
18. *Loro non <u>capiscono</u> la spiegazione del professore.*
19. *La Boston University <u>costruisce</u> un nuovo dormitorio.*
20. *Gli studenti <u>fanno una domanda</u> in classe.*
21. *Io preferisco bere il caffè espresso.*
22. *I compagni di stanza non <u>pulite</u> spesso.*
23. *Tu e Mario fate <u>una gita</u>.*
24. *Preferisco <u>fare una pausa</u> dopo la lezione.*
25. *Giovanna <u>è al verde</u>.*

Exercise 15: Translation

1. *Voglio uscire stasera.*
2. *Conosci John?*
3. *Usciamo con gli amici di tuo figlio.*
4. *Non vogliamo andare alla festa.*
5. *Sai che John studia l'italiano?*
6. *Non puoi guardare la televisione adesso! Devi fare gli esercizi d'italiano!*
7. *Perché John e Michael non vengono stasera?*
8. *Devi avere fame. Vuoi un po' di pizza?*
9. *Non posso studiare perché devo restituire il libro alla biblioteca.*
10. *Non capisco. Puoi ripetere la domanda?*

Part 5: Reflexive and Reciprocal Verbs, Possessives, and the Present Progressive

Exercise 1: Reflexive or Not?

1. not reflexive
2. reflexive
3. not reflexive
4. not reflexive
5. reflexive
6. reflexive
7. reflexive
8. reflexive
9. not reflexive
10. not reflexive

Exercise 2: Listening for Reflexive Verbs

alzarsi (to get up)
io mi alzo
tu ti alzi
lui si alza
lei si alza
Lei si alza
noi ci alziamo
voi vi alzate
loro si alzano
Loro si alzano

mettersi (to put on)
io mi metto
tu ti metti
lui si mette
lei si mette
Lei si mette
noi ci mettiamo

voi vi mettete
loro si mettono
Loro si mettono

divertirsi (to have fun)
io mi diverto
tu ti diverti
lui si diverte
lei si diverte
Lei si diverte
noi ci divertiamo
voi vi divertite
Loro si divertono
Loro si divertono

Exercise 3: Picking Out the Reflexive Pronouns

1. *Giovanni **si** alza molto presto.*
2. *Elena ed io vogliamo svegliar**ci** alle otto.*
3. No reflexive verb.
4. *È importante divertir**si**.*
5. ***Vi** fermate al bar a prendere un caffè?*

Exercise 4: Listening Comprehension

1. *Mi addormento presto tutte le sere.*
2. *Non ti preoccupare! Ci sentiamo presto!*
3. *Dobbiamo prepararci per il nostro viaggio in Italia!*
4. *Mio padre non si sente molto bene.*
5. *Vi fermate al bar a prendere un caffè?*

Exercise 5: Conjugating Reflexive Verbs

	svegliarsi	mettersi	sentirsi
io	mi sveglio	mi metto	mi sento
tu	ti svegli	ti metti	ti senti
lui	si sveglia	si mette	si sente
lei	si sveglia	si mette	si sente
Lei	si sveglia	si mette	si sente
noi	ci svegliamo	ci mettiamo	ci sentiamo
voi	vi svegliate	vi mettete	vi sentite
loro	si svegliano	si mettono	si sentono
Loro	si svegliano	si mettono	si sentono

Exercise 6: Change the Subject

1. *Quando Gianni e Teresa vanno ad una festa si divertono molto.*
2. *Gianni e Teresa devono svegliarsi presto perché devono partire prima delle nove.*
3. *Gianni e Teresa sono contenti perché si sposano l'anno prossimo.*
4. *Gianni e Teresa non si sentono molto bene.*
5. *Gianni e Teresa si fermano al bar a prendere da bere.*

Exercise 7: Reflexive or Not?

1. *Io* sveglio *i bambini perché devono andare a scuola.*
2. *Noi* ci divertiamo *alla festa.*
3. *Tu* lavi *la macchina perché è sporca.*
4. *Giovanni* si mette *una cravatta perché ha una riunione importante.*
5. Vi fermate *al bar a prendere un caffè?*

Exercise 8: Reflexive or Reciprocal?

1. reflexive
2. reciprocal
3. reciprocal
4. reflexive
5. both

Exercise 9: Forming Reciprocal Verbs

1. *Io e Marco ci vediamo.*
2. *Tu e tuo nonno vi scrivete.*
3. *Massimo e Monica si salutano.*
4. *Elena ed io ci sposiamo.*
5. *Tu e i tuoi amici vi vedete ogni sabato sera.*

Exercise 10: Using Possessive Adjectives

1. *il mio libro*
2. *la nostra macchina*
3. *i Loro amici*
4. *il vostro anniversario*
5. *la sua casa*
6. *il suo computer*
7. *la loro famiglia*
8. *il tuo amico*
9. *il Suo cane*
10. *la sua ragazza*

Exercise 11: Article or No Article?

1. *il mio libro*
2. *la loro sorella*
3. *i nostri amici*
4. *mio padre*
5. *la Sua casa*
6. *i miei fratelli*
7. *la vostra famiglia*
8. *mia cugina*
9. *i nostri cugini*
10. *il suo ragazzo/suo ragazzo*

Exercise 12: Number and Gender of Possessive Adjectives

1. *Io vedo mio fratello ogni giorno.*
   Io vedo mia sorella ogni giorno.
   Io vedo i miei amici ogni giorno.
   Io vedo i miei cugini ogni giorno.
   Io vedo mia madre ogno giorno.
   Io vedo i miei nonni ogni giorno.

2. *I Loro amici non possono venire alla festa.*
   Il Loro padre non può venire alla festa
   Il Loro fratello non può venire alla festa.
   Le Loro sorelle non possono venire alla festa.
   La Loro amica non può venire alla festa.
   Il Loro zio non può venire alla festa.

3. *La tua casa non è troppo grande.*
   La tua casa non è troppo grande.
   Il tuo albero di Natale non è troppo grande.
   Il tuo tavolo non è troppo grande.
   I tuoi uffuci non sono troppo grandi.
   Le tue case non sono troppo grandi.

4. *Sua zia fa le spese il sabato.*
   I suoi nipoti fanno le spese il sabato.
   Il suo fidanzato fa le spese il sabato.
   Le sue figlie fanno le spese il sabato.
   Suo fratello fa le spese il sabato.
   I suoi amici fanno le spese il sabato.

Exercise 13: Express in Italian

1. *I miei fratelli e sua sorella sono buoni amici.*
2. *Puoi chiamare mio padre stasera.*
3. *Suo zio si chiama Pietro.*
4. *Mia moglie ed io usciamo con i suoi amici sabato.*
5. *Conosci i miei cugini?*

Exercise 14: Correct Use of Possessive Adjectives

1. *Noi invitiamo i tuoi fratelli alla festa.*
2. *I tuoi fratelli sono nella stanza di tuo fratello.*
3. *Linda e Mario parlano alla loro cara zia.*
4. *Il suo fratellino è in Italia e i suoi cugini sono in Francia.*
5. *Il loro zio è molto ricco. Il mio è povero.*
6. *La nostra macchina giapponese è dal meccanico.*
7. *Le sue figlie fanno un viaggio in Italia.*
8. *Il tuo ragazzo non lavora il sabato e la domenica.*
9. *Oggi c'è una festa a casa dei miei parenti.*
10. *Tu vedi tutti i tuoi cugini?*

Exercise 15: Identifying the Pronoun

1. his
2. ours
3. yours
4. theirs
5. yours
6. yours
7. yours
8. mine
9. ours
10. theirs

Exercise 16: From Noun to Pronoun

Answers vary.

1. *I miei escono…*
2. *Le mie…*
3. *La mia è…*
4. *Il mio…*
5. *I miei…*
6. *Le mie…*
7. *La mia…*
8. *Le mie…*
9. *La mia…*
10. *Il mio…*

Exercise 17: Making a Sentence Negative

1. *Non ti diverti quando esci con i tuoi amici.*
2. *Non ci siamo annoiati alla conferenza.*
3. *Mio padre non si sente molto bene.*
4. *Mio fratello non vuole sposarsi l'anno prossimo.*
5. *I miei amici non si arrabbiano quando non voglio uscire.*
6. *Le tue sorelle non si salutano dopo la festa.*
7. *Il loro zio non vuole svegliarsi presto domani mattina.*
8. *Non ci vediamo la settimana prossima.*
9. *Tu e Marianna non vi preparate per il viaggio.*
10. *Non mi addormento quando lui parla.*

Exercise 18: Working with Reflexive Verbs

1. *I miei amici non vogliono svegliar<u>si</u> presto.*
2. *Noi non riusciamo ad addormentar<u>ci</u> perché c'è troppo rumore.*
3. *<u>Ti</u> alzi presto domani mattina?*
4. *Come <u>si</u> chiama suo fratello?*
5. *Mio padre <u>si</u> arrabbia quando lascio la porta aperta.*
6. *<u>Ci</u> divertiamo molto quando andiamo a casa sua.*
7. *<u>Mi</u> devo preparare per il viaggio.*
8. *Giovanni <u>si</u> innamora facilmente.*
9. *I ragazzi <u>si</u> annoiano a scuola.*
10. *Tu e Gabriella <u>vi</u> vedete spesso?*

Exercise 19: Guess the Meaning

1. young horse
2. small piece
3. small pain
4. humble, cheap dress
5. small church

Exercise 20: *Stare*

io sto
tu stai
lui sta
lei sta
Lei sta
noi stiamo
voi state
loro stanno
Loro stanno

Exercise 21: Forming the Gerund

1. *cantando*
2. *perdendo*
3. *telefonando*
4. *giocando*
5. *partendo*
6. *vedendo*
7. *aprendo*
8. *scrivendo*
9. *leggendo*
10. *mangiando*

Exercise 22: From Present to Progressive

1. *Sto guardando un film.*
2. *Mio fratello sta aprendo la finestra.*
3. *Stiamo telefonando ai nostri amici.*
4. *I tuoi amici stanno giocando a tennis.*
5. *Il treno sta partendo dalla stazione.*
6. *Che cosa stai scrivendo?*
7. *Marco sta leggendo il giornale.*
8. *Tu e Lisa state mangiando la pizza.*
9. *Noi stiamo correndo.*
10. *State ascoltando la musica?*

Exercise 23: Listening Comprehension

1. progressive
2. present
3. present
4. progressive
5. present
6. progressive
7. present
8. progressive
9. present
10. progressive

Exercise 24: Answering Questions

Answers vary.

Exercise 25: Translation

1. I get bored
2. they are getting married
3. you get up
4. you get angry
5. we get ready
6. I apologize
7. you see yourselves or you see each other
8. he washes up
9. we fall asleep
10. you feel

Exercise 26: Changing the Subject

1. *tu*
   Ogni giorno tu ti alzi alle sette. Ti lavi e ti vesti veloce-
   mente: ti metti i jeans e una t-shirt e ti prepari per uscire.
   Torni a casa alle quattro e ti metto a studiare. La sera
   guardi la TV. Vai a letto alle dieci e ti addormenti subito.

2. *Marco*
   Ogni giorno Marco si alza alle sette. Si lava e si
   veste velocemente: si mette i jeans e una t-shirt
   e si prepara per uscire. Torna a casa alle quat-
   tro e si mette a studiare. La sera guarda la TV.
   Va a letto alle dieci e si addormenta subito.

3. *mio fratello ed io*
   Ogni giorno mio fratello ed io ci alziamo alle sette.
   Ci laviamo e ci vestiamo velocemente: ci met-
   tiamo i jeans e una t-shirt e ci prepariamo per
   uscire. Torniamo a casa alle quattro e ci mettia-
   mo a studiare. La sera guardiamo la TV. Andia-
   mo a letto alle dieci e ci addormentiamo subito.

4. *tu e tua sorella*
   Ogni giorno tu e tua sorella vi alzate alle sette. Vi lavate
   e vi vestite velocemente: vi mettete i jeans e una t-shirt
   e vi preparate per uscire. Tornate a casa alle quat-
   tro e vi mettete a studiare. La sera guardate la TV.
   Andate a letto alle dieci e vi addormentate subito.

5. *Giovanni e suo fratello*
   Ogni giorno Giovanni e suo fratello si alzano alle sette.
   Si lavano e si vestono velocemente: si mettono i jeans
   e una t-shirt e si preparano per uscire. Tornano a casa
   alle quattro e si mettono a studiare. La sera guardano la
   TV. Vanno a letto alle dieci e si addormentano subito.

Exercise 27: Translation Practice

1. *Domanda: A che ora ti svegli quan-*
   do devi andare a lavorare?
   Risposta: Answers vary.
2. *Domanda: A che ora ti alzi il sabato?*
   Risposta: Answers vary.
3. *Domanda: Che cosa ti metti quando hai freddo?*
   Risposta: Answers vary.
4. *Domanda: Come ti prepari per un viaggio?*
   Risposta: Answers vary.
5. *Domanda: Ti diverti quando esci con i tuoi amici?*
   Risposta: Answers vary.
6. *Domanda: Ti fermi ad un bar prima di andare in ufficio?*
   Risposta: Answers vary.
7. *Domanda: Ti arrabbi quando i tuoi amici non chiamano?*
   Risposta: Answers vary.

8. *Domanda: Ti innamori facilmente?*
   Risposta: Answers vary.
9. *Domanda: Vuoi sposarti?*
   Risposta: Answers vary.
10. *Domanda: A che ora ti addormenti la sera?*
    Risposta: Answers vary.
11. *Domanda: Pranzi con i tuoi amici di tanto in tanto?*
    Risposta: Answers vary.
12. *Domanda: Che cosa fai quando vuoi*
    divertirti il venerdì sera?
    Risposta: Answers vary.
13. *Domanda: Che cosa ti metti quando devi*
    andare in un ristorante elegante?
    Risposta: Answers vary.
14. *Domanda: Quante volte alla settima-*
    na parli con i tuoi genitori?
    Risposta: Answers vary.
15. *Domanda: Quante volte al mese man-*
    gi in un ristorante elegante?
    Risposta: Answers vary.

Exercise 28: Conjugation Practice

1. *arrabbiarsi*
   io mi arrabbio
   tu ti arrabbi
   lui si arrabbia
   lei si arrabbia
   Lei si arrabbia
   noi ci arrabbiamo
   voi vi arrabbiate
   loro si arrabbiano
   Loro si arrabbiano

2. *innamorarsi*
   io mi innamoro
   tu ti innamori
   lui si innamora
   lei si innamora
   Lei si innamora
   noi ci innamoriamo
   voi vi innamorate
   loro si innamorano
   Loro si innamorano

3. *mettersi*
   io mi metto
   tu ti metti
   lui si mette
   lei si mette
   Lei si mette
   noi ci mettiamo
   voi vi mettete
   loro si mettono
   Loro si mettono

Exercise 29: A Day in the Life

Answers vary.

Exercise 30: The Present Progressive

1. *Maria si sta svegliando.*
2. *I miei amici stanno mangiando al ristorante in centro.*
3. *Noi stiamo giocando a tennis.*
4. *Mio fratello sta andando in bicicletta.*
5. *Io e mia sorella stiamo prendendo un caffè.*
6. *Tu e Massimo state aprendo la porta del garage.*
7. *Simone e Alessio stanno studiando nella camera da letto?*
8. *Che cosa stai leggendo, tu?*
9. *Il cameriere sta servendo la minestra.*
10. *Tutti i suoi amici stannno ascoltando la musica.*

Part 6: Indirect and Direct Object Pronouns, Demonstrative Adjectives

Exercise 1: Transitive or Intransitive?

1. *leggere*   transitive
2. *arrivare*   intransitive
3. *restituire*   transitive
4. *mangiare*   transitive
5. *andare*   intransitive
6. *bere*   transitive
7. *prendere*   transitive
8. *venire*   intransitive
9. *offrire*   transitive
10. *partire*   intransitive

Exercise 2: Identifying the Direct Object

1. *Marco sta scrivendo una lettera ai suoi nonni.*
2. *Oggi a pranzo voglio mangiare un panino.*
3. No direct object
4. No direct object
5. *La mia amica parla italiano, francese, e russo.*
6. *Io e mia moglie abbiamo molti amici.*
7. *Tu conosci John?*
8. No direct object

Exercise 3: Circling the Object

1. *Non voglio prendere il caffè dopo cena.*
2. *I ragazzi stanno ascoltando la musica.*
3. *Il postino porta la posta ogni giorno alle ore tredici.*
4. *I miei zii portano una torta a casa nostra stasera.*
5. *Tutti i miei amici sanno cantare le canzoni napoletane.*
6. *Tu suoni la chitarra.*

7. *Non so fare spaghetti alla carbonara.*
8. *Sto leggendo La Divina Commedia.*
9. *Io preferisco l'estate.*
10. *A che ora finisci i tuoi compiti?*

Exercise 4: Something's Not Right

1. *A colazione bevo il caffè con un po' di latte. Bevo il caffè quando vado in ufficio. Dopo pranzo, bevo il caffè senza zucchero. Ogni tanto bevo il caffè con un po' di anisetta. Il sabato sera vado con mia moglie a mangiare in un ristorante. Dopo cena beviamo il caffè.*
2. *Ogni giorno a pranzo mangio la pizza. A volte mangio la pizza con i funghi. A volte mangio la pizza con il salamino piccante. Mi piace mangiare la pizza quando esco con i miei amici, ma di solito loro non vogliono mangiare la pizza. Quando mangio la pizza bevo la birra.*
3. *Io leggo molti libri. Leggo i libri quando finisco di lavorare. Leggo i libri quando finisco di mangiare. Il sabato vado in una libreria e compro due o tre libri. A casa tengo i libri sugli scaffali. Mi piace leggere i libri.*
4. *Io scrivo molte lettere. Scrivo lettere agli amici in Italia. Scrivo lettere ai cugini a Londra. Scrivo lettere ogni giorno. Scrivo lettere mentre bevo il caffè. Mando molte lettere ma non ricevo molte lettere. Non ricevo lettere perché gli amici non scrivono lettere.*

Exercise 5: Picking Out the Direct Object Pronoun

1. *Inviti i tuoi zii a cena.*
2. *Mi metto una cravatta quando vado a mangiare fuori.*
3. *Mio fratello ha una BMW.*
4. *Penso di comprare una casa in campagna.*
5. *Ricevo molte email dai miei amici.*
6. *Faccio un viaggio in Italia quest'estate.*
7. *Vado a trovare mio cugino in Italia.*
8. *Mio cugino studia storia dell'arte all'Università di Napoli.*
9. *Non frequenta tutte le lezioni.*
10. *Prendo il caffè a colazione tutte le mattine.*

Exercise 6: From Noun to Pronoun

1. *Io la bevo.*
2. *Lo prendi con lo zucchero.*
3. *Lo vedo ogni giorno.*
4. *Le voglio conoscere.*
5. *Gli studenti le capiscono.*
6. *Io lo leggo.*
7. *Lui vuole vederci.* or *Lui ci vuole vedere.*
8. *Noi lo aspettiamo.*
9. *La volete ascoltare.* or *Volete ascoltarla.*
10. *Maria le conosce.*

Exercise 7: Using Direct Object Pronouns

1. *Vado a prendere un caffè.*
   Vado a prenderlo.
2. *Sta scrivendo una lettera.*
   La sta scrivendo.
3. *Marco non mangia la carne.*
   Marco non la mangia.
4. *Tu e Luisa capite l'italiano.*
   Tu e Luisa lo capite.
5. *Non voglio lasciare un messaggio.*
   Non lo voglio lasciare. or Non voglio lasciarlo.
6. *Compro i biglietti domani mattina.*
   Li compro domani mattina.
7. *Mio padre beve il Chianti.*
   Mio padre lo beve.
8. *Vedo te e Maria.*
   Vi vedo.
9. *Marco parla a me e a Giuseppe.*
   Marco ci parla.
10. *Porto Massimo e Simone alla festa.*
    Li porto alla festa.

Exercise 8: Something's Not Right

1. *A colazione bevo il caffè con un po' di latte. Lo bevo quando vado in ufficio. Quando finisco di mangiare, lo bevo senza zucchero. Ogni tanto lo bevo con un po' di anisetta. Il sabato sera vado con mia moglie a mangiare in un ristorante. Quando finiamo di mangiare lo beviamo.*
2. *Ogni giorno a pranzo mangio la pizza. A volte la mangio con i funghi. A volte la mangio con il salamino piccante. Mi piace mangiarla quando esco con i miei amici, ma di solito loro non vogliono mangiarla. Quando la mangio bevo la birra.*
3. *Io leggo molti libri. Li leggo dopo il lavoro. Li leggo dopo cena. Il sabato vado in libreria e ne compro due o tre. A casa li tengo sugli scaffali. Mi piace leggerli.*
4. *Io scrivo molte lettere. Le scrivo ai miei amici in Italia. Le scrivo ai cugini a Londra. Le scrivo ogni giorno. Le scrivo mentre bevo il caffè. Ne mando molte ma non ne ricevo molte. Non le ricevo perché i miei amici non le scrivono.*

Exercise 9: Finding the Indirect Object

1. *Do il libro al mio amico.*
2. *Puoi telefonare a mio padre stasera.*
3. *Non vuole chiedere soldi a suo padre.*
4. *Penso di regalare un orologio a mio fratello per il suo compleanno.*
5. *Mando molte email ai miei cugini in Italia.*
6. *Il pizzaiolo fa una pizza per il cliente.*
7. *Mando una lettera a lui.*
8. *Restituisco la penna a Lei.*

9. *Compro dei fiori per te e Maria.*
10. *Tommaso dice le bugie a noi.*

Exercise 10: Use of Pronouns

1. *Le telefono stasera.*
2. *Gli mando una lettera.*
3. *Non gli chiedo dei soldi.*
4. *Tu e Maria gli restituite il libro.*
5. *Il professore spiega loro la regola. or Il professore gli spiega la regola.*
6. *Non offriamo loro un caffè. or Non gli offriamo un caffè.*
7. *Il bambino gli chiede aiuto.*
8. *Giuseppe e Patricia ci consigliano un film.*
9. *Non ti presto la macchina.*
10. *Marcello gli dice le bugie. or Marcello dice loro le bugie.*

Exercise 11: Using Indirect Object Pronouns

1. *Do dei consigli ai miei amici. Gli do dei consigli. or Do loro dei consigli.*
2. *Presto la macchina a te. Ti presto la macchina.*
3. *Porto dei fiori a voi. Vi porto dei fiori.*
4. *Martina dice le bugie a sua madre. Martina le dice le bugie.*
5. *Telefono a Davide e Maria stasera. Gli telefono stasera. or Telefono loro stasera.*
6. *Compro un regalo per mio fratello. Gli compro un regalo.*
7. *Voglio parlare a te e a Sara. Vi voglio parlare. or Voglio parlarvi.*
8. *Signora Baldini, posso parlare con Lei? Le posso parlare. or Posso parlarLe?*
9. *Gli spaghetti al pomodoro piacciono a me. Mi piacciono gli spaghetti al pomodoro.*
10. *A noi piace la pizza. La pizza ci piace.*

Exercise 12: Double Verb Constructions with Pronouns

1. *Le voglio vedere stasera. or Voglio vederle stasera.*
2. *Sì, ti posso telefonare stasera. or Sì, posso telefonarti stasera.*
3. *Sì, la voglio bere quando finisco di mangiare. or Sì, voglio berla quando finisco di mangiare.*
4. *Sì, la voglio ascoltare. or Sì, voglio ascoltarla.*
5. *Sì, mi piace ascoltarla.*
6. *Sì, a Stefano piace mangiarli. or Gli piace mangiarli.*
7. *Sì, li so fare. or Sì, so farli.*
8. *Sì, li voglio studiare. or Sì, voglio studiarli.*
9. *Li voglio fare stasera. or Voglio farli stasera.*
10. *Sì, la voglio fare a casa tua. or Sì, voglio farla a casa tua.*

Exercise 13: Double Verb Constructions

Use of *dovere*, *potere*, and *volere* will vary.
1. *Faccio gli spaghetti stasera. Non voglio farli. or Non li voglio fare.*

2. *Marco chiede il conto. Marco non lo deve chiedere.* or *Marco non vuole chiederlo.*
3. *Chi paga il conto? Chi lo vuole pagare?* or *Chi vuole pagarlo?.*
4. *Porti tuo fratello stasera. Non lo vuoi portare.* or *Non vuoi portarlo.*
5. *Guardiamo la partita alle otto. Non la possiamo guardare.* or *Non possiamo guardarla.*
6. *Parlo alla mia amica. Le devo parlare.* or *Non devo parlarle.*
7. *Vediamo i nostri amici stasera. Non li possiamo vedere.* or *Non possiamo vederli.*
8. *Tu e Marisa non mangiate la pizza? Tu e Marisa non la volete mangiare.* or *Tu e Marisa non volete mangiarla.*
9. *Marco non ascolta suo padre. Marco non lo vuole ascoltare.* or *Marco non vuole ascoltarlo.*
10. *Massimo telefona a Monica. Massimo non le può telefonare.* or *Massimo non può telefonarle.*

Exercise 14: Double Object Pronouns

1. *Glieli do.* or *Li do loro.*
2. *Io me la lavo ogni mattina.*
3. *Gliele mandiamo.*
4. *Sì, te le presto.*
5. *Te la regaliamo.*
6. *Glielo porto.* or *Lo porto loro.*
7. *Noi ce la mettiamo.*
8. *Ce li preparano.*
9. *Mio padre gliela dà.*
10. *Te le scrivo.*

Exercise 15: Double Object Constructions

Use of *dovere*, *potere*, and *volere* will vary.
1. *Restiuisco la penna a te. Te la voglio restituire.* or *Voglio restituirtela.*
2. *Do la ricetta al farmacista. Gliela do.* or *Devo dargliela.*
3. *Mostro i libri ai clienti. Glieli posso mostrare.* or *Li posso mostrare loro.* or *Posso mostraglieli.* or *Posso mostrarli loro.*
4. *Pietro offre un caffè a me e a Tommaso. Pietro ce lo vuole offrire.* or *Pietro vuole offrircelo.*
5. *Loro portano la torta a mia madre. Loro gliela devono portare.* or *Loro devono portargliela.*
6. *Io e Gabriella spediamo i pacchi a te e a tuo fratello. Io e Gabriella ve li possiamo spedire.* or *Io e Gabriella possiamo spedirveli.*
7. *Ti consiglio un buon film. Te lo voglio consigliare.* or *Voglio consigliartelo.*
8. *Eugenio regala l'orologio a suo nipote. Eugenio glielo vuole regalare.* or *Eugenio vuole regalarglielo.*
9. *Non chiedo soldi a mio padre. Non glieli posso chiedere.* or *Non posso chiederglieli.*

10. *Marcello chiede aiuto a te e a Michele. Marcello ve lo deve chiedere.* or *Marcello deve chiedervelo.*

Exercise 16: Practicing with *Quello*

1. *Quegli uomini stanno chiaccherando un po' troppo.*
2. *Quando penso a quegli anni, mi viene la nostalgia.*
3. *Mi piace tantissimo quella nuova macchina.*
4. *Vuole comprare quello studio in via Panzani.*
5. *Non ho ancora visto quel film.*
6. *Quelle pizze sono buone.*
7. *A mia moglie piacciono quei fiori.*
8. *Luigino sta parlando con quel suo amico.*
9. *Tu conosci quelle ragazze?*
10. *Quell'autobus si ferma davanti alla biblioteca?*

Exercise 17: Practicing with *Questo*

1. *Questi ragazzi sono antipatici.*
2. *Pensiamo di andare a Venezia quest'estate.*
3. *Mi piace tantissimo questa nuova macchina.*
4. *Non voglio leggere questo libro.*
5. *Ho già visto questo film.*
6. *Non posso mangiare queste lasagne.*
7. *A mia moglie piacciono questi fiori.*
8. *Non facciamo un viaggio quest'anno.*
9. *Tu conosci questa ragazza?*
10. *Questo autobus si ferma davanti alla biblioteca?*

Exercise 18: Translation Exercise

1. *Lui compra quei bei fiori per sua moglie.*
2. *Vuole andare a Roma quest'estate.*
3. *Questi libri sono troppo pesanti.*
4. *Ho troppi appuntamenti questa settimana.*
5. *Quei film italiani sono molto interessanti.*
6. *Non posso bere questa birra perché è troppo calda.*
7. *Quegli uomini parlano di politica.*
8. *Voglio vedere quel film con mio padre.*
9. *Questi bambini si annoiano troppo facilmente.*
10. *Quell'idea è molto interessante.*

Exercise 19: This and That

1. *Queste signore sono italiane, ma quelle sono…*
2. *Quell'uomo è ricco, ma questo è…*
3. *Questi ragazzi studiano l'italiano, ma quelli studiano…*
4. *Queste idee sono poco chiare, ma quelle sono…*
5. *Quei film sono noiosi, ma questi sono…*
6. *Quegli studenti sono pigri, ma questi…*
7. *Questa pizza è calda, ma quella…*
8. *Quelli grigi sono brutti, ma questi sono…*
9. *Questo ragazzo legge il giornale, ma quello legge…*
10. *Quel libro è interessante, ma questo è…*

Exercise 20: Days and Dates

1. *Il giorno di San Valentino è il quattordici febbraio.*
2. *Il giorno di Natale è il venticinque dicembre.*
3. *Il mio compleanno è…*
4. *Il giorno della Festa della mamma è il quattordici maggio.*
5. *Il giorno dell'indipendenza americana è il quattro luglio.*

Exercise 21: Answering Questions

1. *Domanda: Qual è la data di oggi?*
   Risposta: Oggi è…
2. *Domanda: Quand'è il tuo compleanno?*
   Risposta: Il mio compleanno è…
3. *Domanda: Quand'è il primo giorno d'estate?*
   Risposta: Il primo giorno d'estate è il ventuno giugno.
4. *Domanda: Quand'è il Giorno del ringraziamento?*
   Risposta: Il Giorno del ringraziamento è il venti… novembre.
5. *Domanda: Quand'è Capodanno?*
   Risposta: Capodanno è il primo gennaio.

Exercise 22: The Weather and the Seasons

1. *Domanda: Quali sono i mesi di primavera? D'estate? D'inverno? D'autunno?*
   Risposta: I mesi di primavera sono marzo, aprile e maggio. I mesi d'estate sono giugno, luglio e agosto. I mesi d'inverno sono dicembre, gennaio e febbraio. I mesi d'autunno sono settembre, ottobre e novembre.
2. *Domanda: Che tempo fa nella tua città in estate?*
   Risposta: D'estate nella mia città…
3. *Domanda: Che tempo fa a Boston a dicembre?*
   Risposta: A Boston a dicembre fa freddo e nevica.
4. *Domanda: Che tempo fa a Los Angeles a marzo?*
   Risposta: A Los Angeles a marzo fa bel tempo.
5. *Domanda: Che tempo fa a Miami a dicembre?*
   Risposta: A Miami a dicembre fa bel tempo.

Exercise 23: More Practice with Double Object Pronouns

1. *Glielo do.* or *Lo do loro.*
2. *Glieli mandiamo.*
3. *Te la regaliamo.*
4. *Noi ce la mettiamo.*
5. *Luigino gliela sta portando.*

Exercise 24: Indirect Object or Direct Object?

1. *Noi lo leggiamo.*
2. *Voi gli parlate.* or *Voi parlate loro.*
3. *La ragazza la compra.*
4. *Gino le telefona.*

Exercise 25: The Months

1. *gennaio*
2. *febbraio*
3. *marzo*
4. *aprile*
5. *maggio*
6. *giugno*
7. *luglio*
8. *agosto*
9. *settembre*
10. *ottobre*
11. *novembre*
12. *dicembre*

Exercise 26: More on the Adjective *Quello*

1. *Quel libro è interessante.*
2. *Quei libri sono interessanti.*
3. *Quello studente è intelligente.*
4. *Quegli studenti sono intelligenti.*
5. *Quell'amica è studiosa.*
6. *Quelle amiche sono studiose.*
7. *Quella ragazza è simpatica.*
8. *Quelle ragazze sono simpatiche.*

Exercise 27: More on the Adjective *Questo*

1. *Questo libro è interessante.*
2. *Questi libri sono interessanti.*
3. *Quest'amico è studioso.*
4. *Quest'amica è studiosa.*
5. *Questa ragazza è simpatica.*
6. *Queste ragazze sono simpatiche.*

Exercise 28: Answering Questions

1. *Oggi è il…*
2. *Oggi è…*
3. *Domani è…*
4. *Siamo in…*
5. *Il mio compleanno è in/a…*
6. *Oggi fa bel tempo (brutto tempo).*
7. *Il giorno dell'independenza è il quattro luglio.*
8. *Halloween è il trentun ottobre.*
9. *L'ultimo giorno dell'anno è il trentuno dicembre.*
10. *Io preferisco…*

Exercise 29: Translation Exercise

1. *Oggi è il primo aprile.*
2. *È il quattordici luglio duemilasette.*
3. *Abito qui dal tre marzo duemila.*
4. *Martedì prossimo è il primo giorno di primavera.*
5. *Piove molto a Boston in/ad aprile.*

Part 7: The Impersonal Si, Piacere, Commands

Exercise 1: Impersonal or Passive Voice

1. passive
2. impersonal
3. impersonal
4. impersonal
5. passive
6. passive
7. impersonal
8. passive
9. passive
10. passive

Exercise 2: Translation Exercise

1. Italian is spoken in Italy.
2. One must pay attention!
3. They say that it will rain tomorrow.
4. You can't smoke in public places.
5. English beers are drunk in that place.
6. Four languages are spoken in Switzerland.
7. You spend a little and eat very well in that restaurant.
8. A warm summer is foreseen.
9. Italian is studied at the university.
10. Used items can be purchased in that store.

Exercise 3: From Personal to Impersonal

1. *Se si studia molto, si impara molto.*
2. *Si dice che nevicherà stasera.*
3. *Si va a teatro stasera?*
4. *Si spende poco in quel ristorante.*
5. *Si dice che Roma sia caotica.*
6. *Si deve fare attenzione!*
7. *Non si può fare così.*
8. *Scusi, non si può fumare qui.*
9. *Si mangia molto bene in quel ristorante.*
10. *Si parte alle otto.*

Exercise 4: From Active to Passive Voice

1. *Si vende la macchina.*
2. *Si bevono i vini italiani.*
3. *Si dice la verità.*
4. *Si spendono tutti i soldi.*
5. *Si dicono le bugie.*
6. *Si fa la pizza in quel ristorante.*
7. *Non si devono mangiare gli spinaci.*
8. *Si spiegano le regole del gioco.*
9. *Si mangiano gli spaghetti alla carbonara.*
10. *Si vendono libri usati.*

Exercise 5: Impersonal or Passive?

1. *Si dice che sia vero.*
2. *Si legge il giornale.*
3. *Si vendono macchine usate.*
4. *Si spendono tanti soldi.*
5. *Si dicono le bugie.*
6. *Si accetta la carta di credito.*
7. *Non si ha più pazienza.*
8. *Non si può lasciare la macchina davanti alla stazione.*
9. *Se si vuole imparare, si deve studiare.*
10. *Si affittano camere.*

Exercise 6: The Impersonal *Si* with Adjectives

1. *Quando si è giovani non si hanno molte preoccupazioni.*
2. *Quando si è ricchi non si è sempre felici.*
3. *Quando si è stanchi non si può lavorare.*
4. *Quando si è tristi non si ragiona.*
5. *Quando si è onesti si dice la verità.*

Exercise 7: Identifying and Transforming Reflexive Verbs

1. *Mi diverto al mare.* becomes *Ci si diverte al mare.*
2. *Si deve preparare per il viaggio.* becomes *Ci si deve preparare per il viaggio.*
3. *Non si alza molto presto.* becomes *Non ci si alza molto presto.*
4. *Ti svegli presto ogni mattina.* becomes *Ci si sveglia presto ogni mattina.*
5. *Vi alzate prima o poi.* becomes *Ci si alza prima o poi.*
6. *Si annoiano facilmente.* becomes *Ci si annoia facilmente.*
7. *Mi arrabbio spesso.* becomes *Ci si arrabbia spesso.*
8. *Si innamorano raramente.* becomes *Ci si innamora raramente.*
9. *Mi lavo ogni mattina.* becomes *Ci si lava ogni mattina.*
10. *Mi vesto in fretta.* becomes *Ci si veste in fretta.*

Exercise 8: Identifying the Subject

1. *Mi piace Michele.*
2. *Ti piacciono le birre irlandesi?*
3. *A Mario piace la pizza.*
4. *A Giovanni e Angela piace cucinare.*
5. *Vi piacciono i film di Roberto Benigni.*
6. *A Maria piacciono loro.*
7. *A loro piace Maria.*
8. *Gli piacciono i miei amici.*
9. *Al gatto piace giocare con lo spago.*
10. *A voi piacciono i biscotti della nonna.*

Exercise 9: *Piace* or *Piacciono?*

1. *Mi piacciono gli spaghetti al pomodoro.*
2. *Ti piace leggere?*
3. *A Mario piacciono i racconti di Alberto Moravia.*
4. *Ai miei genitori piace andare a teatro.*

5. *Non mi <u>piace</u> il tuo atteggiamento.*
6. *Ai nostri amici <u>piacciono</u> i vostri amici.*
7. *Ti <u>piacciono</u> i vini italiani?*
8. *Mi <u>piace</u> l'arrosto di vitello.*
9. *Non le <u>piace</u> la tua fidanzata.*
10. *Ci <u>piacciono</u> le lasagne della nonna.*

Exercise 10: Sentence Building

1. Pasta is pleasing to us.
2. The movie is pleasing to you and John.
3. Going out on Friday nights is pleasing to us.
4. She is pleasing to him,
5. But he is not pleasing to her.
6. All of Bob Dylan's songs are pleasing to me.
7. Their professor is pleasing to them.
8. Taking walks is pleasing to my grandparents.
9. Working is not pleasing to my uncle.
10. Ice cream is pleasing to my brother's kids.
11. Your friends are pleasing to us.

Exercise 11: Translation Exercise

1. *Ci piace la pasta.*
2. *Vi piace il film.*
3. *Ci piace uscire il venerdì sera.*
4. *Gli piace lei,*
5. *ma non le piace lui.*
6. *Mi piacciono tutte le canzoni di Bob Dylan.*
7. *Gli piace il loro professore.*
8. *Fare le passeggiate piace ai miei nonni.*
9. *A mio zio non piace lavorare.*
10. *Ai figli di mio fratello piace il gelato.*
11. *Ci piacciono i tuoi amici.*

Exercise 12: Logical Endings

Answers may vary. Possible answers are given.
1. *Mia madre non va alla festa, perché non le piacciono le feste.*
2. *I miei genitori non vengono a cena, perché non gli piace mangiare a casa nostra.*
3. *Telefoni a Gabriella, perché ti piace.*
4. *Mangi al ristorante stasera, perché ti piace mangiare fuori.*
5. *Michele e Maria vanno in treno, perché non gli piace viaggiare in aereo.*
6. *Non voglio parlare con Alberto, perché non mi piace.*
7. *Non abbiamo voglia di studiare, perché non ci piace il professore.*
8. *Pietro vuole comprare una nuova cravatta, perché gli piace vestirsi elegantemente.*
9. *Tu e Bruno non preparate la cena, perché non vi piace cucinare.*
10. *Non mangiamo al ristorante cinese, perché non ci piace la cucina cinese.*

Exercise 13: Likes and Dislikes—Informal

1. *Ti piacciono le lasagne?*
2. *Ti piace sciare?*
3. *Ti piace il tiramisù?*
4. *Ti piacciono i film di Roberto Rossellini?*
5. *Ti piace il vino rosso?*

Exercise 14: Likes and Dislikes—Formal

1. *Le piacciono le lasagne?*
2. *Le piace sciare?*
3. *Le piace il tiramisù?*
4. *Le piacciono i film di Roberto Rossellini?*
5. *Le piace il vino rosso?*

Exercise 15: Conjugating *Mancare*

io manco
tu manchi
lui/lei/Lei manca
noi manchiamo
voi mancate
loro/Loro mancano

Exercise 16: Sentence Building

1. Our friends are lacking to us.
2. Your uncle is lacking to you and John.
3. My father is lacking to me.
4. She is lacking to him,
5. But he is not lacking to her.
6. We are lacking to them.
7. You and Michele are lacking to me.
8. We are lacking to my grandparents.
9. Their uncle is lacking to them.
10. My sister is lacking to my brother.

Exercise 17: Translation Exercise

1. *Ci mancano i nostri amici.*
2. *Vi manca vostro zio.*
3. *Mi manca mio padre.*
4. *Gli manca lei,*
5. *ma non le manca lui.*
6. *Gli manchiamo.*
7. *Mi mancate tu e Michele.*
8. *Manchiamo ai nostri nonni.*
9. *Gli manca il loro zio.*
10. *Mia sorella manca a mio fratello.*

Exercise 18: Forming Informal Commands

ascoltare	*prendere*
tu: Ascolta!	*tu: Prendi!*
noi: Ascoltiamo!	*noi: Prendiamo!*
voi: Ascoltate!	*voi: Prendete!*

dormire
tu: Dormi!
noi: Dormiamo!
voi: Dormite!

finire
tu: Finisci!
noi: Finiamo!
voi: Finite!

Exercise 19: Your New Coworker

Answers will vary. Possible answers are given.
1. *Prendi il treno alla stazione!*
2. *Compra un nuovo stereo da Best Buy!*
3. *Arriva quando vuoi!*
4. *Parcheggia la macchina nel parcheggio vicino alla stazione!*
5. *Appendi il cappotto nel mio ufficio!*

Exercise 20: Now in the Plural

Answers will vary. Possible answers are given.
1. *Prendete il treno alla stazione!*
2. *Comprate un nuovo stereo da Best Buy!*
3. *Arrivate quando volete!*
4. *Parcheggiate la macchina nel parcheggio vicino alla stazione!*
5. *Appendete il cappotto nel nostro ufficio!*

Exercise 21: Forming Formal Commands

ascoltare
(Lei): Ascolti!
(Loro): Ascoltino!

prendere
(Lei): Prenda!
(Loro): Prendano!

dormire
(Lei): Dorma!
(Loro): Dormano!

finire
(Lei): Finisca!
(Loro): Finiscano!

Exercise 22: Your New Neighbor

Answers will vary. Possible answers are given.
1. *Noleggi una macchina alla Hertz!*
2. *Venda i libriusati alla libreria in centro!*
3. *Vada al bar qui vicino!*
4. *Lavi i vestiti a casa mia!*
5. *Prenda il gelato in gelateria!*

Exercise 23: Now in the Plural

Answers will vary. Possible answers are given.
1. *Noleggino una macchina alla Hertz!*
2. *Vendano i libriusati alla libreria in centro!*
3. *Vadano al bar qui vicino!*
4. *Lavino i vestiti a casa mia!*
5. *Prendano il gelato alla gelateria!*

Exercise 24: From Affirmative to Negative

1. *Compra il giornale!* becomes *Non comprare il giornale!*
2. *Metti le chiavi sul tavolo!* becomes *Non mettere le chiave sul tavolo!*
3. *Porta tuo fratello a scuola!* becomes *Non portare tuo fratello a scuola!*
4. *Finisci i tuoi compiti!* becomes *Non finire i tuoi compiti!*
5. *Dormi!* becomes *Non dormire!*
6. *Bevi il caffè!* becomes *Non bere il caffè!*
7. *Presta la macchina a tuo fratello!* becomes *Non prestare la macchina a tuo fratello!*
8. *Sveglia i bambini alle otto!* becomes *Non svegliare i bambini alle otto!*
9. *Prendi quel libro!* becomes *Non prendere quel libro!*

Exercise 25: Forming Commands

1. *Non pulire!*
2. *Leggiamo!*
3. *Non parcheggino!*
4. *Non lasciate!*
5. *Ascolta!*
6. *Non aspettiamo!*
7. *Sentano!*
8. *Prenda!*
9. *Non parli!*

Exercise 26: Commands with Irregular Verbs

1. *Sii generoso!*
2. *Va' a sciare!*
3. *Sta' zitto!*
4. *Da' un dollaro!*
5. *Abbi pazienza!*
6. *Va' a giocare!*
7. *Fa' colazione!*
8. *Di' qualcosa in italiano!*

Exercise 27: Commands with Irregular Verbs

1. *Non essere generoso!*
2. *Non andare a sciare!*
3. *Non stare zitto!*
4. *Non dare dei soldi ad un amico!*
5. *Non avere pazienza!*
6. *Non andare a giocare!*
7. *Non fare colazione!*
8. *Non dire qualcosa in italiano!*

Exercise 28: Commands with Irregular Verbs

1. *Sia ragionevole!*
2. *Vada a fare le spese!*
3. *Faccia attenzione!*
4. *Stia attento/a!*
5. *Abbia pazienza!*
6. *Dica "Buon giorno"!*
7. *Faccia colazione!*
8. *Dica qualcosa in italiano!*

Exercise 29: Imperatives with Pronouns

1. *Sì, dilla!*
2. *No, non mi telefonare!*
3. *Sì, fatela!*
4. *Sì, divertitevi!*
5. *Sì, svegliali!*

Exercise 30: Imperatives with Pronouns

1. *Sì, lo prepari!*
2. *No, non gliela dia!*
3. *Sì, li portino!*
4. *Sì, lo faccia!*
5. *Si alzi alle due!*

Exercise 31: I Command You!

1. Don't talk!
2. Let's go to the party!
3. Don't tell me a lie!
4. Please, close the door!
5. Hey, boys, don't make noise!
6. Wake up!
7. Lend the car to him!
8. Don't get mad!

Exercise 32: Make It Positive

1. *Dimmelo!*
2. *Fate così!*
3. *Leggete quel libro!*
4. *Ascoltalo!*
5. *Rispondi loro!* or *Rispondigli!*

Exercise 33: A Suggestion, a Command

1. *Vieni qui!*
   Come here!
2. *Smettila!*
   Stop it!
3. *Stai zitto!*
   Be quiet!
4. *Legga questo libro!*
   Read this book!
5. *Non bere l'acqua del rubinetto!*
   Don't drink the water from the faucet!
6. *Mangiamo la pizza stasera!*
   Let's eat pizza tonight!
7. *Non mi dire bugie!*
   Don't tell me lies!
8. *Mangia gli spaghetti!*
   Eat some spaghetti!
9. *Ascolta i tuoi genitori!*
   Listen to your parents!
10. *Fate attenzione!*
    Pay attention!

Exercise 34: Imperative Forms of Irregular Verbs

andare
(tu): Va'! or Vai!
(Lei): Vada!
(noi): Andiamo!
(voi): Andate!
(Loro): Vadano!

dare
(tu): Da'! or Dai!
(Lei): Dia!
(noi): Diamo!
(voi): Date!
(Loro): Diano!

fare
(tu): Fa'! or Fai!
(Lei): Faccia!
(noi): Facciamo!
(voi): Fate!
(Loro): Facciano!

stare
(tu): Sta'! or Stai!
(Lei): Stia!
(noi): Stiamo!
(voi): State!
(Loro): Stiano!

dire
(tu): Di'!
(Lei): Dica!
(noi): Diciamo!
(voi): Dite!
(Loro): Dicano!

avere
(tu): Abbi!
(Lei): Abbia!
(noi): Abbiamo!
(voi): Abbiate!
(Loro): Abbiate!

essere
(tu): Sii!
(Lei): Sia!
(noi): Siamo!
(voi): Siate!
(Loro): Siano!

venire
(tu): Vieni!
(Lei): Venga!
(noi): Veniamo!
(voi): Venite!
(Loro): Vengano!

Exercise 35: To Like or Not To Like

1. *Mi piace la pasta.*
2. *Ti piacciono gli spaghetti al pomodoro?*
3. *Gli piacciono le lasagne.*
4. *Le piace il caffè.*
5. *Gli piace la torta.*
6. *A voi piacciono i ravioli.*
7. *A me piace l'insalata verde.*
8. *A noi piacciono le mele.*
9. *A Maria piacciono i romanzi di Alberto Moravia.*
10. *A Giacomo piace il prosciutto crudo.*

Part 8: The Passato Prossimo and the Imperfetto

Exercise 1: *Avere* and *Essere* in the Present Tense

avere	*essere*
io ho	sono
tu hai	sei
lui/lei/Lei ha	è
noi abbiamo	siamo
voi avete	siete
loro/Loro hanno	sono

Exercise 2: Past Participles—Regular or Irregular?

1. *speso*
2. *scritto*
3. *risposto*
4. *preso*
5. *perduto* or *perso*
6. *messo*
7. *letto*
8. *conosciuto*
9. *chiuso*
10. *chiesto*
11. *bevuto*
12. *fatto*
13. *andato*
14. *venuto*
15. *diventato*
16. *restato*
17. *stato*
18. *stato*
19. *morto*
20. *arrivato*
21. *partito*
22. *ritornato*
23. *entrato*
24. *uscito*
25. *salito*
26. *sceso*
27. *caduto*
28. *nato*
29. *offerto*
30. *detto*
31. *aperto*
32. *veduto* or *visto*

Exercise 3: Sentence Analysis

Sentence Infinitive Past Participle *avere/essere*
1. *Trovate dieci dollari per strada.*
   trovare — *trovato* — *avere*
2. *Andiamo a un concerto di Bob Dylan.*
   andare — *andato* — *essere*
3. *Comprano il nuovo romanzo di Umberto Eco.*
   comprare — *comprato* — *avere*
4. *Giochi a tennis ogni giorno.*
   giocare — *giocato* — *avere*
5. *Esco tutte le sere.*
   uscire — *uscito* — *essere*
6. *Incontri una persona famosa.*
   incontrare — *incontrato* — *avere*
7. *Ritorniamo a casa alle 4 di mattina.*
   ritornare — *ritornato* — *essere*
8. *Vengo a piedi.*
   venire — *venuto* — *essere*
9. *Mio fratello dà una bottiglia di vino a mio padre.*
   dare — *dato* — *avere*
10. *Sono una persona fortunata.*
    essere — *stato* — *essere*
11. *Non rispondiamo mai alle email*
    rispondere — *risposto* — *avere*
12. *Arrivate in ufficio in ritardo.*
    arrivare — *arrivato* — *essere*
13. *Marcello dorme tutto il giorno.*
    dormire — *dormito* — *avere*
14. *Vediamo molti film italiani.*
    Vedere — *veduto* or *visto* — *avere*

Exercise 4: From Present to Past

1. *Avete trovato dieci dollari per strada.*
2. *Siamo andati/e a un concerto di Bob Dylan.*
3. *Hanno comprato il nuovo romanzo di Umberto Eco.*
4. *Hai giocato a tennis ogni giorno.*
5. *Sono uscito/a tutte le sere.*
6. *Hai incontrato una persona famosa.*
7. *Siamo ritornati/e a casa alle 4 di mattina.*
8. *Sono venuto/a a piedi.*
9. *Mio fratello ha dato una bottiglia di vino a mio padre.*
10. *Sono stato/a una persona fortunata.*
11. *Non abbiamo mai risposto alle email.*
12. *Siete arrivati/e in ufficio in ritardo.*
13. *Marcello ha dormito tutto il giorno.*
14. *Abbiamo visto (or veduto) molti film italiani.*

Exercise 5: From Present to Past

1. *Io ho mangiato la pizza.*
2. *Maria è andata all'università venerdì scorso.*
3. *Noi siamo usciti/e sabato sera.*
4. *Ho bevuto il caffè a colazione.*
5. *Gli studenti sono arrivati in classe alle 4.15.*
6. *Le sue amiche sono restate a casa stasera.*
7. *Non ho avuto tempo.*
8. *Loro hanno detto sempre la verità.*
9. *Voi avete fatto attenzione in classe.*
10. *Lei ha letto molti libri.*
11. *Maria e Marco sono partiti alle 8.00.*
12. *Tu hai dormito molto.*
13. *Noi siamo stati dei bravi studenti.*

Exercise 6: Questions about Your Past

Answers will vary. Possible answers are given.
1. *Domanda: Che cosa hai fatto sabato scorso? Hai fatto le spese?*
   Risposta: Sono andato al cinema sabato scorso con mia moglie. Poi siamo andati a mangiare in un ristorante. Io non ho fatto le spese.
2. *Domanda: Racconta di un viaggio che hai fatto. Dove sei andato? Con chi? Hai visitato un museo? Hai visto dei monumenti? Hai mangiato in un ristorante straordinario? Hai viaggiato in treno, in macchina o in aereo?*
   Risposta: L'anno scorso io e mia moglie siamo andati in Italia. Abbiamo visitato Venezia e Firenze. Siamo andati alla Galleria degli Uffizi a Firenze, e al Guggenheim a Venezia. Abbiamo mangiato in un ristorante straordinario a Venezia. Si chiama «Pizzeria al Profeta». Abbiamo viaggiato in aereo e in treno.
3. *Domanda: Hai mai fatto un viaggio in Italia? Inghilterra? Germania? Spagna? Quali città hai visitato? Che cosa hai visto?*
   Risposta: Ho fatto un viaggio in Inghilterra un paio di anni fa. Ho visitato Londra. Ho visto Piccadilly Circus e Buckingham Palace.
4. *Domanda: Hai mai visto un film italiano? Quale film hai visto?*

*Risposta: Ho visto un film italiano l'altra
sera. Ho visto «La Tigre e la Neve».*

5. *Domanda: Hai mai mangiato in un ristorante lussuoso? Che cosa hai mangiato? Che
cosa hai bevuto? Quanto hai speso?*
*Risposta: La settimana scorsa ho mangiato al ristorante Grille 23 a Boston. Ho mangiato una bistecca
e ho bevuto del vino rosso. Ho speso $300 dollari.*

6. *Domanda: Hai mai conosciuto una persona famosa? Chi? Quando l'hai conosciuta?*
*Risposta: Ho conosciuto Yoko Ono un paio
di anni fa quando ho visitato Londra.*

7. *Domanda: Che cosa hai fatto l'estate scorsa? Hai fatto
un viaggio? Dove? Hai letto molto? Hai dormito molto?*
*Risposta: Non ho fatto un viaggio l'anno scorso.
Ho lavorato tutta l'estate e ho letto molti libri.*

Exercise 7: Translation Exercise

1. *Sono molto stanco/a, perché non
ho dormito la notte scorsa.*
2. *Perché? Sei uscito/a?*
3. *No, ho lavorato fino alle 8.*
4. *A che ora sei tornato/a a casa?*
5. *Io devo andare a lavorare alle 7 domani mattina.*
6. *Sai che io sono andato/a a teatro venerdì sera?*
7. *Abbiamo visto una commedia di Carlo Goldoni.*
8. *Ti piace viaggiare? Sei andato/a in vacanza l'anno
scorso? Sei andato in macchina, in treno, in aereo?*

Exercise 8: Reflexive Verbs in the Past Tense

1. *Noi ci siamo svegliati/e molto presto.*
2. *Vittoria si è preparata per il viaggio.*
3. *Luisa e Francesca si sono annoiate alla festa.*
4. *Fabio e Giuseppe si sono divertiti molto.*
5. *Tu e Luisella vi siete arrabbiati/e.*
6. *I ragazzi non si sono sentiti bene oggi.*
7. *Le bambine si sono lavate le mani.*
8. *Sara si è innamorata di Filippo.*
9. *Ti sei riposato/a questo weekend?*
10. *Mi sono fermato/a al bar a prendere un caffè.*

Exercise 9: Reciprocal Constructions in the Past Tense

1. *Io e la mia ragazza ci siamo visti.*
2. *Angela e suo cugino si sono scritti.*
3. *Io e mia madre ci siamo parlati/e.*
4. *Marco e Angela si sono telefonati.*
5. *Giuseppe e i suoi amici si sono chiamati.*

Exercise 10: Working with Object Pronouns in the Past Tense

1. *Li ho letti.*
2. *L'abbiamo mangiata.*

3. *L'hanno guardata.*
4. *Li hai dati.*
5. *L'hai letto.*
6. *Le abbiamo mangiate.*
7. *Le hanno cercate.*
8. *Ci ha visti/e.*
9. *Le ha comprate.*
10. *L'avete voluto vedere.*
11. *Non l'ha capita.*
12. *L'abbiamo fatta domenica sera.*
13. *Non li avete potuti ascoltare.*
14. *Vi abbiamo cercati/e.*

Exercise 11: From Present to *Imperfetto*

1. *Io ascolto un disco di Elvis.*
Io ascoltavo un disco di Elvis.
2. *Noi fumiamo delle sigarette.*
Noi fumavamo delle sigarette.
3. *Gregorio beve la birra.*
Gregorio beveva la birra.
4. *Simone lava le macchine.*
Simone lavava le machine.
5. *Io ricevo un messaggio da Massimo una volta alla settimana.*
Io ricevevo un messaggio da Massimo una volta alla settimana.
6. *Noi dormiamo molto il sabato e la domenica.*
Noi dormivamo molto il sabato e la domenica.
7. *Loro devono mangiare la frutta.*
Loro dovevano mangiare la frutta.
8. *I ragazzi dormono durante il film.*
I ragazzi dormivano durante il film.
9. *Io vado all'università.*
Io andavo all'università.

Exercise 12: Conjugating the *Imperfetto*

andare (to go):

io andavo	*noi andavamo*
tu andavi	*voi andavate*
lui/lei/Lei andava	*loro/Loro andavano*

ricevere (to receive):

io ricevevo	*noi ricevevamo*
tu ricevevi	*voi ricevevate*
lui/lei/Lei riceveva	*loro/Loro ricevevano*

costruire (to build):

io costruivo	*noi costruivamo*
ti costruivi	*voi costruivate*
lui/lei/Lei costruiva	*loro/Loro costruivano*

Exercise 13: Translating Exercise with the *Imperfetto*

1. *Io parlavo con i tuoi amici.*
2. *Tu giocavi a baseball con tuo nonno.*
3. *Lui dormiva mentre il suo capo parlava.*
4. *Quando avevo 10 anni, bevevo molta aranciata.*
5. *Non diceva una bugia.*
6. *Erano belli/e.*
7. *Mentre io leggevo il giornale, mia moglie parlava con suo fratello.*
8. *Facevo la spesa il sabato.*

Exercise 14: *Passato Prossimo* or *Imperfetto?*

1. *Ieri pomeriggio, mentre <u>leggevo</u>, mio fratello <u>ascoltava</u> la musica.*
2. *"Marcello, con chi <u>parlavi</u> quando io <u>sono arrivato/a</u>?" "<u>Parlavo</u> con Martina."*
3. *La settimana scorsa io e mia moglie <u>siamo andati</u> nel Vermont, perché <u>faceva</u> bel tempo e volevamo vedere le foglie che <u>cambiavano</u> colore.*
4. *Quando Michele <u>aveva 12 anni, frequentava</u> la scuola media.*
5. *L'anno scorso mio fratello <u>ha venduto</u> la casa perché <u>ha trovato</u> un nuovo lavoro a Boston.*
6. *Il weekend scorso io <u>sono dovuto</u> andare a Philadelphia, perché il mio capo non si sentiva bene.*
7. *Il volo <u>è partito</u> alle 8 e noi <u>siamo arrivati</u> all'aeroporto alle 8 e 15.*
8. *Non abbiamo potuto andare alla festa ieri sera, perché <u>abbiamo dovuto</u> andare a vedere mio padre.*
9. *Ieri sera Federico <u>ha conosciuto</u> mio fratello.*
10. *Mentre noi guardavamo il film, loro <u>parlavano</u> al telefono.*

Exercise 15: The *Trapassato Prossimo*

1. *Avevo mangiato la pasta.*
2. *Eravamo andati in spiaggia.*
3. *Vi eravate visti l'anno scorso.*
4. *Il signor Gianni aveva chiamato la polizia.*
5. *Tu avevi saputo la verità.*
6. *Non aveva visto il film.*
7. *Mi ero svegliato presto.*
8. *Avevi già letto quel libro.*
9. *Avevamo ascoltato musica tutta la sera.*
10. *Si erano innamorati.*

Exercise 16: Listening Comprehension

Answers will vary. Possible answers are given.
1. *Domanda: Da quanto tempo studi l'italiano?*
   Risposta: Studio l'italiano da 6 mesi.
2. *Domanda: Da quando abiti in questa casa?*
   Risposta: Abito in questa casa dal 2000.

3. *Domanda: Da quante settimane non vedi tuo fratello?*
   Risposta: Non vedo mio fratello da due settimane.
4. *Domanda: Da quanti giorni fai gli esercizi sull'imperfetto?*
   Risposta: Li faccio da due settimane.
5. *Domanda: Da quanto tempo non vai in un ristorante cinese?*
   Risposta: Non vado in un ristorante cinese da tre mesi.
6. *Domanda: Da quanti anni hai la patente di guida?*
   Risposta: Ho la patente di guida da vent'anni.
7. *Domanda: Da quanto tempo non fumi le sigarette?*
   Risposta: Non fumo da dieci anni.
8. *Domanda: Da quanto tempo suoni uno strumento musicale?*
   Risposta: Suono la chitarra da un mese.
9. *Domanda: Da quanti anni guardi i Simpsons?*
   Risposta: Guardo i Simpsons da otto anni.
10. *Domanda: Da quanti anni bevi il caffè?*
    Risposta: Bevo il caffè da vent'anni.

Exercise 17: Past or Present?

1. *Ieri mattina Marco si è svegliato alle 7 e si è alzato alle 7 e 30. Ha preparato la colazione per suo figlio ed è andato in ufficio, dove ha lavorato tutto il giorno.*
2. *Stasera io voglio andare al cinema con il mio amico. Il mio amico si chiama Giovanni. Normalmente lui si annoia al cinema. Questa volta io e Giovanni ci divertiamo sicuramente, perché andiamo a vedere un film divertentissimo. Dopo il film ci fermiamo al bar a prendere un caffè.*
3. *Due giorni fa io mi sono alzato/a molto tardi, poi mi sono lavato/a e mi sono vestito/a velocemente, perché non volevo arrivare tardi al lavoro. Il mio capo è molto simpatico, ma io non posso arrivare tardi al lavoro, perché lui si arrabbia facilmente!*

Exercise 18: Answering Questions in Italian

Answers will vary. Possible answers are given.
1. *Mi sono svegliato/a alle otto stamattina.*
2. *Ieri pomeriggio ho letto un libro.*
3. *La notte scorsa mi sono addormentato/a alle undici.*
4. *Sono stato/a in Florida due anni fa.*
5. *Ho visto «Amarcord» di Fellini.*

Exercise 19: Time Expressions in the Past

1. *Sono andato a studiare in biblioteca ieri sera.*
2. *Ho visto i miei genitori la settimana scorsa.*
3. *Ho letto la «Divina Commedia» nove anni fa.*
4. *Ho lavato la macchina martedì scorso.*
5. *Ho conosciuto tua sorella ieri.*

Exercise 20: Translation Exercise

1. *Marco e Angela si sono sposati.*

2. *John si è arrabbiato, perché i suoi amici non hanno chiamato.*
3. *Non ho ancora fatto colazione.*
4. *Io e i miei amici non ci vediamo mai.*
5. *La notte scorsa mi sono addormentato/a alle undici.*
6. *Hanno guardato la televisione tutta la sera.*
7. *Ho lavorato tutti i sabati per tre mesi, perché volevo guadagnare molti soldi.*
8. *Ha pagato lui il caffè, perché non avevamo soldi.*
9. *La conferenza incomincia alle otto di mattina.*

Exercise 21: From Present to Past

1. *Marcello le ha comprate.*
2. *Tu e Vincenzo l'avete fumato.*
3. *Io e Simone l'abbiamo comprata.*
4. *Li ho visti al ristorante.*
5. *Federico e i suoi amici l'hanno ordinata.*
6. *Tu l'hai bevuto.*
7. *Simone non li ha ascoltati.*
8. *Il signor Gianni l'ha chiamata.*
9. *La polizia li ha cercati.*

Exercise 22: A Love Story

Il mese scorso, Mary, una ragazza canadese, <u>ha fatto un viaggio</u> in Sicilia. Mary <u>ha preso</u> il volo dall'aeroporto di Toronto ed <u>è arrivata</u> a Palermo. Mary <u>ha fatto una passeggiata</u> e <u>ha comprato</u> dei vestiti nei negozi di Palermo. Mary <u>ha visto</u> il Palazzo dei Normanni e le catacombe dei Cappuccini. Il giorno dopo <u>faceva brutto tempo</u>, così Mary <u>ha passato</u> la giornata in albergo. Quella sera Mary <u>ha mangiato</u> in una piccola trattoria. Nella trattoria Mary <u>ha conosciuto</u> un bel cameriere siciliano. Il cameriere <u>si chiamava</u> Piero. Quella sera, Mary e Piero <u>sono andati</u> al cinema a vedere un film di Roberto Benigni e a ballare per tre ore in discoteca. Il giorno dopo Mary <u>è tornata</u> in Canada. Piero <u>è rimasto</u> a Palermo, ma <u>ha scritto</u> una lettera d'amore a Mary. Quando Mary <u>è arrivata</u> a casa, <u>ha trovato</u> la lettera di Piero. <u>Ha letto</u> la lettera di Piero, e gli <u>ha telefonato</u> per invitarlo a Toronto.

Exercise 23: Further into the Past

1. *La settimana scorsa mia moglie <u>ha letto</u> il libro che io le <u>avevo regalato</u> l'anno scorso.*
2. *Luisella non <u>è andata</u> in Germania, perché <u>aveva visitato</u> Amburgo l'anno scorso.*
3. *Marcello non ha mangiato con noi, perché aveva <u>fatto colazione</u> dai suoi nonni.*
4. *Quando io <u>ho chiamato</u> mio fratello, lui era già partito.*
5. *Alessio non è venuto al cinema, perché <u>aveva visto</u> il film la settimana scorsa.*

Exercise 24: Translation

1. *Quando Dante ha scritto la« Divina Commedia», Charles Dickens non aveva ancora scritto «David Copperfield».*
2. *Mi ero già addormentato quando è arrivato.*
3. *Non ho comprato la farina oggi, perché mia moglie l'aveva comprata ieri.*
4. *Abbiamo cucinato/dato una cena per gli amici che avevamo conosciuto in Italia.*
5. *Non ho letto il libro ieri sera, perché l'avevo letto il mese scorso.*

Exercise 25: When I Was a Child

Answers will vary. Possible answers are given.
1. *Quando ero piccolo…non ero molto studioso. Preferivo giocare con i miei amici.*
2. *Quando ero piccolo…andavo a scuola tutti i giorni.*
3. *Quando ero piccolo…non avevo un computer.*
4. *Quando ero piccolo…andavo al mare con i miei genitori.*
5. *Mia madre aveva paura quando… io e mio fratello nuotavamo.*
6. *Quando avevo quindici anni…fumavo le sigarette.*
7. *Quando avevo sedici anni…ho cominciato a guidare.*
8. *Quando avevo diciotto anni…sono andato in Italia per la prima volta.*

Part 9: The Future Tense, the Conditional Mood, the Subjunctive

Exercise 1: Recognizing the Simple Future Tense

1. *tu dormirai*
2. *loro berranno*
3. *io vorrò*
4. *noi parleremo*
5. *tu studierai*
6. *loro saranno*
7. *lui pagherà*
8. *tu avrai*
9. *io dirò*
10. *voi farete*

Exercise 2: From Present to Future

1. *I ragazzi non andranno in Italia.*
2. *Tu berrai il vino a cena.*
3. *Domani sera io starò a casa.*
4. *To riceverai molte email.*
5. *Mio figlio diventerà famoso.*
6. *Non verremo a casa tua domani sera.*
7. *Vorrò fare un viaggio in Italia.*
8. *Tu e Anna potrete dormire da noi.*
9. *Balleremo tutta la sera.*
10. *Preferirò andare a Roma.*

Exercise 3: In the Future

1. *Io e Marianna <u>mangeremo</u> in un ristorante cinese.*
2. *I miei fratelli <u>andranno</u> a fare le spese*
3. *Lei <u>guarderà</u> la TV stasera.*
4. *Tutti i ragazzi <u>metteranno</u> i libri sul tavolo.*
5. *Mio nipote <u>avrà paura</u> del cane.*
6. *Io <u>sarò al verde</u> la prossima settimana.*
7. *I medici <u>saranno</u> certi della diagnosi.*
8. *Tu e Marta <u>berrete</u> il vino al ristorante stasera.*
9. *Anna* dirà *la verità a suo padre.*
10. *Tutti i miei amici <u>preferiranno</u> andare in macchina.*

Exercise 4: Talking about Your Future

Answers will vary. Possible answers are given.

1. *Sì, farò un viaggio quest'estate.*
2. *Andrò a Londra.*
3. *Sì, leggerò una guida turistica prima di partire.*
4. *No, non vedrò i miei amici questo weekend.*
5. *Avrò 65 anni quando finirò di lavorare.*
6. *Non so chi sarà il prossimo presidente degli Stati Uniti.*
7. *Preparerò la cena appena arriverò a casa domani.*
8. *Farò le spese alle otto sabato mattina.*
9. *Mangerò gli spaghetti stasera per cena.*
10. *Farò un viaggio in Italia l'anno prossimo.*

Exercise 5: Recognizing the Future Perfect

1. *sarai partita* you will have left
2. *avrò mangiato* I will have eaten
3. *saremo andati* we will have gone
4. *avrete bevuto* you will have drunk
5. *saranno diventati* they will have become
6. *avrà dormito* it will have slept
7. *avranno creduto* they will have believed
8. *sarà potuta tornare* she will have been able to return
9. *avremo ascoltato* we will have listened
10. *avrai fatto* you will have made/done

Exercise 6: Will Have

1. *Il mio amico <u>avrà preparato</u> una bella cena.*
2. *Tutti i miei cugini <u>avranno preso</u> il caffè al bar.*
3. *Tu ed io <u>avremo guidato</u> da Firenze a Roma.*
4. *Tu e Larissa <u>avrete aspettato</u> per due ore.*
5. *Giorgio e Lorenzo <u>avranno sentito</u> il rumore.*
6. *Tutti gli studenti <u>avranno finito</u> l'esame.*
7. *Mia nonna <u>avrà ricevuto</u> il regalo che le abbiamo mandato.*
8. *Tu sarai <u>andato/a</u> al supermercato.*
9. *I ragazzi <u>saranno ritornati</u> a casa.*
10. *Voi <u>vi sarete svegliati/e</u> molto presto stamattina.*

Exercise 7: Recognizing the Conditional

1. *tu partiresti*

2. *io berrei*
3. *tu mangeresti*
4. *io abiterei*
5. *loro farebbero*
6. *noi saremmo*
7. *io darei*
8. *loro starebbero*
9. *io direi*
10. *tu puliresti*

Exercise 8: Correct Translation

1. *vorrei* I would like
2. *sognerebbe* she would dream
3. *arriveresti* you would arrive
4. *dormirebbe* he would sleep
5. *finirebbero* they would finish
6. *sarei* I would be
7. *porteresti* you would bring
8. *andremmo* we would go
9. *dareste* you would give
10. *scriverei* I would write

Exercise 9: Conditional Situations

1. *Io <u>mangerei</u> a casa tua, ma non ho tempo.*
2. *I miei cugini <u>dormirebbero</u> da noi, ma devono partire stasera.*
3. *Marco <u>darebbe</u> la mancia al cameriere, ma è al verde.*
4. *Mia madre mi <u>regalerebbe</u> un orologio.*
5. *Io <u>aprirei</u> la finestra, ma non ho caldo.*
6. *Che cosa <u>penserebbe</u> tuo padre?*
7. *Noi <u>vorremmo</u> un arrosto di vitello.*
8. *Loro <u>partirebbero</u> alle otto, se avessero i biglietti.*
9. *Mio figlio <u>si sveglierebbero</u> presto.*
10. *Tu e Giorgio <u>aspettereste</u> l'autobus.*

Exercise 10: The Conditional Perfect

1. *<u>Avrei comprato</u> una macchina.*
2. *<u>Avremmo letto</u> il libro.*
3. *Voi non <u>avreste dovuto</u> mangiare prima delle otto.*
4. *Anna e Carlo <u>avrebbero aiutato</u> il figlio.*
5. *<u>Avresti fatto</u> le lasagne per cena.*
6. *<u>Avrebbe detto</u> sempre la verità.*
7. *Non <u>avrei avuto</u> tempo.*
8. *Mi <u>sarei vestito/a</u> in fretta.*
9. *Gaetano <u>avrebbe mangiato</u> gli spaghetti.*
10. *Tu e Marcello <u>sareste tornati</u> presto.*

Exercise 11: Recognizing the Conditional Perfect

1. *saremmo partiti* we would have left
2. *avrebbe comprato* she would have bought
3. *si sarebbe scusata* she would have apologized
4. *avreste preferito* you would have preferred

5. *sarebbero venute* they would have come
6. *avresti portato* you would have brought
7. *avrei chiamato* I would have called
8. *avremmo guadagnato* we would have earned
9. *saresti stato* you would have been
10. *avrebbero lasciato* they would have left

Exercise 12: What Do You Think?

Answers may vary. Possible answers are given.

1. *Io penso che la guerra sia inevitabile.*
2. *I miei genitori vogliono che io vada a cena.*
3. *Il mio miglior amico crede che io sia sincero.*
4. *È necessario che mio fratello compri una nuova macchina.*
5. *Ho paura che abbiano dimenticato la torta.*
6. *È importante che tutti facciano attenzione.*
7. *Può darsi che la conferenza cominci alle otto.*
8. *Il mio capo desidera che io faccia la presentazione.*
9. *Noi siamo sicuri che oggi sia venerdì.*
10. *Gli americani vogliono che ci sia l'assicurazione sanitaria per tutti.*

Exercise 13: Present Indicative or Present Subjunctive?

1. *Noi vogliamo andare al cinema stasera.*
   Present indicative.
2. *Lui pensa che voglia venire anch'io.*
   Present subjunctive.
3. *È impossibile sapere la verità.*   Present indicative.
4. *Avete paura che lui vada da solo*   Present subjunctive.
5. *Bisogna che gli studenti studino di più.*
   Present subjunctive.
6. *Sono sicuro che Marco viene stasera.*
   Present indicative.
7. *Siamo contenti che nostro padre si senta bene.*
   Present subjunctive.
8. *I miei amici non credono nell'astrologia.*
   Present indicative.
9. *È importante che tutti capiscano le regole.*
   Present subjunctive.
10. *È ora che tu compri un orologio.*   Present subjunctive.

Exercise 14: From Present to Past in the Subjunctive

1. *Non sono sicuro che lui capisca.*
   *Non sono sicuro che lui **abbia capito**.*
2. *È possibile che Marcello vada in macchina.*
   *È possibile che Marcello **sia andato** in macchina.*
3. *Tu hai paura che io lasci il libro a casa.*
   *Tu hai paura che io **abbia lasciato** il libro a casa.*
4. *Mio padre è contento che mia madre vada dal dottore.*
   *Mio padre è contento che mia madre **sia andata** dal dottore.*
5. *Sembra che voi andiate.*
   *Sembra che voi **siate andati**.*

6. *Sono felice che tu compri una nuova macchina.*
   *Sono felice che tu **abbia comprato** una nuova macchina.*
7. *Loro dubitano che io dica la verità.*
   *Loro dubitano che io **abbia detto** la verità.*
8. *Tu e Marcello pensate che la conferenza cominci alle nove.*
   *Tu e Marcello pensate che la conferenza **sia cominciata** alle nove.*
9. *Io e mio fratello crediamo che nostro cugino dica una bugia.*
   *Io e mio fratello crediamo che nostro cugino **abbia detto** una bugia.*
10. *È possibile che loro vendano la casa.*
    *È possibile che loro **abbiano venduto** la casa.*

Exercise 15: Recognizing Verb Tenses and Moods

1. *Io dormo fino alle undici sabato mattina.*
   Present tense
2. *Noi siamo contenti che lui abbia dormito bene ieri notte.*
   Past subjunctive
3. *Tu dormirai bene stanotte.*   Future
4. *Avremmo dormito da mio fratello ma lui non ha lo spazio.*   Future perfect
5. *Marco dormirebbe per delle ore, ma deve lavorare.*
   Conditional
6. *Io e mia moglie dormivamo quando mio fratello ha chiamato.*   Imperfect (*imperfetto*)
7. *Maria dormirà a casa nostra stasera.*   Future
8. *Non ho seguito il tuo discorso perché non avevo dormito bene la notte scorsa.*
   Pluperfect (*trapassato prossimo*)
9. *Tu e tuo fratello dormireste in un albergo ma gli alberghi sono pieni.*
   Conditional
10. *Non vuole che tu dorma troppo.*   Present subjunctive

Exercise 16: Recoginzing Verb Tenses

1. Imperfect (*imperfetto*)
2. Perfect tense (*passato prossimo*)
3. Imperfect (*imperfetto*)
4. Conditional
5. Pluperfect tense (*trapassato prossimo*)
6. Present subjunctive
7. Conditional
8. Conditional perfect
9. Imperfect (*imperfetto*)
10. Future perfect

Exercise 17: Practicing Verb Tenses

1. *Io vorrei.*
2. *Noi diamo.*
3. *Voi berrete.*
4. *Loro abbiano chiesto.*

5. *Tu avrai preferito.*
6. *Lui sarebbe andato.*
7. *Io mi sveglierei.*
8. *Lei faccia.*
9. *Noi staremo.*
10. *Tu avresti avuto.*

Exercise 18: More Tense and Mood Practice

1. I would like a dish of spaghetti with tomato sauce.
2. My sisters will have already left.
3. I don't believe that it is true.
4. I would have liked to see the movie with you.
5. We will take your car this evening.
6. We would like to accompany you to the supermarket.
7. All of the boys will go to Rome this summer.
8. It is impossible that Alberto did not understand.
9. You would have wanted to come with us.
10. It will rain tomorrow.

Part 10: The Final Exam

Exercise 1: Some Basic Questions

Answers will vary. Possible answers are given.

1. *Domanda: Come ti chiami?*
   Risposta: Mi chiamo…
2. *Domanda: Come stai oggi?*
   Risposta: Sto bene.
3. *Domanda: Di dove sei?*
   Risposta: Sono di…
4. *Domanda: Com'è la tua città?*
   Risposta: La mia città non è molto grande.
5. *Domanda: Ci sono molti ristoranti nella tua città?*
   Risposta: Ci sono molti ristoranti nella mia città.
6. *Domanda: C'è un museo nella tua città?*
   Risposta: Non c'è un museo nella mia città.
7. *Domanda: Che ore sono?*
   Risposta: Sono le otto di sera.
8. *Domanda: Tu hai un marito o una moglie?*
   Risposta: Sì, ho una moglie.
9. *Domanda: Come si chiama?*
   Risposta: Si chiama…
10. *Domanda: Com'è tuo marito/tua moglie?*
    (cinque aggettivi)
    Risposta: È bella, giovane, intelli-gente, simpatica e bruna.
11. *Domanda: Quali lingue parli?*
    Risposta: Parlo inglese e italiano.

Exercise 2: *Avere* and *Essere*

1. *Lucia e io <u>abbiamo</u> una bicicletta bianca.*
2. *Boston <u>è</u> una bella città.*
3. *Maria e Giovanni <u>sono</u> studenti.*
4. *Tu e Davide <u>siete</u> di Roma.*
5. *Luciano e Luca <u>hanno</u> una bella stanza.*
6. *Noi <u>siamo</u> intelligenti.*
7. *Il <u>bambino ha</u> tre anni.*
8. *Tu <u>hai</u> un esame oggi?*
9. *Voi <u>avete</u> molti CD di Bob Dylan?*
10. *Lei, Signor Salvi, <u>ha</u> il libro d'italiano?*

Exercise 3: The Indefinite Article

1. *Ecco <u>una</u> piazza.*
2. *Ecco <u>un</u> amico.*
3. *Ecco <u>uno</u> stadio.*
4. *Ecco <u>una</u> stazione.*
5. *Ecco <u>uno</u> zaino.*
6. *Ecco <u>un</u>'amica.*

Exercise 4: The Definite Article

1. *l'università*	*le università*
2. *l'edificio*	*gli edifici*
3. *la penna*	*le penne*
4. *il libro*	*i libri*
5. *l'autobus*	*gli autobus*
6. *l'auto*	*le auto*
7. *la classe*	*le classi*
8. *la conversazione*	*le conversazioni*

Exercise 5: Adjective Agreement

1. *L'automobile di papà è <u>grigia</u>.*
2. *Marco ha due amici <u>inglesi</u>.*
3. *I cani di Antonio sono <u>vecchi</u>.*
4. *Gli occhi di Marcello sono <u>verdi</u>.*
5. *Mario è una persona <u>simpatica</u>.*
6. *Luisa e Marco sono alti e <u>biondi</u>.*

Exercise 6: Adjective Placement

1. *Marcello ha una Ford <u>gialla</u>.*
2. *Ci sono <u>molti</u> ristoranti in centro.*
3. *Lei ha una casa <u>bianca</u>.*
4. *Carlo e Marco sono <u>buoni</u> amici.*
5. *Lui è un bel ragazzo.*
6. *È un esame <u>lungo</u>.*
7. *Io e Giovanna siamo nella <u>stessa</u> classe.*
8. *Ho una macchina <u>tedesca</u>.*
9. *Giovanni è un <u>vecchio</u> amico.*
10. *Abbiamo <u>pochi</u> amici in Florida.*
11. *Marcello è un <u>buono</u> studente.*
12. *Marco ha due amici <u>giapponesi</u>.*

13. *Papà ha una <u>nuova</u> automobile.*
14. *Marcello ha degli amici <u>simpatici</u>.*

Exercise 7: Article/Adjective/Noun Formation

1. *Carmella è <u>una cara amica</u>.*
2. *Marcello ha <u>una Ferrari rossa</u>.*
3. *Lui è <u>un giovane professore</u>.*
4. *<u>Molte città italiane</u> hanno delle belle piazze.*
5. *In Piazza dei Nobili c'è <u>un nuovo ristorante</u>.*
6. *Lei ha <u>un libro interessante</u>.*
7. *<u>Gli stessi studenti</u> sono in classe.*
8. *<u>L'altro giorno</u> ho visto un film con Roberto Benigni.*
9. *<u>La Casa Bianca</u> è a Washington, D.C.*
10. *L'italiano è <u>una bella lingua</u>.*
11. *Papà mangia <u>nel nuovo ristorante in centro</u>.*
12. *Ci sono <u>molti alberi nel giardino</u>.*

Exercise 8: *Bello*

1. *Che bella cosa!*
2. *Che bel giorno!*
3. *Che begli occhi!*
4. *Che bel libro!*
5. *Che bello stadio!*
6. *Che bei capelli!*
7. *Che bell'edificio!*
8. *Che begli uffici!*

Exercise 9: *Buono*

1. *Sono <u>buoni</u> consigli.*
2. *È un <u>buon</u> caffè.*
3. *È una <u>buon</u>'abitudine.*
4. *È un <u>buon</u> libro.*
5. *È un <u>buon</u> albergo.*

Exercise 10: Possessive Adjectives

1. *Questa sera noi invitiamo <u>i tuoi fratelli</u> alla festa.*
2. *<u>I tuoi libri</u> sono nella stanza <u>di tuo fratello</u>.*
3. *Linda e Mario parlano <u>alle loro zie</u>.*
4. *<u>Suo fratello</u> è in Italia e <u>i suoi cugini</u> sono in Francia.*
5. *<u>I miei libri</u> sono <u>sul suo tavolo</u>.*
6. *<u>La nostra macchina</u> è dal meccanico.*
7. *<u>Le sue figlie</u> fanno un viaggio in Italia.*
8. *<u>Tuo cugino</u> non lavora il sabato e la domenica.*
9. *Sai che Marco non va alla festa con <u>la sua ragazza</u>?*
10. *Tu vedi <u>le sue macchine</u>?*
11. *<u>Il loro nonno</u> vuole bene <u>ai suoi nipoti</u>.*
12. *Penso di comprare dei fiori per <u>la mia cara zia</u>.*
13. *<u>I miei esami</u> sono difficili.*
14. *Gli studenti non fanno <u>i loro compiti</u>.*
15. *<u>I suoi figli</u> sono intelligenti.*
16. *<u>Le loro amiche</u> non vengono con noi.*

Exercise 11: Verbs in the Present Tense

1. *Noi <u>cerchiamo</u> il numero di telefono del professore.*
2. *Gli studenti <u>hanno torto</u>.*
3. *Loro <u>stanno per</u> finire l'esercizio.*
4. *Maria <u>finisce</u> il compito.*
5. *Questo semestre loro <u>abitano</u> nel dormitorio.*
6. *Tu e Marco <u>ripetete</u> la spiegazione.*
7. *I bambini <u>nuotano</u> nella piscina.*
8. *Tu e Maria <u>guardate</u> la televisione.*
9. *Voi <u>conoscete</u> la fidanzata di Marcello.*
10. *Io <u>voglio</u> andare al concerto di Bob Dylan.*
11. *La lezione d'italiano <u>comincia</u> alle 4.*
12. *Tu <u>restituisci</u> il libro al professore.*
13. *I camerieri <u>servono</u> il caffè ai clienti.*
14. *Voi <u>lavorate</u> in ufficio.*
15. *Noi <u>chiudiamo</u> la finestra.*
16. *Tu <u>pensi</u> a tuo fratello?*
17. *Io <u>aspetto</u> il treno.*
18. *Noi <u>giochiamo</u> a tennis oggi.*
19. *Io <u>vengo</u> alla festa domani sera.*
20. *Loro <u>escono</u> spesso con le loro amiche.*
21. *Tu <u>dici</u> sempre la verità?*
22. *Io non <u>so</u> se Giovanni è uno studente.*
23. *Non mi <u>piacciono</u> gli spaghetti alla carbonara.*
24. *Marco non <u>riesce</u> a capire la tua domanda.*
25. *Tu <u>fai una gita</u> quest'estate?*

Exercise 12: Wanting

Answers will vary. Possible answers are given.

1. *Voglio andare al cinema. Non posso perché devo studiare.*
2. *Voglio andare in vacanza. Non posso perché devo lavorare.*
3. *Voglio leggere un libro. Non posso perché devo andare a letto.*
4. *Voglio suonare la chitarra. Non posso perché devo preparare la cena.*
5. *Voglio andare a sciare. Non posso perché devo aiutare mio fratello.*

Exercise 13: *Andare, Fare, Stare, Dare*

1. *Come stai tu oggi?*
2. *Quando date una festa voi?*
3. *Noi andiamo in Italia ogni anno.*
4. *Che cosa fai tu sabato sera?*
5. *Io do del tu ai miei amici.*

Exercise 14: Verb Conjugations

	Restituire	Vedere	Dormire	Parlare
io	restituisco	vedo	dormo	parlo
tu	restituisci	vedi	dormi	parli
lui/lei/Lei	restituisce	vede	dorme	parla
noi	restituiamo	vediamo	dormiamo	parliamo
voi	restituite	vedete	dormite	parlate
loro/Loro	restituiscono	vedono	dormono	parlano

	Mangiare	Bere	Andare	Fare
io	mangio	bevo	vado	faccio
tu	mangi	bevi	vai	fai
lui/lei/Lei	mangia	beve	va	fa
noi	mangiamo	beviamo	andiamo	facciamo
voi	mangiate	bevete	andate	fate
loro/Loro	mangiano	bevono	vanno	fanno

Exercise 15: Translation

1. *Luca e Mario imparano a parlare italiano.*
2. *Sono di Providence. Penso ai miei amici a Providence.*
3. *Tu hai caldo e il caffè è freddo.*
4. *Tu e Maria avete voglia di mangiare.*
5. *Che macchina hai?*
6. *Quali lingue parli?*
7. *La domenica Anna va in chiesa con Maria.*
8. *Leggo un libro sulla storia italiana.*
9. *Dopo cena Giulia fa una passeggiata e poi fa una telefonata a Maria.*
10. *Mi dispiace, ma domenica vado al cinema con Cristina.*
11. *Conosci John?*
12. *Usciamo con gli amici di tuo figlio.*
13. *Devi avere fame. Vuoi della pizza?*
14. *Sai che il mio amico John è uno studente?*
15. *Non puoi guardare la TV adesso. Devi
studiare per il tuo esame.*

Exercise 16: Answering Questions

Answers will vary. Possible answers are given.
1. *Domanda: Leggi molto?*
   Risposta: Io leggo molto.
2. *Domanda: Dove mangi a pranzo? Che cosa mangi? Con
   chi mangi? Bevi il caffè quando finisci di mangiare?*
   *Risposta: Mangio in ufficio. Di solito mangio un panino. Man-
   gio da solo. Non bevo il caffè quando finisco di mangiare.*
3. *Domanda: Esci domani sera?*
   Risposta: Sì, esco domani sera.
4. *Domanda: Hai mai detto una bugia di convenienza?*
   Risposta: Sì ho detto qualche bugia di convenienza.
5. *Domanda: Sai chi è Marcello Mastroianni?*
   Risposta: So chi è.
6. *Domanda: A che ora sei andato/a a dormire ieri sera?*
   Risposta: Sono andato a dormire alle undici.

7. *Domanda: Ti piace viaggiare?*
   Risposta: Mi piace viaggiare.
8. *Domanda: Sei andato/a in vacanza l'anno scorso?*
   Risposta: Sono andato in Francia l'anno scorso.
9. *Domanda: Dove sei nato/a?*
   Risposta: Sono nato a Providence.
10. *Domanda: Che cosa hai mangiato a cena ieri sera?*
    Risposta: Ho mangiato l'arrosto di vitello.

Exercise 17: Direct Object Pronouns

1. *Simone compra le sigarette.* Simone le ha comprate.
2. *Noi leggiamo una rivista.* Noi l'abbiamo letta.
3. *Io vedo Marco e i suoi amici.* Io li ho visti.
4. *Voi bevete l'acqua.* Voi l'avete bevuta.
5. *Gli studenti chiudono i libri.* Gli studenti li hanno chiusi.
6. *Tu e Marco fumate un sigaro.* Tu e Marco l'avete fumato.
7. *Io compro una maglietta.* Io l'ho comprata.
8. *I suoi amici ordinano la grappa.* I suoi amici l'hanno
   ordinata.

Exercise 18: Direct and Indirect Object Pronouns

1. *Gli ho parlato stamattina.*
2. *L'ho cercato.*
3. *Hanno dimenticato di telefonargli.*
4. *Non li hai visti.*
5. *Non l'ho guardata ieri sera.*
6. *Li ha ordinati.*
7. *Le avete viste sabato sera.*
8. *Abbiamo telefonato loro.*
9. *L'ho incontrata al ristorante.*

Exercise 19: Double Object Pronouns

1. *Domanda: Quando ti metti una giacca?*
   Risposta: Me la metto quando ho freddo.
2. *Domanda: Ti lavi la faccia tutte le mattine?*
   Risposta: Me la lavo tutte le mattine.
3. *Domanda: Quando ti metti un grosso maglione di lana?*
   Risposta: Me lo metto quando nevica.
4. *Domanda: Quando ti metti la maglietta leggera?*
   Risposta: Me la metto quando vado al mare.
5. *Domanda: Quando si lavano la faccia i bambini?*
   Risposta: Se la lavano quando finiscono di mangiare.
6. *Domanda: Hai dato il libro a Paolo?*
   Risposta: Sì, gliel'ho dato.
7. *Domanda: Hai prestato la tua macchina a tuo fratello?*
   Risposta: No, non gliel'ho prestata.
8. *Domanda: Hai mandato l'email ai tuoi nonni?*
   Risposta: Sì, gliel'ho mandata.
9. *Domanda: A che ora ti sei preparato/a la colazione oggi?*
   Risposta: Me la sono preparata alle otto.
10. *Domanda: Dai il libro a Mariella?*
    Risposta: Glielo do.

Exercise 20: The *Passato Prossimo*

1. *Venerdì scorso la mia famiglia è partita per New York in treno.*
2. *Mio padre e mia madre hanno viaggiato in seconda classe.*
3. *Il mio amico ha portato un po' di vino bianco.*
4. *Noi abbiamo bevuto il vino durante il viaggio.*
5. *Io ho dormito durante il viaggio.*
6. *Quando il treno è arrivato, noi siamo scesi dal treno.*
7. *Io ho voluto prendere un taxi.*
8. *I miei genitori hanno telefonato al fratello di mio padre.*
9. *Maria e suo fratello sono usciti venerdì sera.*
10. *Mio zio è morto l'anno scorso.*
11. *Le mie due sorelle sono entrate e hanno trovato una sorpresa.*
12. *Io sono nato/a nel mese di ottobre.*
13. *Tu e Maria siete andati/e a sciare l'anno scorso.*
14. *Loro hanno lavorato sabato scorso.*
15. *Maria e Elena non sono state a Milano.*

Exercise 21: Now or Then?

1. *Ieri mattina Marco si è svegliato alle 7 e si è alzato alle 7 e 30. Poi ha preparato i bagagli per il viaggio ed è andato all'aeroporto, dove ha preso il volo per la Sardegna.*
2. *Stasera io voglio andare al cinema con un mio amico. Il mio amico si chiama Giovanni. Normalmente lui si annoia al cinema. Questa volta io e Giovanni ci divertiamo sicuramente perché andiamo a vedere un film divertentissimo. Dopo il film ci fermiamo al bar a prendere un caffè.*
3. *Due giorni fa io ho lavorato fino a tardi e sono tornato a casa alle undici. Ho mangiato velocemente, perché avevo molta fame. Sono andato a letto alle undici e e mezza e mi sono addormentato subito.*

Exercise 22: Answering Questions in the *Passato Prossimo*

Answers will vary. Possible answers given.

1. *Domanda: A che ora ti sei svegliato/a stamattina?*
   Risposta: Mi sono svegliato alle otto stamattina.
2. *Domanda: Hai mai visto un film italiano? Come si chiama? Ti è piaciuto?*
   Risposta: Sì, ho visto «La vita è bella». Mi è piaciuto molto.
3. *Domanda: Hai già festeggiato il tuo compleanno quest'anno?*
   Risposta: Sì, ho già festeggiato il mio compleanno quest'anno.
4. *Domanda: Ti innamori raramente?*
   Risposta: Mi innamoro raramente.
5. *Domanda: Leggi velocemente? Quante pagine leggi in un'ora?*
   Risposta: Leggo cento pagine in un'ora.
6. *Domanda: Sei mai stato/a in Florida? Quanto tempo fa?*
   Risposta: Sono stato in Florida due anni fa.
7. *Domanda: Sei andato/a a vedere i tuoi genitori il mese scorso?*
   Risposta: Sono andato a vedere mia madre il mese scorso.
8. *Domanda: A che ora ti sei addormentato/a la notte scorsa?*
   Risposta: Mi sono addormentato alle undici.
9. *Domanda: Che cosa hai fatto ieri pomeriggio?*
   Risposta: Ho guardato un film.

Exercise 23: Conjugation across the Tenses

Conjugate the verb *arrabbiarsi* in the requested tenses.

present	future
io mi arrabbio	*io mi arrabbierò*
tu ti arrabbi	*tu ti arrabbierai*
lui/lei/Lei si arrabbia	*lui/lei/Lei si arrabbierà*
noi ci arrabbiamo	*noi ci arrabbieremo*
voi vi arrabbiate	*voi vi arrabbierete*
loro/Loro si arrabbiano	*loro/Loro si arrabbieranno*

imperfetto	present conditional
io mi arrabbiavo	*io mi arrabbierei*
tu ti arrabbiavi	*tu ti arrabbieresti*
lui/lei/Lei si arrabbiava	*lui/lei/Lei si arrabbierebbe*
noi ci arrabbiavamo	*noi ci arrabbieremmo*
voi vi arrabbiavate	*voi vi arrabbiereste*
loro/Loro si arrabbiavano	*loro/Loro si arrabbierebbero*

passato prossimo	past subjunctive
io mi sono arrabbiato/a	*io mi sia arrabbiato/a*
tu ti sei arrabiato/a	*tu ti sia arrabbiato/a*
lui/lei/Lei si è arrabbiato/a	*lui/lei/Lei si sia arrabbiato/a*
noi ci siamo arrabbiati/e	*noi ci siamo arrabbiati/e*
voi vi siete arrabbiati/e	*voi vi siate arrabbiati/e*
loro/Loro si sono arrabbiati/e	*loro/Loro si siano arrabbiati/e*

Exercise 24: Translation Exercise

1. *Domanda: Ti fermi a un'edicola prima di andare in ufficio?*
   Risposta: Sì, mi fermo a un'edicola prima di andare in ufficio.
   Conditional: Mi fermerei a un'edicola prima di andare in ufficio.
2. *Domanda: Ti arrabbi quando i tuoi amici non chiamano?*
   Risposta: Sì, mi arrabbio quando i miei amici non chiamano.
   Passato Prossimo: Mi sono arrabbiato quando i miei amici non hanno chiamato.
3. *Domanda: Dove ti piace mangiare?*
   Risposta: Mi piace mangiare a casa.
   Imperfetto: Mi piaceva mangiare a casa.

4. *Domanda: Ti sei divertito/a venerdì sera?*
   Risposta: Non mi sono divertito/a venerdì sera.
   Conditional Perfect: Mi sarei divertito/a venerdì sera.
5. *Domanda: Quante volte alla settimana parli con i tuoi genitori?*
   Risposta: Parlo con mia madre due volte alla settimana.
   Future Perfect: Avrò parlato con mia madre due volte alla settimana.

Exercise 25: Reciprocal Construction

1. *Marco e il suo amico si sono parlati.*
2. *Elena e suo cugino si sono visti.*
3. *Io e mio padre ci siamo scritti.*
4. *Giorgio e il suo compagno si sono telefonati.*
5. *Giuseppe e i suoi amici si sono chiamati.*

Exercise 26: *Passato Prossimo* or *Imperfetto*?

1. *Ieri pomeriggio tu e Maria <u>avete parlato</u> con i ragazzi che <u>giocavano</u> a calcio.*
2. *Quando io e mia moglie <u>siamo usciti</u> stamattina, il nostro gatto <u>dormiva</u> ancora.*
3. *Il mese scorso, tu e Lisa siete andati in Italia. Voi <u>vi siete divertiti</u> molto.*
4. *Quando loro <u>sono partiti</u>, <u>erano le otto e trenta</u>.*
5. *Ieri a mezzogiorno Anna si <u>è fermata</u> al ristorante, perché <u>aveva fame</u> e sete.*
6. *Quando noi <u>siamo arrivati</u> in biblioteca stamattina, <u>pioveva</u>.*
7. *Giovedì scorso io e Luciano <u>siamo andati</u> in spiaggia, perché <u>era</u> una bella giornata.*

Exercise 27: The Future Tense

1. *Io non <u>farò attenzione</u> a quello che dice il professore.*
2. *Marco non <u>potrà</u> uscire, perché deve studiare.*
3. *Marcello, tu <u>avrai sete</u>.*
4. *Voi <u>dovrete</u> fare attenzione in classe.*
5. *Io <u>do del tu</u> agli amici.*
6. *Io non <u>berrò</u> il caffè a colazione.*
7. *Noi <u>avremo paura</u>.*
8. *Loro <u>prepareranno</u> la colazione per i bambini.*
9. *Tu <u>scriverai</u> molte lettere agli amici?*
10. *Io <u>risponderò</u> al telefono.*
11. *Voi <u>partirete</u> da casa.*
12. *I ragazzi <u>si sveglieranno</u> molto presto.*
13. *Tu e Maria <u>riceverete</u> molte email.*
14. *Gianni <u>offrirà</u> un caffè al professore.*
15. *Tu <u>crederai</u> negli UFO?*
16. *Tutti gli studenti <u>dormiranno</u> durante il viaggio.*
17. *Che cosa <u>chiederai</u> tu?*
18. *La studentessa <u>aprirà</u> il libro a pagina diciannove.*
19. *I ragazzi <u>seguiranno</u> il discorso.*
20. *Mi <u>piacerà</u> molto rivedere Parigi*

Exercise 28: The Present Conditional

1. *Io e mia moglie <u>costruiremmo</u> una nuova casa, se avessimo i soldi.*
2. *Lo studente <u>farebbe una domanda</u> in classe, ma è troppo timido.*
3. *Loro <u>darebbero del Lei</u> al professore.*
4. *Loro <u>finirebbero</u> le lasagne, ma non hanno più fame.*
5. *I ragazzi non <u>capirebbero</u> il discorso.*
6. *Il mio amico <u>pulirebbe</u> più spesso, se avesse tempo.*
7. *Tu faresti <u>una pausa</u> dopo la lezione.*
8. *Lui <u>preferirebbe</u> il caffè italiano.*
9. *Giovanni <u>studierebbe</u>, se avesse tempo.*
10. *L'avvocato <u>spiegherebbe</u> la legge al cliente.*
11. *I miei amici <u>pagherebbero</u> il caffè.*
12. *Noi <u>impareremmo</u> l'italiano.*
13. *Tu <u>torneresti</u> in Italia l'anno prossimo.*
14. *Marco e Angela <u>andrebbero</u> alla festa di Giovanni.*
15. *Io mi alzerei molto tardi.*

Exercise 29: *Piacere*

1. *Gli siamo piaciuti molto.*
2. *Non ci piacciono i film stranieri perché non ci piace leggere i sottotitoli.*
3. *Sono usciti ieri sera. Lei non gli è piaciuta, ma lui è piaciuto a lei.*
4. *Non le piacciono i suoi amici, perché bevono troppa grappa.*
5. *Mi piace lavare la macchina il sabato. Lavoro la domenica.*
6. *A Marco e Lisa piace uscire.*
7. *Non gli piacciamo perché non ci conoscono.*
8. *Mi piacerebbe mangiare in quel ristorante.*
9. *Potrei andare alla festa, ma non mi piacciono le feste.*
10. *Mi sarebbe piaciuto il professore ma non mi ha dato un buon voto.*

Exercise 30: *Corretto o Incorretto?*

1. *Io abito a Roma.*
2. *Noi abbiamo mangiato nel nuovo ristorante.*
3. *Ho preso un caffè al bar.*
4. *Pierino studiava l'italiano.*
5. *Marcello e Maria avevano letto il libro.*
6. *Quella signora avrà sessant'anni.*
7. *Io e mia moglie andremmo in Italia.*
8. *Penso che lui sia un amico di Claudio.*
9. *Mio fratello non crede che io sia andato/a alla festa.*
10. *È importante che tu vada stasera.*

Exercise 31: Listening and Translating

1. *Andrò in Italia l'anno prossimo.*
   I will go to Italy next year.

2. *Vorrei andare a cena con te, ma non posso perché devo studiare.*
   I would go to dinner with you, but I can't because I have to study.
3. *L'anno scorso abbiamo fatto un viaggio in Florida.*
   Last year we took a trip to Florida.
4. *Marco avrebbe detto una bugia.*
   Marco would have told a lie.
5. *Maria e sua madre facevano una passeggiata ogni domenica.*
   Maria and her mother used to take a walk every Sunday.
6. *Mentre io studiavo mio fratello ha telefonato a sua moglie.*
   While I was studying, my brother telephoned his wife.
7. *Se ti ho chiamato è perché ti volevo parlare.*
   If I called you it is because I wanted to talk to you.
8. *Abitiamo a Boston da un anno.*
   We have been living in Boston for a year.
9. *Che ore sono? Saranno le sette.*
   What time is it? It must be seven o'clock.
10. *Dovevo studiare tutti questi verbi!*
    I had to study all these verbs!
11. *Puoi aiutarmi?*
    Can you help me?
12. *Avrebbero voluto fare un viaggio.*
    They would have liked to take a trip.
13. *Studiavamo in biblioteca.*
    We used to study in the library.
14. *Ho imparato a parlare italiano.*
    I learned to speak Italian.

Exercise 32: From Indicative to Subjunctive

1. *Noi pensiamo che Mario e Silvia si siano sposati l'anno scorso.*
2. *È possibile che Gianni si sia arrabbiato.*
3. *Sembra che non abbiano ancora fatto colazione.*
4. *Peccato che i miei amici ed io non ci vediamo mai.*
5. *Pare che Tino abbia mangiato la torta.*

Index

A

Adjectives
    demonstrative adjectives, 129, 147–51, 156–57
    invariable adjectives, 19–20
    and noun agreement, 13–18
    placement of, 15–16
    possessive adjectives, 106–10
    as quantifying words, 16–18
    suffixes for, 113–14
Adverbs, 16–18, 89–91
Affirmative commands, 176, 180–82
Alighieri, Dante, xi, xii
Andare (to go), 57–59, 281
Answer key, 304–35
Articles, 11–13, 19–21
Ascoltare (to listen), 55–56
Aspettare (to wait), 55–56
Avere (to have), 27, 31–35, 194, 279–80

B

Barzini, Luigi, xi
Bello (beautiful, handsome, nice), 39
Bere (to drink), 80, 281–82
Buono (good), 38–39

C

Campanilismo, xii
Capire (to understand), 82
C'è, 36
Cercare (to look for), 282
Che ora è?, 68–70
Che ore sono?, 68–70
Ci sono, 36
Com'è?, 37
Come sono?, 37
Commands, 161–91
Common nouns, 2–3. *See also* Nouns
Conditional mood, 225, 233–39
Conditional perfect tense, 236–39
Conjugations. *See also* Verbs
    first conjugation verbs, 49–74
    second conjugation verbs, 50, 75–94
    third conjugation verbs, 50, 75–94
Conoscere (to know), 86–87

D

Da quando?, 213
Da quanto tempo?, 213
Dare (to give), 57–59, 282
Dates, 152
Days of week, 44–45, 152

Definite articles, 12–13, 19, 21
Demonstrative adjectives, 129, 147–51, 156–57
Dialects, xi–xii
Diphthongs, 191
Direct object, 129–36, 155
Direct object pronouns, 129–36
Dire (to say, to tell), 83, 282–83
Divine Comedy, xi
Dormire (to sleep), 76, 226, 233, 280–81
Double object pronouns, 143–46, 155
Double verb constructions, 56, 141–43
Dovere (to have to, must), 84–85, 283

E

Ecco!, 36–37
English-to-Italian glossary, 296–303
Essere (to be), 27–31, 35, 194, 279–80
Exam, 251–78

F

Fare (to do, to make), 57–60, 284
Feminine nouns, 3–6